New Testament

Johannes Nissen

New Testament
and Mission

Historical
and Hermeneutical
Perspectives

4th edition

PETER LANG

Frankfurt am Main · Berlin · Bern · Bruxelles · New York · Oxford · Wien

Bibliographic Information published by the Deutsche Nationalbibliothek
The Deutsche Nationalbibliothek lists this publication in the Deutsche Nationalbibliografie; detailed bibliographic data is available in the internet at <http://www.d-nb.de>.

Based on the Danish Version of "Ordet tog bolig iblandt os", Forlaget ANIS, Copenhagen 1996.

ISBN-10: 3-631-56097-4
ISBN-13: 978-3-631-56097-6
US-ISBN 0-8204-8781-3

© Peter Lang GmbH
Europäischer Verlag der Wissenschaften
Frankfurt am Main 1999
4th edition 2007
All rights reserved.

Printed in Germany 1 2 3 4   6 7

www.peterlang.de

Preface to the first edition

In 1996 I published a book in Danish on New Testament and mission which forms the basis of the present volume. Although the content and outline are essentially the same, the English version is not a direct translation. Some minor changes and additions have been made for the following reasons.

In the first place the present book is aimed at an international circle of readers. In consequence, more literature is surveyed and the number of references to the scholarly debate on New Testament and mission has increased.

Secondly, I also wanted to consider new books and articles which have appeared since the Danish version was published. The debate on the character of mission is a continuing process. It is my hope that this publication will make a contribution to the biblical foundation of mission.

Biblical quotations are from the New Revised Standard Version (NRSV) unless otherwise stated.

Special thanks are due to Lektor Edward Broadbridge, who read and corrected the English text, and to Jytte Kløve, secretary at the Department for Biblical Studies, for her help in the preparation of the typescript of this book.

I am also grateful to the Faculty of Theology at Aarhus University and to Aarhus University Research Foundation for financial support for the linguistic revision. Finally, I would like to thank Verlag Peter Lang for its readiness to publish this book.

Aarhus, May 1999   Johannes Nissen

Note to the second edition

The reception of *New Testament and Mission* by biblical scholars, missiologists and students alike has been sufficiently rewarding to warrant a second edition. The subject of mission on a biblical basis in a modern multi-religious context is clearly undergoing a revitalizing process, to which this second edition, with the addition of a few minor linguistic corrections from the first edition, is a modest contribution.

Aarhus, May 2002   Johannes Nissen

Note to the third and fourth editions

The third edition (2003) and fourth edition (2006) follow the second edition with no changes to the text.

Aarhus, September 2006   Johannes Nissen

Contents

1. **Introduction: Aim and method of this study** 13

   1. Biblical scholarship and missiology 13
   2. Text and experience 13
   3. Historical meaning and contemporary significance 15
   4. Perspectives, paradigms and models 16
   5. Mission and missions 16
   6. Questions of definitions 17
   Notes 19

2. **Mission as disciple-making: The Gospel of Matthew** 21

   Introduction 21
   I. A Re-reading of the "Great Commission" 21
      1. The term "mission command" 21
      2. Focus on the locality or the task? 22
   II Mission in Matthew: Its motivations and content 23
      1. All authority 23
      2. Two mission strategies in conflict 23
      3. Jesus' compassion for the harassed and helpless 24
      4. The content of mission: God's kingdom and his justice 25
   III. The subjects and addressees of mission 26
      1. Missionary discipleship 26
      2. The church as mission 27
      3. The Jews and the nations 27
      4. The centripetal and the centrifugal mission 27
      5. The little ones 28
   IV. Hermeneutical Perspectives 29
      1. Evangelism and Christian education 29
      2. Mission – not manipulation 29
      3. Mission in Christ's way 30
      4. Justice as an integral part of mission 32
      5. The church as mission 32

6. Christ's presence among the little ones 32
Notes 33

3. **Crossing boundaries: Mission in Mark's Gospel** 37

Introduction 37
I.   The Kingdom of God and the crossing of boundaries 38
    1. The Gospel as a mission text 38
    2. The inclusive character of the Kingdom 38
    3. Crossing boundaries in Galilee 39
    4. Crossing boundaries in Jerusalem 41
II. The Kingdom and the way 41
    1. The call to discipleship 41
    2. Discipleship as a learning process 42
    3. Mission from the empty tomb 43
III. Hermeneutical perspectives 44
    1. A corrective to a triumphant mission 44
    2. An open-ended story – an unfinished mission 44
    3. Mission from the periphery 45
Notes 46

4. **The liberating ministry of Jesus and the Acts of the Spirit: The**
   mission perspectives of Luke-Acts 49

Introduction 49
I.   The proclamation of the Jubilee – the Gospel of Luke 50
    1. The "Great Commission" 50
    2. Jesus' proclamation in the synagogue of Nazareth 50
    3. The Jubilee as a new beginning 52
    4. Good news to the rich? 54
    5. Towards a sharing of common resources 54
II. Holy Spirit, mission and community 55
    1. The universal scope of salvation 55
    2. The boundary-breaking role of the Holy Spirit 56
    3. The function of meals and households in Luke's mission 57
    4. The Holy Spirit and the community of ownership 58
    5. Spirit, baptism and miracles 59
III. Mission and dialogue in Acts 60
    1. The missionary speeches 60
    2. Paul's speech at the Areopagus – failure or success? 61

3. The context of the Areopagus speech 62
4. The content of the speech: points of contact, continuity, critique
    and contradiction 63
5. Dialogue in Ephesus 65
IV. Hermeneutical perspectives 66
    1. Good news to the poor – and to sinners 66
    2. Towards a prophetic-critique hermeneutics 67
    3. The Year of the Jubilee and the debt crisis 68
    4. The Holy Spirit in mission 69
    5. The message and method in dialogue 69
Notes 71

5. **Sent into the world: Mission and incarnation in the Fourth Gospel** . 75

Introduction 75
I. Mission as sending 75
    1. The sending of the Son 76
    2. The sending of the disciples 77
    3. The sending of the Spirit 79
    4. Mission and mutual love 80
II. Christ as God's universal invitation 81
    1. "Come and see" 81
    2. The Prologue 82
    3. Inclusive and exclusive aspects of Johannine christology 83
    4. Mission as dialogue and witness 84
        a. On rebirth (Jesus and Nicodemus) 85
        b. On living water (Jesus and the Samaritan woman) 87
III. Hermeneutical perspectives 89
    1. A trinitarian perspective 89
    2. In dialogue with various religious traditions 90
    3. An incarnational model of mission 91
    4. "I am the way" 92
    5. The role of the Holy Spirit in mission 92
Notes 93

6. Constrained by the love of God: Paul's foundation and practice of mission 99

Introduction 99
I. The motivation for Paul's mission 100
    1. Paul's conversion and call 100
    2. The universal scope of salvation (Romans) 101
    3. Ministers of reconciliation (2 Corinthians) 103
    4. Firmness and flexibility (1 Corinthians) 105
        a. The basic principles 106
        b. The flexibility 107
        c. Cross and culture 108
II. Paul's missionary strategy and his communities 109
    1. Different forms of mission in early Christianity 109
    2. Paul's missionary strategy 110
    3. Conflicting roles of missionaries 110
    4. In Christ – a new community 111
    5. The collection 113
    6. The encounter between Christians and non-Christians:
        belief and practice 113
    7. Theological and christological aspects of Paul's answer 115
III. Hermeneutical perspectives 116
    1. The double apostolate 116
    2. Urban mission 117
    3. The collection as a model for partnership 118
    4. Integrity and openness 120
    5. Rejection, inclusion or...? 121
Notes 122

7. Proclamation and confrontation: The witness to powers and authorities – Colossians and Ephesians 127

Introduction 127
I. Colossians 127
    1. The situation of the Colossians 127
    2. Liberation from the tyranny of the powers 128
    3. Reconciliation in Christ 129
II. Ephesians 131
    1. The religious background of the epistle 131
    2. All things reconciled in Christ 131
    3. The reconciliation of Jews and Gentiles 133

    4. The conflict with the powers 134
    5. The missionary task of the church 135
III. Hermeneutical perspectives 136
    1. Christ as the Lord of the universe 136
    2. The importance of reconciliation 137
    3. New humanity and cultural identity 137
    4. Mission to "foreign" structures 138
    5. Holy war or mission of peace? 140
Notes 140

8. **Hope and witness: Mission in 1 Peter and the Book of Revelation** . . 143

Introduction 143
I. The witness of hope – 1 Peter 144
    1. The situation of the readers 144
    2. God's household and God's people 145
    3. The calling to do good 146
II. Prophetic witness – the Book of Revelation 147
    1. The background 147
    2. Conflict with the surrounding culture 148
    3. The cosmic Christ and the renewal of the creation 149
III. Hermeneutical perspectives 151
    1. Christians and the state – conformity or non-conformity? 151
    2. The mission of hope 153
Notes 154

9. **Mission, culture, and dialogue: New Testament perspectives and
    present challenges** 157

Introduction 157
I. Plurality and unity in mission 157
    1. Incarnation and contextualization 157
    2. The plurality of the Bible as a positive challenge 159
    3. Some tendencies in recent mission theology 160
    4. Major lines in the New Testament understanding of mission 161
II. Gospel and cultures 163
    1. Inculturation 163
    2. Christ and culture 165
    3. Church, cross and culture 166
    4. Criteria for discernment of the spirits 167

III. Bible and dialogue 169
   1. Three models for dialogue 169
     a. Exclusivism 170
     b. Inclusivism 170
     c. Pluralism 171

   2. The uniqueness and the universality of Christ 172
   3. A trinitarian approach to mission 174
   4. Mission on the way 174
Notes 176

Bibliography 181

1.

Introduction:
Aim and method of this study

1. Biblical scholarship and missiology

In recent years there has been a growing interest in the biblical foundation for mission. It is a problem, however, that biblical scholars and missiologists are often ignoring each other's work.[1]

Biblical scholars tend to emphasize the diversity of the biblical message and the historical character of each text. The implication of this is that the interpreters are hesitant to draw any conclusions as to the relevance of the texts for today's mission.

By contrast, missiologists tend to err in the opposite direction. They are inclined to overlook the rich diversity of the biblical texts and therefore to reduce the biblical motivation for mission to one single idea or text. Missiologists tend far too easily to read back into the Bible aspects of the missionary enterprise in which they are involved today.

In order to establish a fruitful dialogue between biblical scholarship and missiology we must give up the traditional division of labour between the historical exegesis and systematic theology. For many years historical criticism has been the dominant model of interpretation. According to this model, the task of the scholar is to uncover the original meaning of the Bible by means of linguistic and historical analysis. Professional interpreters have to jettison all bias so as not to distort the Bible's original meaning with modern questions. When they have completed their job of putting together the package of "original meanings" of the relevant texts, they hand this "baton" over to the other theologians to "apply" it to the contemporary world.

This model has been seriously called into question by the recognition that no interpreter can understand any text without prejudgments formed from his or her own context. Therefore, an increasing number of biblical scholars realize that they are dependent upon other theologians (including missiologists) just as these other theologians depend upon them.

2. Text and experience

A new model of interpretation has emerged. It is based on the belief that deepest insight and relevance lie neither in the original meaning of the Bible alone nor in the contemporary context but in the to-and-fro of question and answer between them. This model of interpretation is that of a conversation.[2]

The relationship between text and context can be understood as the fusion of two horizons. The text represents the first horizon, and the context of the interpreter is the second horizon. The ultimate goal of this model of interpretation as conversation is to fuse these horizons in a way that is true to the past and relevant to the present.[3] It is in this fusion of horizons that biblical scholars and other theologians meet and actually supplement each other.

The aim of this study is to contribute to such a conversation between biblical scholarship and missiology. This is reflected in the outline of the book. All chapters except one have two parts. The first part offers a historical description of the theology of mission in the various New Testament writings. The second part consists of hermeneutical reflections.

This structure of each chapter might create the impression that historical analysis and hermeneutical reflections are two separate processes of work. This, however, is not the case. It is not as though the relation between historical analysis and hermeneutics can be solved by way of direct "application" of the texts. One can use historical criticism to reconstruct more or less accurately the missiologies, implicit in the various traditions of the Bible, but one can not ask it to provide us with a biblical founded missiology for our times. Historical criticism will tell us what Matthew, John or Paul thought about mission, not what *we* must think about mission in our concrete historical situation.[4]

What we need is an interaction between text and contemporary experience.[5] Our way of reading the text is effected by the time in which we live. Even if we try to be as historical accurate as possible we come to the Bible with some specific questions. As can be seen from the following chapters, my own approach is in keeping with this new method of interpretation. One has only to look at my selection of issues and topics and at the way in which I am asking questions. From the works I have consulted it can be seen that I have learned much from third world theologians as well as missiologists.

We should note that the dialogue between text and experience has already begun in the Bible itself. The Bible is by definition an open book, that is a book open to the ongoing process of transmission and interpretation. The transmission and interpretation of biblical traditions of faith which can be observed in the Bible remain normative. But this canonized interpretative process gives also freedom for new theological thinking and new prophetic action.[6]

The ongoing interpretation is characterized by a re-reading of the traditions of the past. New situations forced reexamination and recasting of the tradition, and they provided the believing community with a dynamic and living traditional base upon which to build and in terms of which to understand its past in the light of its changing presents and futures.[7]

The first Christians avoided two pitfalls which could be characterized as "traditionalism" and "situationalism". While the "traditionalists" tend to apply biblical texts in a normative way directly to the present situation, the "situationalists" tend to forget the past.

Contrary to both methods we have to study the old texts in the light of questions and hopes of our situation *and* vice versa. H.-R. Weber has made a helpful distinction between what he calls "proof-text" and "clue-text".[8] He points out that the way need not always go from the old text to the present situation, as is current in much traditional Bible studies. In fact, the early Christians more often went the other way: from their own time and its unintelligible events back to the old biblical texts (which in their case was the "Old Testament"), in order to understand the meaning of what happened in their time and become involved in it as believers. This is not a "proof-text"-method, but rather a "clue-text"-method. Biblical texts and perspectives function as clues, as guides, suggesting lines of inquiry, initiating new trains of thought and motivating action.

3. Historical meaning and contemporary significance

In the past hermeneutics has been occupied predominantly with how texts serve to pass on *information*. Today the focus has shifted to the question of how texts might have a *transformative* role.[9] "Historical objectivity is not a reconstruction of the past in its unrepeatable factuality, it is the truth of the past in the light of the present".[10] The task of the interpreter is "not only to ask about the past and present of a text in the light of the past and present of its readers and hearers, but especially *to ask about its future, its transforming effect* upon those that come into contact with it."[11]

We cannot jump to some privileged place of neutrality or complete objectivity. It is from within our life-worlds, that we engage in the reading task. This however raises some important questions[12]: If our own life-worlds are the starting point for reading the Bible, will we not find in its pages only that for which we are looking? Can we as readers have interests and still be open to challenges from the text?

Any use of Scripture must face the risk that the biblical text just becomes a mirror reflecting back what we want it to say. Therefore, some method must be used which allows the text to speak its piece, to function as a window through which we see something besides our own thoughts.[13]

If meaning were not in some sense "there" in the text, how could texts ever challenge, inform, or transform their readers? How could the text ever criticize a dominant ideology?[14] D. J. Bosch rightly notices that "Good exegesis is produced where the exegete's own horizon has been opened in the way the biblical author's horizon was opened. The text remains the firm point of orientation. But understanding is not merely a reproductive process but a creative one. In fact, it may generate different valid interpretations in different readers, but they should all still be consonant with the intention of the text."[15]

Here it might be useful to make a distinction between a text's *meaning* ("Sinn") and its *significance* ("Bedeutung").[16] A given text has only one meaning which is the author's meaning (what the author intended to say), but it can have many significances. The significance is the result of the *application* (and *appropriation*) of the text in a *new* situation.

From this it follows that it is as important to establish what the text *means* today (its significance) as it is to find out what it *meant* in the first century. Though the major task of biblical scholars is to investigate the text in its original setting, they can benefit much from missiologists and others in asking new questions and thereby often discovering new aspects of the text. They will also get a better understanding of the way in which the text functioned at its beginning.

In today's mission our goal cannot be to imitate the specific things Jesus and the first Christians did; rather we must take the model of incarnation itself to hear and discover anew, *as they did*, how to express and embody the gospel *in our context*.

4. Perspectives, paradigms and models

The use of the term "perspective" in the subtitle of this book signalizes the importance of the interaction between the historical and the hermeneutical dimension in our reading of the New Testament. In recent years two other terms: "paradigm" and "model" have been used in a similar way to characterize this interaction.[17] It is presupposed that the renewal of biblical studies can contribute to the renewal of mission, and conversely the renewal of mission can provide new perspectives and understanding of the scriptures.

Both terms have at least two aspects in common. The first aspect is descriptive. Paradigms and models reflect the experience, the belief and the value of a specific community. The second aspect is normative. Paradigms and models are somehow imperative. They give a pattern or perspective on the life of the readers.

The term "paradigm" might also have a subjective element. D. J. Bosch has compared a paradigm with a map. He states: "I recognize that different theological interpretations, including my own, reflect different contexts, perspectives and biases". This is not the same as regarding all theological positions as equal. "I realize that my theological approach is a "map", and that map is never the actual "territory". Although I believe that my map is best, I accept that there are other types of maps and also that, at least in theory, one of those may be better than mine..."[18]

Although there are many common elements in "perspective", "paradigm" and "model" I prefer the first term. As I take it, this term has three dimensions: (1) a historical-descriptive dimension, (2) a normative dimension and (3) a subjective dimension. All three dimensions are important.

As noted previously we are asking specific questions to the texts. We are looking at them from a specific point of view, a specific angle. In short, we are all looking at the texts through our lenses. But we cannot suppose that our contemporary concerns are directly reflected in the first-century experiences. Therefore, we must ask seriously whether the issues to which the first Christians speak apply to our situations.[19] Sometimes the answer will be negative, sometimes it will be positive. Either way, there is a request for a careful analysis of whether our situation is analogous and similar to the one addressed by a biblical text.

5. Mission and missions

There is always the danger of reductionism. For many Christians the so-called "Great Commission" in Matt 28:18-20 has become the only biblical foundation for mission. In other cases priority is given to Paul's mission, which is conceived of as itinerant mission. However, the mission in the New Testament is not reducible to Matthew or John or Paul. On the contrary, the correlation of all these currents of thoughts lends them mutual illumination and balance.[20]

A missiologically relevant reading of the Bible will not lead to any universal missiology but (as in the New Testament itself) to a variety of missiological

16

perspectives.[21] Different theologies of mission do not necessarily exclude each other; "they form a multicolored mosaic of complementary and mutually enriching as well as mutually challenging frames of reference."[22] Instead of trying to formulate one uniform view of mission we should rather attempt to chart the contours of "a pluriverse of missiology in a universe of mission" (Soares-Prabhu).

Of course, the existence of more than one mission theology raises the question of a unity within the diversity.[23] There may be diversity and sometimes even theological disagreement within the Bible. Such diversity should not be glossed over too easily. The *necessity* and *validity* of different expressions of the gospel have to be accepted by the Christians[24] because "the diversity of thought within the Bible reflects the diversity of God's actions in different historical situations and the diversity of human response to God's actions".[25]

It is anachronistic to attempt to base all modern "missionary" efforts on the Bible, that is, to seek biblical precedents or literal mandates for all our missionary activities. Mission today must rather be seen as arising from something fundamental, from the basic movement of God's people toward the world – more precisely, toward the numerous peoples who have not (yet) accepted God's new covenant in Jesus Christ. This movement must be understood as a way of following God who sent and "gave his Son, so that everyone, who believes in him may not perish but may have eternal life" (John 3:16).[26]

Here it might be useful to distinguish between *mission* and *missions*. The first refers primarily to the *missio Dei* (God's mission), that is, God's self-revelation as the One who loves the world, God's involvement in and with the world.[27] *Missions* (the *missiones ecclesiae*: the missionary venture of the church) refer to particular forms, related to specific times, places, or needs, of participation in *missio Dei*.

6. Questions of definitions

"New Testament and mission" can be defined in two ways both of which are relevant for this study. The first way is about the "biblical foundations" or "biblical grounding", the second is about the content of mission.

Following M. Spindler one can distinguish between three kinds of questions that must be asked in a biblical grounding of mission[28]:

(1)   *Why* mission? That is, the *reasons* that make mission both possible and necessary.

(2)   *How* must the church carry out mission? That is, the *methods* of missionary action in and according to the Bible.

(3)   *What* is mission? That is the *essence* of mission.

All of these are relevant when we try to define the term "mission" and all are raised in the various chapters of this book.

The second question relates more specifically to our understanding of the term "mission". It should be distinguished from the related term "evangelism".[29]

17

Although mission and evangelism are linked together and inextricably interwoven in theology and praxis, mission has a broader meaning. Mission is the church sent into the world, to love, to serve, to preach, to teach, to heal, to liberate.[30]

Traditionally, New Testament mission is defined as Gentile mission. Scholars have asked particularly about the church's *universal* mission.[31] This aspect is certainly very important. However, a more comprehensive definition is required. The New Testament material points to various aspects all of which might play a role today. At least four aspects can be discerned[32]:

(1)   Mission is *being sent out* (especially the Fourth Gospel).

(2)   Mission is *making disciples* of all nations (cf. the Gospel of Matthew).

(3)   Mission is *deliverance and emancipatory action* (cf. the Gospel of Luke).

(4)   Mission is *witness* (especially the Acts of the Apostles and the Fourth Gospel).

Choosing *one* biblical concept as the focus for a study on the "biblical foundations for mission" is bound to lead to distortions, since the New Testament comprises a variety of missionary theologies and approaches.[33]

The present study attempts to do justice to this plurality. Yet a certain selection of perspectives and issues is inevitable. I shall conclude this introduction by indicating some limitations of my work.

a. The greatest demarcation is that there is no section on mission in the Old Testament. It would therefore be misleading to characterize the book as a biblical theology of mission. The limitation to the New Testament is primarily due to the size of the book. Moreover, the New Testament is the most important source for a Christian theology of mission.

b. Some readers would perhaps miss a special section on Jesus and mission. However, such a section would not correspond to the idea of this study, which is an examination of various New Testament writings and their missiology. To be sure, the "omission" of such a chapter is not due to a scepticism as to say something about the historical Jesus. On the contrary, in my estimation Jesus' proclamation of God's kingdom and the boundary-breaking nature of his ministry is foundational for mission in the New Testament. This is also reflected in the Gospels. They are both a *window* to the historical Jesus and a *mirror* of the life and thinking of each evangelist and his community.

c. A few New Testament books are not examined. This includes the letter to the Hebrews, the Johannine letters and the Pastoral letters (cf. the introduction to chapter 8).

18

Notes

1   For the following description of the relation between text and interpreter see also Bosch 1986.
2   Cf. Levison & Pope-Levison 1995, 329-330.
3   See Gadamer 1990, 101-121 and 293-326; Thiselton 1980, 10-23.
4   Cf. Soares-Prabhu 1986, 86.
5   Without this interaction we will have a "theology from above" which neglects the present contexts of mission, or we will have a "theology from below" which uses the Bible to illustrate and validate a predetermined activity. There is a need for a perspective simultaneously involving a view from above and from below. Cf. van Engen 1996, 37-41.
6   See Weber 1989, 25-26.
7   Cf. Acthemeyer 1980, 128.
8   Weber n.d, 13. For further reflections see also Nissen 1984, 121-124.
9   Cf. Green 1995, 413.
10 Nolan 1977, 4.
11 Costas 1979, 24. Italics added.
12 Cf. Green 1995, 417.
13 Cf. Swartley 1983, 183ff.
14 Cf. Vanhoozer 1995, 317.
15 Bosch 1986, 76.
16 For this distinction see Ricoeur 1973, espec. 194-195.
17 Bosch 1991 and Arias (& Johnson) 1992. These works from two missiologists have been very helpful for the present study.
18 Bosch 1991, 187.
19 To the problem of analogy between two historical situations and the question of a correlation see McDonald, 1993, 224-227. – Seldom will any biblical context be fully analogues to any modern situation. We would prefer to speak of putting biblical materials and modern situations into dialogue rather than into analogues. Cf. Birch & Rasmussen 1976, 194.
20 Cf. Legrand 1990, 6-7.
21 Cf. Soares-Prabhu 1986, 87.
22 Bosch 1991, 8.
23 For further reflections on this issue see chapter 9 of this study.
24 Cf. Dunn 1977, 32.
25 Quoted from the Bristol report on hermeneutics (Faith and Order) entitled "The Significance of the Hermeneutical Problem for the Ecumenical Movement", published in The Bible 1980, 32.
26 Cf. Spindler 1995, 125.
27 For further reflections on *Missio Dei* see chapter 9, III.3.
28 Spindler 1995, 126.

29 For a helpful discussion of the relation between "mission" and "evangelism" see Bosch 1991, 409-419; Klaiber 1997, 24-27. Both authors perceive mission to be wider than evangelism. Bosch, however, presents a theology of mission, while Klaiber investigates the biblical call for "conversion" in the sense of personal decision in evangelism and discusses questions of pastoral care and ecclesiology that arise following conversion.

30 This comprehensive understanding of mission is often defined by the threefold task of the church: witness (*martyria*), service (*diakonia*) and communion (*koinonia*).

31 See, for instance, Senior & Stuhlmueller 1983, 2.

32 Cf. Spindler 1995, 127-131.

33 Cf. Legrand 1990, 5-7; Bosch 1986, 67-68.

2.

Mission as disciple-making:
The Gospel of Matthew

Introduction

Any description of mission in the Gospel of Matthew must begin with the so-called "Great Commission" in Matt 28:16-20. It is also commonly assumed that this text has offered the most powerful motivation for mission throughout the centuries. However, it has been demonstrated that it was not used as basis for mission until the end of the 17th century.[1]

But the fact that Matt 28:16-20 is considered to be *the* most important mission text has to some extent complicated the understanding of it.[2] The text is often taken out of its context and read as an autonomous decree which speaks directly to our own situation. Where this occurs, the Great Commission is easily degraded to a mere slogan, or used as a pretext for what we have in advance decided, perhaps unconsciously, it should mean.

Such a reading of the text is based on questionable exegesis because it ignores the results of the critical study of the Gospels, which have shown convincingly that Matt 28:16-20, as it now stands, is a composition of the evangelist. In fact, the text is a summary of – and a key to understanding – the entire Gospel.[3]

I. A Re-reading of the "Great Commission"

1. The term "mission command"
The use of the text in modern time has obscured the original meaning in two directions. The first relates to the use of the definite article in *the* "Great Commission", a misleading term, since there are at least four different versions of the "last commission" (Matt 28:16-20; Mark 16:14-20; Luke 24:44-47; and John 20:19-23). In addition there is a reference to a mission command in the pre-Easter material in the Gospels, e.g. Matt 10:5-16.

Furthermore, the idea that Matt 28:16-20 is a *command* must be challenged.[4] Protestant mission has often emphasized in a one-sided manner *obedience* as a motive for mission. However, the parallels in Luke 24 and John 20 are not to be interpreted as commands. If the last commission is interpreted thus, it is easily placed in the context of legalism. Mission is then depersonalized and the "command" soon becomes a marching order of a Christian militia, engaged in a holy war.

When the first Christians did engage in mission, it was simply an expression of the inner law of their lives. It has been argued convincingly that the early Christian mission was an essential result of Pentecost,[5] the event that was its driving force.

The "debt" (or "obligation") which Paul had to Greeks and non-Greeks alike (Rom 1:14) was the debt of *gratitude*, not of duty. In the same way mission in Matt 28 must be seen as a *consequence* of Jesus' authority: "To me is given..."

2. Focus on the locality or the task?

The second point is connected to the understanding of the words "Go therefore and make disciples..." The phrase "go therefore" has acquired particular importance in Western missionary thinking. Some scholars emphasize the imperative element, e.g. J. Blauw: "The fact that this *participium* is put first...places the emphasis on going, on travelling. One will have to pass Israel's boundaries consciously and intentionally to be able to fulfil the order".[6]

The participle is probably a redundant auxiliary participle, of a kind frequent in Semitic writings added for emphasis or style, but with no denotative value whatever.[7] The accent of the command is not on the going out: "The image is rather one of a teacher seated and imparting instruction than that of a messenger coursing to the furthest corner of the earth".[8] "Make disciples" is the imperative and carries the main emphasis.[9] The commandment bears on the *formation of disciples*, not on their departure.

But due to the standard Western translations of the Greek participle *poreuthentes* as "Go ye (therefore)!", a peculiar conception of mission developed.[10] The emphasis tended to be on the "going" rather than on the "making disciples". The locality, not the task, determined whether one was a missionary or not; a missionary was a person who was sent by an agency in one locality to go and work in another. The greater distance between these two places, the clearer it was that the individual was a missionary.

If, however, we translate *poreuthentes* not as a separate command, but as adding emphasis and urgency to *matheteusate* ("make disciples"), a different picture of mission emerges. It then refers to bringing people to Jesus as Lord, wherever they may be. Mission then loses its preoccupation with the geographical component and becomes mission in six continents.

What I have argued so far is that both *poreuthentes* and *matheteusate* refer to *one* event. This is also clear from the structure of the Great Commission. The text has the form of a three-step proclamation:

a.   A revelatory statement: "All authority..." (v. 18).

b.   A mission command: "go(ing) therefore...make disciples of all the nations...baptizing them...teaching them..." (vv. 19-20a).

c.   A concluding promise: "I am with you always..." (v. 20b).

In what follows I shall not give a detailed analysis of Matt 28:16-20. Instead I shall try to discuss various questions relevant to the issue of mission in the Gospel of Matthew and in so doing I shall discuss other mission texts in the Gospel.

II. Mission in Matthew: Its motivations and content

1. All authority
It is natural to begin with the question of the motivations for mission. Here the christological thrust of the summary must be noticed. Jesus dominates all its three steps in the final commission. It is *his* authority which is the basis of mission. Mission means to teach what *he* has commanded. And it is sustained by *his* supportive presence.[11]

The word authority (Greek: *eksousia*) plays a significant role in Matt 28:16-20. What is new in relation to the Gospel narrative is not the fact of Jesus' authority, but its extension: now he is invested with all the authority of the Father and reigns over "heaven and earth", i.e. over the total reality. Jesus' authority manifests itself in action in very specific ways.[12] In Matthew's Gospel *eksousia* is the power to:

a.   teach authoritatively about God's will, esp. 5:17-48; 7:28-29;

b.   forgive sins and re-establish community with God, 9:6;

c.   cast out demons, heal all sickness, re-establish the physical integrity of people, 10:1; cf. 9:35;

d.   (this power) is given to the disciples. esp. ch. 10 (and to men: 9:8).

The setting of the Great Commission is important. The story takes place on a mountain, the common place of revelation in Matthew. Here it signifies the place where Jesus manifests his authority as Son of God and the kingdom of heaven breaks into human history through incarnation. The mountain is mentioned in other texts as well.[13] Of special interest is the reference to the mountain in the temptation story in 4:1-11.

2. Two mission strategies in conflict
It is suggestive to compare the Great Commission in Matt 28 with this temptation story. What Satan proposes in Matt 4 is an effective missionary strategy with miracles and public relations that would prove Jesus' divine uniqueness beyond all question. But Jesus says no. In Matthew this encounter has a special dimension, for in a sense all the things that Satan suggests and the offers he makes will come to pass – in due time, and for others![14]

There are some striking parallels to Matt 28:16-20:[15] in both cases we find the motif of the mountain. Similarly we find the word to "give" indicating the origin of power. In both texts the power question is addressed, "authority, power", being used in one case, and the "kingdom" in the other. Both make the universal aspect essential (cf. the use of the word "all") and finally, in both passages the verb "to fall on one's knees, to adore" appears.

Thus, we have placed at the beginning and at the end of Jesus' ministry two texts which describe alternative understandings of his mission as Son of God, alternative methods to incarnate the kingdom of heaven. One is the *devil's strategy*: Satan proposes to Jesus that he manifest his divine sonship and the kingly authority of the Father by ruling the whole earth as its new political overlord, dominating all kingdoms of the world. Jesus could thus *impose* God's kingdom and justice by means of political power, introduce theocracy, and avoid the suffering of the cross. No freedom is left for people in this strategy; they would submit to Jesus in the same way as they now submit to political kings (Matt 20:20-28). And that kind of power would have its origin in the "gift" from Satan and would be available to Jesus only if he adored the devil.

Jesus' answer is absolutely clear and allows for no compromise: *God's strategy* and will is not that Jesus be a political, a theocratic, a triumphant Messiah – as many people, even the disciples, expected (cf. Matt 16:21-23). The mission of Jesus, the Son of God, who is also the expected king of Israel, is to manifest and incarnate God's kingdom by reigning not from above – as the devil suggests – but as Immanuel, as "God with us" (Matt 1:23; 28:20). The resurrection does not install Jesus "above" us as King or Lord or heavenly Son, but confirms that he is Son of God as Immanuel, as king dwelling among us.[16]

God's strategy differs from that of the devil in its conception of suffering and misery.[17] In the first temptation Jesus is asked to change stones into bread. The words in Matt 4:4 are uttered *by* a hungry person. They are *not* addressed to hungry persons. As noted by K. Stendahl: "Jesus answered: 'Human beings do not live by bread alone', but he never said that to hungry people. Them he fed".[18] By rejecting the temptation of the devil, Jesus acts in solidarity with those who hunger. He himself lived at subsistence level.

The central message of the second and third temptation could be summarized in a similar way. Thus the second temptation points forward to the cross, cf. the mocking words of the bypassers at the cross, Matt 27:42: "He saved others; he cannot save himself". This is the temptation to forget the cross and not to show solidarity with those who suffer. Matt 4:5-7 reflects the idea that the Kingdom of God cannot be implemented by mighty and triumphalist acts. The Kingdom of God has been inaugurated in the *suffering* of Christ – in his solidarity with all those who suffer.

In short, Jesus was tempted to abuse his strength, his gifts, his relation to the Father. It was the temptation of triumphalism, forgetting or bypassing the cross.

3. Jesus' compassion for the harassed and helpless

According to Matthew mission is also motivated in Jesus' compassion. From the beginning Matthew underscores the real nature of Jesus' Messiahship. He is "*God with us*" (1:23). He is with his people in their suffering (cf. 8:17) and prayer (18:20).

The same idea of his presence is also stressed in the final words of the resurrected Christ, who promises to be *with* his disciples to the end of the world (28:20). Jesus' presence among people takes the form of compassion.[19] This is a dominant motif in chs. 8 and 9 where Matthew has a number of healing stories. He concludes this section with a summary statement on the teaching and healing of Jesus (9:35), adding: "When he saw the crowds, he had compassion for them, because they were harassed and helpless, like sheep without shepherd" (9:36).

It is this compassion which constitutes the basis of his mission. In the following chapter Matthew records that Jesus sent the twelve disciples to Israel (10:5-16). Furthermore, it is evident that this compassion goes beyond sentiment. Jesus had a messianic mission to the common people which consisted of liberating them from their suffering and their fatalistic resignation to suffering.[20]

By putting the missionary charge immediately after 9:36 Matthew indicates that the disciples in their mission must share the compassion of Jesus for the lost sheep.[21] This is entirely in line with the parable in 25:31-46, which insists that the nations of the world will meet Jesus when they deal with his hungry, thirsty, persecuted, sick, imprisoned, and naked "brethren".

4. The content of mission: God's kingdom and his justice

What then is the content of mission? According to Matt 28:20 the disciples are to teach others "to obey everything that I have commanded you". But where are the disciples and the readers to find everything that Jesus has commanded? The verb "command" (*entellesthai*) occurs here in the aorist, so the reference is not to a *new* revelation, but to what the earthly Jesus has already taught his followers. G. Bornkamm rightly notes that the resurrected and elevated One makes the word of the earthly Jesus normative for the church of all times until the end of the world.[22]

For Matthew teaching is by no means merely intellectual enterprise – as it was for the ancient Greeks and is for us. Jesus' teaching is an appeal to his listeners' will, not primarily to their intellect; it is a call for a concrete decision to follow him and to submit to God's will.[23]

What, then, is God's will? Particularly two texts are illustrative. The first one is the double love commandment, 22:34-40. Notice also the similarity of language between the Great Commission and the story of the rich young man (19:17): "If you wish to enter into life, keep (*tereson*) the commandments (*tas entolas*)".

The second passage is the Sermon on the Mount, which indicates that discipleship for Matthew means the willingness to live according to the ethics of the Kingdom. The disciples are to seek God's kingdom and his justice (6:33). The two key concepts are the kingdom and the justice (or righteousness). God's kingdom means a life of righteousness and justice which surpasses the life practised by the Pharisees (5:20). The exhortation to love our enemies forms the culmination of Jesus' ethic of God's kingdom (5:43-48). This exhortation more than any other command reflects the true nature of Jesus' boundary-breaking ministry.

The Greek word used for "righteousness" or "justice" (*dikaiosyne*) is not exhausted at the personal level of spirituality and behaviour. It has to do with the social order of God in the world. "God's will on earth as in heaven", includes what social order of God in the world. "God's will on earth as in heaven", includes what we today call the "structures" of society. So mission has to do with justice – in persons, communities, and nations.[24]

It is clear from these and other texts (e.g. 25:31-46) that we cannot do without the neighbour. As J. Matthey says, "According to Matthew's Great Commission, it is not possible to make disciples without telling them to practice God's request of justice for the poor. The love commandment, which is *the* basis for the churches' involvement in politics, is an integral part of the mission commandment".[25]

III. The subjects and addressees of mission

1. Missionary discipleship

Who are the subjects or carriers of mission according to Matthew? The theme of discipleship is central to Matthew's Gospel and to his understanding of the church and mission. The verb *matheteuein* only occurs four times in the New Testament (13:52; 27:57; 28:19 and Acts 14:21). The dominant assertion in Matt 28:19 is that disciples are to be made.[26] The two participles "baptizing" and "teaching" are clearly subordinate to "make disciples".

In Matt 28:19-20 the concept of discipleship has a double meaning. On the one hand it characterizes a Christian existence after Easter; on the other hand it points back to the pre-Easter period. This twofold aspect can be described in the following way: Discipleship before Easter is the model for discipleship after Easter just as Jesus himself is the model for the first disciples (cf. 10:24-25).

Matthew conceived mission not as a course of indoctrination but as an incorporation of ever new members into the *learning community.*[27] Discipleship after Easter has to be inspired by what it meant to be a disciple before Easter, which implied: vicarious poverty, a greater righteousness, the way to the cross by acknowledging and following the one who lived and interpreted the will of God.

The content and conditions of discipleship in the lifetime of Jesus are illustrated most clearly in the mission discourse in Matt 10:1-42.[28] In its essence it probably reflects the historical Jesus, although part of the discourse also is marked by the situation of the Matthean community.[29]

The mandate given to the disciples in ch. 10 includes a call for poverty and simple lifestyle. What is demanded from Jesus is an attitude: freedom from acquisitiveness (mission must not become a source of gain) and a trust in providence so absolute that it can wholly dispense with even the minimum of material resources. Poverty and powerlessness are for Matthew an absolutely indispensable part of Christian mission.[30]

To become a disciple of Jesus *after Easter* involves sharing with him his death and resurrection on his march to the final revelation of his messianic kingdom. He commands his followers to make disciples; that is, to move them to surrender to his liberating authority and to volunteer for the march already en route to a new order of things, namely his kingdom.[31]

2. The church as mission

The mission discourse in ch. 10 and the final commission in ch. 28 are usually considered to be the two most important mission texts in the first Gospel. Matt 5:13-16 is a third text the significance of which for Matthew's theology of mission has largely been overlooked.

In this passage the disciples are described as the salt of the earth and the light of the world. The words in 5:13-16 are not just to individual followers of Jesus but to the Christian community as a whole. The ultimate basis of the church's mission is the witness of its community life and praxis. This mission is fulfilled first of all by living visibly as the church. The text also shows that genuine mission will lead people to give glory to God (5:16).[32]

The church has a central role in Matthew's theology. He is the only one among the evangelists to use the word *ekklesia* (16:18; cf. 18:17). The church is the subject of mission – not only in the sense that it proclaims the gospel, but also in the sense that it lives it. This does not mean that Matthew conceives of the church as an ideal community. It is a church where the "weeds" are together with the "wheat" (13:24-30), a church where there are hypocrites, false prophets (7:15; 24:11), and false messiahs (24:24).

It seems as if the church which was called for mission had many internal problems.[33] That God can use such a fragile fellowship in his mission is something of a miracle.[34] This miracle has to do with the promise which concludes the last commission: "I am with you always, to the end of the age".

3. The Jews and the nations

Finally we must ask who are the addressees of mission? In the final commission they are identified as "all nations" (28:19). This term is commonly interpreted universally as referring to all people. Some scholars, however, have questioned this interpretation, suggesting that the words "all nations" (*panta ta ethne*) refer to all people excluding the Jews. In that case Matthew is envisaging the termination of any missionary effort among the Jews to concentrate exclusively on the Gentiles.

Although the term *ethnos* ("nation") is used almost exclusively of Gentiles in other parts of the Gospel, it is unlikely that Matthew excludes the Jews altogether. The effect of Jesus' death and resurrection is that all the boundaries have fallen back. Now "all nations" have access to the gospel of the Kingdom. So the Jews are included among "all the nations". But they are no longer a specially privileged people.[35]

4. The centripetal and the centrifugal mission

There are other problems in defining the addressees of mission. The universality of the final commission contrasts strikingly with the particularity of the mission instruction in Matt 10:5-6: "Go nowhere among the Gentiles...", and with Jesus' words in 15:24: "I was sent only to the lost sheep of the house of Israel".

Many attempts have been made to solve this contradiction.[36] The best solution is probably to suppose that Matthew is operating with a two-stage scheme of salvation history implying two stages in the mission of Jesus.[37] The mission of the

27

earthly Jesus is a centripetal mission directed to Israel in the hope that the conversion of his people will inaugurate the "eschatological pilgrimage of nations to the mountain of God" (cf. Isa 2:2; Mic 4:1) and so lead to the salvation of the world.[38]

But the Jews reject this mission (cf. 21:33-46; 22:1-14).[39] Their rejection reaches its climax in the passion narrative, when the "whole people" rejects Jesus as the Messiah (27:25). This leads to the death of Jesus, marking the end of his centripetal mission to Israel. But the vindication of that death by God through the resurrection invests Jesus with "all authority in heaven and on earth" (28:16) and opens the way for a universal post-Easter mission to all nations (28:18-20).

Throughout the whole Gospel, Matthew presents Jesus both as the *Messiah for the Jews* (e.g. 2:2-6; cf. 10:5-6; 15:24) and as the *Messiah for the nations* (e.g. 4:15-16; cf. 2:1-12; 8:5-13). The double christology points to the double target of mission addressees.[40] The kingdom of God is for everybody, for those originally invited and for later arrivals (22:1-10). In the kingdom there are no exclusions – except self-exclusion. If there are those "called" but not "chosen" it is because of their rejection (8:12; 22:5-6) or unfaithfulness or fruitlessness (21:43).

Matthew never says that Jesus actually took the initiative to go out to the Gentiles. They approach him, not he them – the magi, the centurion of Capernaum, the Canaanite woman. Thus the centripetal mission has the character of an *invitation*.[41] Jesus replaces Jerusalem. It is an invitation to share in his blessings, and the invitation is for all: "Come to me, all you that are weary and are carrying heavy burdens, and I will give you rest" (11:28).

The community is called to make disciples of all nations. This task is to be carried out both centripetally, as others are attracted by the community's life of "good works" (5:16), and centrifugally, as disciples go out in active mission to others (so the commission of 28:18-20 which reaffirms and expands on the instructions in ch. 10).[42]

The transition from Matt 10:5-6 to Matt 28:18-20 has often been understood as if Jesus proceeded from a mission to Israel to a mission to the nations – that is as a kind of quantitative augmentation, or a transition from "home" mission" to "foreign" mission. This understanding, however, neglects the fact that to the restriction placed on mission in Matt 10 there is also added an alternative: "go rather to the lost sheep of the house of Israel" (10:6). This means that the mission of Jesus was from the outset intended to go beyond the frontiers to "the miserable ones", to those who were held in no esteem and even were of bad reputation.[43]

5. The little ones

The emphasis on Jesus' partiality for those who are down and lost can be observed throughout the first Gospel. According to Matthew, it was Jesus major motive for mission, cf. 9:36. This movement to compassion in Jesus' heart led to the double movement of mission: the centripetal coming of the little ones, and the centrifugal sending of the disciples.[44]

In God's strange economy *the little ones* are assigned a particular priority both as the objects and as the subjects of mission.[45] The little ones include the poor (5:3;

28

11:5; 19:21), the children (18:2-5; 19:14-15), the weary and overburdened (11:28), "the least ones of all" (25:40.45) and several others. The special concern of Jesus and Matthew for these people means not only that they are not excluded as the addressees of discipleship in the kingdom, but also that they are in fact the privileged addressees of the Great Commission. Universality passes through the particularity of the weakest and the smallest ones in humankind. Globalization is inseparable from contextualization.[46]

IV. Hermeneutical Perspectives

The concept of mission in Matthew's Gospel represents a challenge to recent tendencies in missiology. What then are the hermeneutical consequences of the texts? Besides the critical remarks in the introduction I want to point at the following hermeneutical perspectives.

1. Evangelism and Christian education
Matthew's model of mission has rightly been characterized as "mission as disciple-making" (Bosch), "the mission that makes disciples" (Legrand) or "the Matthean didactic paradigm" (Arias). This didactic model is a challenge to modern conceptions.

We are used to considering mission (or evangelism) and Christian education as two separate activities. While mission is seen as the out-reach activity of the church, Christian education has to do with the inner life of the community.

The idea that evangelism and Christian education are separate in the mission and ministry of the church cannot be derived from the Great Commission. According to Matthew, mission has a catechetical character. Christian education is already evangelism and should be carried out evangelistically. It is no less than the evangelization of each generation, learning together the way of the Kingdom, in a community of disciples, at each stage in life and throughout all of the experiences of life, and in each particular context. Disciples are not born, they are made, and it takes a whole lifetime, with no graduation in sight.[47]

2. Mission – not manipulation[48]
The comparison between the third temptation in Matt 4 and the Great Commission in Matt 28 raises the question: what is the difference between Jesus' rejection of "all the kingdoms of the world and their splendour" (4:8) and his acceptance of "all authority in heaven and on earth" (28:18)?

The satanic temptation is to use a power which is imposed on people. This is manipulation or propaganda. Authentic mission works in a different way. Since it is based on the power of love it presupposes the freedom of the recipient to accept or reject the message, whereas the manipulation denotes an attitude which do not respect the freedom of the recipient. Instead he or she is reduced to a mere object of the message[49].

This distinction between authentic mission and manipulation is related to another distinction – that between a "good master" and a "bad master".[50] The two masters adopt a different attitude to their disciples.

The good master is not interested in a yesman. His message must form the life of the disciples in such a way that they are liberated and will grow in freedom. Contrary to this the bad master has only supporters who are thoroughly dependent on all his words and acts. They are unfree and controlled by him. They become like copies of their master.

A mission which makes the recipient to a copy of the missionary is criticized by Jesus in Matt 23:15: "Woe to you, scribes and Pharisees, hypocrites! For you cross see and land to make a single convert, and you make the new convert twice as much a child of hell as yourselves". A different form of mission is described in the Great Commission in Matt 28:18-20.

The charismatic leader, because of his strongly personal charisma, tends to exercise absolute, personal control over his followers. This is strikingly evident in Hinduism where the guru identifies with the deity itself and calls for the total surrender of the disciples to the Master.[51]

Is the teaching of Jesus of this kind? There is no doubt that we find in it apodictical statements of great power uttered with an authority that goes beyond the authority of the Old Testaments prophets speaking in the name of Yahweh (e.g. Matt 5:21-47). It is certain too that Jesus demanded from his followers an unswerving fidelity to his person, outweighing all other human values and ties: a demand quite unparalleled in the history of his people (e.g. Matt 10:37). In that sense the authority of Jesus is charismatic in nature. To a certain extent it resembles the authority of a guru.

However, freedom was a value for Jesus – precisely because his teaching was not so much the imparting of "sound doctrine" as the communication of a message of love. But there can be no love without freedom – that is why there is always a dialogical element in the teaching of Jesus, a profound respect for the interlocutor, rare in the utterances of charismatic teachers. This appears strikingly in the characteristic form that Jesus chose for his teaching – his parables. The parable is an essentially open-ended, dialogical form. At the same time it is a critical teaching: The listener's world is turned upside-down.[52]

It should also be noted that being a disciple of Jesus does not signify that one has, as it were, arrived. In several parables there is a call to constant vigilance which is intended as a warning against any possible self-exaltation.

3. Mission in Christ's way
The location of Matt 4:1-11 indicates that Jesus right from the beginning of his ministry refused three temptations in his messianic mission: (a) "Feeding the hungry"; (b) "Being spectacular" and (c) "Pursuing political power".[53]

Before Jesus began his public ministry, he was struggling with what that ministry was going to be, and how it was to be carried out. "What came out are certain parameters for mission, his and ours. We know that Jesus turned water into wine and that he fed thousands of people with five loaves and two fish. Yet in the wilderness he refused to turn stone into bread as a characteristic of his mission. We also know that Jesus once walked on water. But he would not jump to safety from a high place in order to offer a spectacular demonstration of his mission. In order to draw the world to himself, Jesus did bow his head. But only on the cross, not in front of the offerings of power and wealth. Today we may not find it easy to contextualize these parameters. But that there are parameters for mission is something the churches must recognize".[54]

The ecumenical document "Mission and Evangelism" (1982) has a paragraph entitled "Mission in Christ's way". It makes the point that an imperialistic crusader's spirit was foreign to Christ. Then it continues: "Churches are free to choose the ways they consider best to announce the Gospel to different people in different circumstances. But these options are never neutral. Every methodology illustrates or betrays the Gospel we announce. In all communications of the Gospel, power must be subordinate to love".[55]

These words may be seen as a critical commentary to the way in which Matt 28:18-20 has been used in the past by colonial missions and still is used today by some mission agencies. Whatever qualities of dedication and compassion individual missionaries may have shown, the colonial mission was part of a grim scenario.[56] Too often it treated people as objects to be converted, rather than as persons created in the image of God.

According to the Japanese theologian K. Koyama this crusader's spirit has changed Christianity into a one-way-traffic-religion. "Often this one-way set-up has been justified by simply quoting the Great Commission of the Risen Lord: 'Go therefore...' (Matt 28:19-20). I do not understand this powerful sentence as an authorization for 'one-way-traffic'. I believe it calls for 'Christ-like-going'. Take note that it says not just 'go' but 'go therefore', that is to say, go on the basis of the life and ministry of Jesus Christ, his love, his self-denial, his hope, his death, his resurrection. Only so are we to make disciples of all nations".[57]

In this interpretation the 'Christ-like going' is not 'one-way-traffic'. It is intensely two-ways. And in this two-way-traffic situation with his people, Jesus gave up his right of way (cf. Matt 20:28).

The church is called to follow Christ's example. Mission in Christ's way means that we must read Matt 28:18-20 together with such texts as Matt 27:41-42 (the temptation on the cross) and with Matt 16:24-25 – where Jesus tells his disciples: "If any want to become my followers, let them deny themselves and take up their cross and follow me". It means that the "crusading mind" has to be replaced by the "crucified mind".[58]

The Great Commission in Matt 28 read in the light of Matt 4:1-11 is to be understood not as a mandate to an aggressive militant mission, obsessed with "making disciples" ("church growth") but as an invitation to "follow Jesus" in mission (church life). Such a following of Jesus can never be a "crusade", an act of violence against religions and cultures, but always as an acting of loving service, carried out in poverty and powerlessness, in dependence on God and in conflict and eventually in persecution (cf. the mission discourse in Matt 10:1-42). Mission, then, is not to be imaged as a "conquest" (winning the world for Christ), nor as a "sale" (selling the gospel), but as light which illuminates the darkness or as salt which gives savour (Matt 5:13-16).[59]

Today we would perhaps speak about "the temptation of secularization, of using worldly means and methods, Madison Avenue techniques for selling the gospel. We all know that it works. But we should learn: one does not sell Jesus as one sells toothpaste. There is the cross, there is the mystery. And there is God's time, the right time."[60] However, the gospel is not for sale, not because it is not worth anything, but because it is too precious. It is so precious that it cannot be bought or sold. It can only be shared freely.[61]

4. Justice as an integral part of mission

As mentioned previously we should not allow ourselves to choose between "righteousness" and "justice" when seeking for the meaning of *dikaiosyne*. Maybe we should translate this term with "justice-righteousness", in an attempt to hold on to both dimensions.[62] According to Matthew justice is the goal of discipleship. He insists on a "higher justice" that exceeds that of the scribes and Pharisees (5:20) "To announce a gospel that is not proclaiming and demanding this 'higher justice' and that ignores or postpones the highest priority of love in God's action is a serious departure from the 'Great Commission,' which sends us back to 'everything Jesus commanded.' "[63]

Particularly in our contemporary world of violence and counter-violence, of oppression from the right and the left, of the rich getting richer and the poor poorer, it is imperative for the church-in-mission to include the "higher justice" of the Sermon on the Mount in its missionary agenda. "Its mission cannot concern itself exclusively with the personal, inward, spiritual and 'vertical' aspects of people's life."[64]

5. The church as mission

One aspect of the Gospel of Matthew which is of crucial importance for the church today is the vision of the church as a visible community of salt and light.

Mission is not only verbal proclamation but healing action as well (cf. Matt 4:32; 9:35), and it strives not just for "church growth" (as if the church were an end in itself) but for the wholeness of creation, that is, for the total and integral liberation of human and cosmic history into the fulness of the eschatological Kingdom (Matt 10:7).[65]

If there are to be Christian disciples in the future, they will need to be made, not simply born. The church, in fact, needs to see itself as Matthew saw it: as a distinct and appealing counter-culture, a city set on a hill, making visible the reality of God's reign in the midst of the old order: a community concerned not so much to root out the weeds in its midst as to cultivate wheat of such quality that others will see it, "and give glory to your Father in heaven" (cf. 5:16).[66]

6. Christ's presence among the little ones

A number of incidents and sayings in the first Gospel emphasize the astonishing fact that the messianic king and son of David had come in lowliness and poverty.

The most famous of these passages is the parable of the last judgment (25:31-46), according to which Christ identifies himself totally with the most miserable among our fellow humans.

In this story the poor and needy are seen as bearers of Christ's presence: "Anything you did for one of my brothers here, however humble, you did for me" (25:40; NEB) There is a debate about "the least of my brethren."[67] Are they disciples or all the poor and outcasts? Superficially Matthew's use of "brethren" might suggest the former and so support a more exclusive reference. There are, however, other factors that need to be taken into account that suggest a more inclusive reference. The most important of these is that at heart of Matthew's christology is the deliberate identification of "God-with-us" with the powerless and the weak rather than the strong.[68]

This text plays a significant role in recent missiology, especially in the theology of liberation. Thus, J. Miguez-Bonino points out that the poor belong to the understanding of the very nature of the church. Therefore, if the identity of the church is to be found in Christ (*ubi Christus, ibi ecclesia*), then we must pay attention to the fact that Christ said that he would be present when his words were remembered and the meal shared, and that he would be present in the poor and the oppressed. The problem is that the church today does not recognize itself in the poor. But this situation is one of lost identity. The church which is not the church of the poor puts in serious jeopardy its churchly character.[69] Christians from the poor countries put a critical question to those among us who live in the rich countries:[70] How did you meet Christ in your needy neighbours? Where did you recognize his face?

Notes

1   Cf. Newbigin 1987, 32.
2   Cf. Bosch 1991, 57; Soares-Prabhu, 1994, 271-272.
3   See, for instance, Bornkamm 1964; Michel 1950/51.
4   Bosch 1983, 219-220; Soares-Prabhu 1994, 272-273.
5   Boer 1961; Allen 1962.
6   Blauw 1962, 86.
7   Matthew frequently uses the verb *poreuomai* in this auxiliary sense, with no distinct meaning of its own; so, for instance, 2:8; 9:13; 11:4.
8   Legrand 1990, 79.
9   Cf. Kasting 1969, 36.
10   Cf. Bosch 1983, 229-230.
11   Cf. Soares-Prabhu 1993, 72.
12   Cf. Matthey 1980, 166-167.
13   This includes among others Matt 5-7 where Jesus teaches and preaches the Kingdom and Matt 17:1-13 where he reveals his glory (the transfiguration).
14   Stendahl 1980, 79.
15   See Matthey 1980, 163-164.

16 Cf. Matthew 1980, 166. See also Nissen 1984, 30.
17 Nissen 1984, 36-37.
18 Stendahl 1980, 79.
19 For further reflections on this issue see Nissen 1984, 64-65; 153-154.
20 Cf. Nolan 1977, 36.
21 Nissen 1984, 47.
22 Bornkamm 1964, 187.
23 Cf. Frankemölle 1982, 127-128.
24 Cf. Arias & Johnson 1992, 25.
25 Matthey 1980, 171.
26 Cf. Legrand 1990, 79.
27 According to Weber 1971, 58-61, discipleship in Matthew´s Gospel is "the way of those called and elected for mission".
28 For a discussion of this passage see Park 1995; Brown 1977.
29 Nissen 1984, 46-47.
30 Cf. Soares-Prabhu 1993, 80-81.
31 Cf. Verkuyl 1978, 107.
32 Cf. Soares-Prabhu 1994, 278-279.
33 Cf. Arias & Johnson 1992, 34.
34 Cf. Matt 28:17, which can be translated as asserting either that *some* disciples doubted or that *all* doubted. Following many commentators I prefer the latter translation. Cf. Matthey 1980, 165: "It is precisely those disciples who submit themselves to him but still have fundamental doubts that Jesus sends out in mission".
35 Cf. Senior & Stuhlmueller 1983, 252.
36 See, for instance, Hahn 1965, 26-28; Frankemölle 1982, 100-102. Bosch 1991, 60.
37 Cf. Soares-Prabhu 1994, 69.
38 Cf. Jeremias 1958, 55-73.
39 On the motif of rejection see Senior & Stuhlmueller 1983, 245-246. The rejection of Israel becomes the paradoxical opening to the nations.
40 Cf. Arias & Johnson 1992, 30.
41 Cf. the title of H.-R. Weber's book on Matthew's theology of mission.
42 Cf. Donaldson 1996, 46-47.
43 Cf. J. Aagaard 1985, 152. The Greek construction of Matt 10:6 can be rendered in two ways. Either it could mean "to the lost sheep *of* Israel" (a partitive genitive) or it could mean "to the lost sheep, namely Israel". See also my comments in Nissen 1984, 47: "Perhaps the ambiguity of the language is intended so that we could say: Jesus and his first followers were sent to Israel as a whole and therefore especially to the lost sheep *within* Israel."
44 Cf. Weber 1971, 35.
45 Cf. Arias & Johnson 1992, 31-32.
46 Cf. Arias & Johnson 1992, 31. Cf. my reflections in Nissen 1984, 170. 177-179: The option for the poor must be seen within a greater framework, the option for Israel which again must be seen within a greater framework: the option for the whole of mankind. Jesus was a "universalist" (he died for mankind), only because he was a "particularist" (his ministry to Israel). And this "particularism" could only be effected because he was a "particularist" in a specific way: in his option for the poor and the disadvantaged.
47 Cf. Arias & Johnson 1992, 19-20.

48　For further reflections on this and the following section see Nissen 1998.

49　Hammar 1975, 48, suggests that the story of the temptation should be seen as a critique of manipulation and propaganda.

50　For this distinction see Thelle 1991, 90.

51　For further references see Soares-Prabhu 1982, 252.

52　Cf. Soares-Prabhu 1982, 255.

53　For this threefold messianic temptation in mission see the notes by C. van Engen, "Congregation and Mission: Basic Course in Theology of Mission" (a series of lectures given at the University of Copenhagen, January 1997). I owe this reference to H. Raun Iversen, co-leader of the course. For similar observations on the temptation story see Crosby 1977, 163-166.

54　Fung 1989, 5.

55　"Mission and Evangelism" 1982, 439.

56　Cf. Bosch 1991, 302-303.

57　Koyama 1979, 53.

58　Cf. Koyama 1979, 54.

59　Cf. Soares-Prabhu 1993, 86.

60　Stendahl 1980, 79-80.

61　Cf. Fung 1989, 8.

62　Cf. Bosch 1991, 71-72. More in detail on the importance of the justice for Matthew's Gospel in Crosby 1988, especially 171ff.

63　Arias & Johnson 1992, 25.

64　Bosch 1991, 70.

65　Soares-Prabhu 1994, 273.

66　Cf. Donaldson 1996, 48.

67　The different opinions are also reflected in the translations. NRSV has "one of the least of these who are members of my family".

68　Cf. Rowland 1995, 174-176; cf. Weber 1971, 43. For arguments in favour of the inclusive understanding see also Nissen 1984, 137-138.

69　Miguez-Bonino 1975, 40-41; cf. de Santa Ana 1977, 20-21.

70　Cf. A. M. Aagaard 1985, 253-254.

3.

Crossing boundaries:
Mission in Mark's Gospel

Introduction

"Go into all the world and proclaim the good news to the whole creation" (Mark 16:15). This text is considered by many to be the mission command par excellence. The command seems to have all the most important elements in mission: Its *content* is summarized in the good news. Its *address* is to the whole world; and its focus is on the *proclamation* as the instrument of mission.

However, the mission command is part of the "longer ending" of Mark (16:9-20), which is an addition intended to bring the conclusion of Mark into line with those of the other Gospels. Moreover, certain promises are added in vv. 16-18: whoever believes and is baptized will be saved; whoever rejects the message will be condemned. And specific signs will accompany those who believe. By using the name of Jesus they will cast out demons; they will speak in tongues; they will pick up snakes in their hands and drink poison unharmed. They are also entrusted with the gift of healing.

Two points should be noticed. First, the "longer ending" contains early Christian tradition which probably gives us an insight into very common and popular views. Similar promises can be found in other parts of the New Testament, e.g. Luke 10:17-19. Doubtless we find in these traditions traces of a "charismatic" oriented mission in early Christianity which may well have formed the background for the work of Paul's opponents in 2 Corinthians.[1]

Second, the vocabulary and theological emphases of these verses run counter to the evangelist's own vocabulary and theology. The "longer ending" promises "signs and wonders", but in Mark 8:11-12 the Pharisees are criticized for demanding "signs". In 13:22-23 Jesus strongly warns his disciples against the "signs and wonders" which are performed by "false Christs and false prophets."[2] Probably both the longer ending and the shorter ending (vv. 9-10) reflect the witness and concerns of churches in the second century, at a time when there was a growing interest in charismatic gifts and miracles.

The genuine Marcan perspective on mission points in another direction. It is an emphasis on the discipleship of the cross (see 8:34-38). W. Klaiber notes that the perspective of the coming mission stands totally under the sign of confessing Jesus even under persecution. The eschatological address in 13:9-14 underlines this. It is not the successive overcoming of Satan by the disciples' authority that forms the horizon for preaching the gospel to all nations, but rather the impending general persecution (13:10).[3]

I. The Kingdom of God and the crossing of boundaries

1. The Gospel as a mission text

The fact that the concluding section with the "Great Commission" is a later addition does not mean that the original form of Mark's Gospel is without mission perspectives. These are especially clear in two ways:

First, Mark's Gospel itself can be seen as a "Great Commission". It is the creation of a new literary genre the aim of which is to communicate the good news of Jesus Christ in narrative form. Jesus and his message are *dynamic*, not static. Mark tells a story which is ongoing. It is a *communication*, involving invitation and response. "The basic story Mark offers his readers is the account of a man driven to communicate a message to others and exercising power on their behalf, even in and through his death."[4]

The ministry of Jesus aims at reaching people. The news spread rapidly, and he was soon spoken of all over the district of Galilee (1:28). The news spread far and wide, and people kept coming to him from all quarters (1:45; 3:7-8). Moreover, Jesus was not alone. Right from the beginning he called his disciples to be fellow-workers (1:16-20).

Secondly, the concepts of *"way" and "journey"* play a significant role in the structure of the Gospel.[5] At the *beginning* of the Gospel John the Baptist is described as proclaiming the "way of the Lord" (1:2-8). The disciples are called to follow the way of Jesus (1:16-20; cf. 2:13-15). Similarly, the disciples in the *middle* of Mark's narrative are moving along a way.[6] Following Jesus means willingness to go the way of the cross (8:34). The disciple with faith is on the way to salvation (10:52).

The *concluding* part of the Gospel confirms the motives of the "way" and "journey". The "way of the Lord", which began in Galilee and moved through opposition, ignorance and even death in Jerusalem will be taken up again by Jesus. At the Last Supper he promises that he will be going before his disciples into Galilee and this promise is reaffirmed to the women at the tomb (14:28; 16:7). So, the risen Jesus will be gathering his community in Galilee in order to continue the way.[7]

The two aspects are closely related to each other. One might even speak of one overall theme: God's kingdom and the "way". In other words, here we have the dual character of Jesus' ministry: invitation and response.

2. The inclusive character of the Kingdom

Mark presents the kingdom of God as the central concept in the proclamation of Jesus. This is made clear in the summary of 1:15: "The time is fulfilled, and the Kingdom of God has come near; repent, and believe in the good news". This verse is the hermeneutical key to the Marcan story and its theology.

The content of the Kingdom is not unfolded by means of a number of Bible references or theological concepts. Instead the reader is invited to follow Jesus on a journey through Galilee. We hear how the Kingdom of God step by step takes hold of people.[8]

Mark emphasizes the powerful acts of Jesus, especially his exorcisms. The first half of the Gospel puts great emphasis on acts and miracles (1:21-8:26). Other characteristic features are Jesus' table fellowship with tax collectors and sinners (2:14-17); his association with lepers (1:40-45); with women (1:30-31; 5:25-34; 12:41-44; 14:3-9; 15:40-41) and with children (10:13-16).

It is noteworthy that Jesus' compassion with these people often led to controversies with those in power. He radically defended the right to life. This is illustrated by the two sabbath conflicts in 2:23-3:6. The stories illustrate a conflict between two understandings of the law. According to Jesus the Pharisees had made the law into a *burden*, whereas it was supposed to be a *service*. For Jesus the sole purpose of the law was the good of human beings. "The sabbath was made for humankind and not humankind for the sabbath" (2:27). The law was but a means, not an end in itself. Where it prevented the satisfaction of a basic need such as hunger, it ceased to have any binding power.

It is significant that Jesus does not relate the observance of the sabbath to the glory and honour of God. He is not saying 'the sabbath is for the honour of God, who alone is the Lord of it.' The reason for his failure to do so can only be that in his eyes the honour of God is the fullness of man, the dignity of man. It is in man's face that the glory of God shines forth.[9] In other words, the will of God is always the dignity of human beings.

If one's own good is sufficient justification for the violation of the sabbath, how much more the good of others. To those who criticized Jesus for healing a man with a withered arm on the sabbath he said: "Is it lawful to do good or to do harm on the sabbath, to save life or to kill?" (3:4). The meaning is clear: If the sabbath is for the good of man, an act of goodness like healing can only be in keeping with the original intention of the law. Any law that forbids doing good to others is by that very fact null and void.[10]

The two stories in 2:23-3:6 indicate that the law has to be the servant of men and women and not their master. Jesus radically defended the right to live. He responded personally, and called his disciples to respond concretely to the most human basic need for food. Jesus used the hermeneutics of life:[11] from the perspective of God's kingdom, there is no more sacred value than human life, and no higher law than human need.

In Mark's Gospel the Kingdom of God is conceived of as boundary crossing. His primary narrative theme is that in Jesus God has intervened human history.[12] In the various manifestations of Jesus' preaching, e.g. the healings, the exorcisms, and the teachings, God's future power invaded and transformed the human present.[13] Jesus' preaching shattered the economic, political, cultic, legal and ethnic boundaries.

3. Crossing boundaries in Galilee

The Gospel of Mark has three major parts. After the prologue in 1:2-13 and the summary of Jesus' proclamation in 1:14-15 comes the first major part in 1:16-8:21, which is a description of his ministry in Galilee. The second part is about the cost of discipleship (8:22-10:52). Although Jesus does not leave Galilean territory until

10:1, the whole section is seen as a journey toward Jerusalem. The scene of the last part is Jerusalem (11:1-16:8).

From this survey it is clear that Galilee has a dominant role in the Gospel. It is here that the chief part of Jesus' kingdom ministry occurs, while Jerusalem is described as a place of opposition, suffering and death. Moreover, the proclamation of the good news is almost exclusively reserved to Galilee. The only two references found in the "Jerusalem" section of the Gospel (13:10; 14:9) refer to *future* preaching to Gentiles.[14]

At that time Galilee was an area of mixed population. It was a cultural crossroads.[15] Because of their impurity Galilean Jews were looked down upon by the Jews from Jerusalem who saw themselves as the heirs of cultural and religious purity. For them "Galilee" was synonymous with "fool"; cf. Nathanael's response in John 1:46. The Marcan Jesus confronted the power centred in Jerusalem with the radical message of the Kingdom of God. If Galilee was the place of the rejected and marginal, Jerusalem represented established power, judgment and death.[16] Not only was it a geographic centre; it was the cultural, social, religious, political, and ideological hub of the entire Jewish world.

L. Legrand has observed that the Galilean ministry represented a frontier ministry. Jesus' activity was all the more peripheral in that it touched especially the humble people, the '*am ha-aretz*', "the people of the land". By proclaiming his gospel in Galilee and to those who lived on the margin of Judaism, Jesus was turning his back on the focus of the life and the expectancies of official Judaism. As Mark 1:38 puts it, Jesus said he must "move on" (NRSV: "go on"). But his moving on was more sociological and religious than geographical.[17]

Galilee symbolizes the universality of the gospel. W. Kelber has drawn attention to the significance of Jesus' journeys around and across the Sea of Galilee. His kingdom ministry on both sides of the lake is Mark's way of depicting the church's mission as inclusive of both Jew and Gentile. "The lake, losing its force as a barrier, is transposed into a symbol of unity, bridging the gulf between Jewish and Gentile Christians. The two are the one. Galilee is no longer ethnically confined to either a Jewish or a Gentile Christian identity, rather "all of Galilee" is where Jewish Christians and Gentile Christians live together in the newness of the Kingdom."[18]

The mission "to the other side" of the lake begins in 4:35 with the story of the sea storm (4:35-41). This is followed by the healing of the demoniac in 5:1-20 which is a mission story taking place in a Gentile territory. The man wanted to be with Jesus (5:19) in the same way as the disciples (3:14). But he was called to a different form of mission: "Go home to your friends, and tell them how much the Lord has done for you, and what mercy he has shown you" (5:19). Thus, he became the first missionary to the Gentiles and the anticipation of the universal model of evangelization by personal witness. "Similar to the conversion of Cornelius in Acts 10, the Gerasene exorcism in Mark 5:1-20 constitutes the crucial watershed of the mission to the Gentiles".[19]

This interpretation of Galilee as the symbol of the universality is reaffirmed in the last part of the Gospel. Jesus will "go before" the disciple "to Galilee" after his

40

resurrection (14:28; cf. 16:7). The community is to be regathered in the very territory where Jesus had first met them and given them a share in his boundary-breaking kingdom ministry. "The community is not to remain in Jerusalem, but to move with renewed awareness and power back to Galilee where the universal mission of the church beckons."[20]

4. Crossing boundaries in Jerusalem

The last part of Jesus' ministry takes place in Jerusalem. Here again we have several examples of his boundary-breaking mission.

In the first place, the story of Jesus' action in the temple is particularly significant. In the pre-Marcan tradition this event might have been seen as a priestly purification of the temple. But in Mark's interpretation, the actions and words of Jesus are a prophetic condemnation of the temple and a signal of a new locus of worship open to Gentiles. Jesus' words "My house shall be called a house of prayer for all the nations" (11:17) has a special emphasis in Mark's Gospel.

Secondly, there is the so-called apocalyptic discourse in Mark 13. This text is another example of the universal character of Jesus' mission: "The good news must first be proclaimed to all nations" (13:10). The time between the existing world and the world to come is characterized as a time for proclamation and witness.

Thirdly, the passion of Jesus is anticipated by a symbolic act: he is anointed by an anonymous woman in Bethany (14:3-9). This woman is depicted as a true disciple. In a sense, what she has done can be characterized as a kind of "Great Commission": "Truly I tell you, wherever the good news is proclaimed in the whole world, what she has done will be told in remembrance of her" (14:9). The remembrance of Jesus is related to the remembrance of this woman. Thereby it is also indicated that the passion narrative had to be a constitutive part of the coming mission.

Fourthly, the curtain of the temple was torn in two from top to bottom (15:39). This is a sign that God's presence is no longer limited to the temple. The admission to God is open for all. The first one to proclaim Jesus as the Son of God is a Gentile centurion!

II. The Kingdom and the way

1. The call to discipleship

Recent scholarship has given considerable attention to Mark's portrayal of the disciples. Some scholars insist that the Gospel was written with a strongly polemical purpose that involved discrediting them as representatives of a type of Christianity.[21] Others view Mark's purpose as being more didactic than polemical and see the disciples' function being to provide the readers with lessons in discipleship. According to this interpretation the failures of the disciples are not intended to invalidate them as fellow disciples with whom the readers associate themselves, but serve as warning examples for the readers.[22]

This latter approach must be recommended. It takes the disciples to be representative figures, symbolic of both positive and negative attitudes in the Marcan community.

The positive role of the disciples is particularly underlined in the account of Jesus' appointment of the Twelve in 3:13-19. Here we have a threefold definition of their function: (1) They are to be specially associated *with Jesus*; (2) they are to be sent out as his emissaries to *proclaim his message*; and (3) they are to exercise his authority in *expelling demons*.[23]

The negative treatment of the disciples is most clearly seen in the passion narratives in chs. 14 and 15. One of them betrays Jesus, and the rest forsake him in cowardice. By contrast, the female followers are depicted more positively (cf. 14:3-9; 15:40-41), although the reference in 16:8 is more ambiguous.

In the central section of the Gospel (8:22-10:52) Mark has linked his teaching on discipleship to three predictions by Jesus of his own suffering, death, and resurrection. Three situations are described and each of these has three components:

(a)   a passion prediction (8:31; 9:31; 10:33-34);

(b)   an account of misguided behaviour on the part of one or more of the disciples (8:32-33; 9:31-34; 10:35-41);

(c)   Jesus' corrective teaching on the true discipleship (8:34-9:1; 9:35-50; 10:42-45).

The meaning of these three sequences is clear and concretely relevant to Mark's community: to believe in the gospel of Christ is to follow him and to follow him is to be willing to suffer with him.[24] According to 13:9-13 believers should expect persecution and pressure from family members, religious leaders, and government officials as they proclaim the gospel during the period between the resurrection and the second coming of Jesus. It is therefore natural to conclude that "Mark wrote in a setting characterized by persecution to people who were suffering".[25]

This is not to say that the Marcan community is an apocalyptic sect. Instead of offering an eschatological timetable or speculative calculation on the basis of a checklist of eschatological woes, Mark 13 focuses on the responsibility of proclaiming the gospel and the opposition that such proclamation receives (vv. 9-13). The worldwide progress of the gospel message is the key eschatological necessity. It is the condition that must be fulfilled "first" for the eschaton to appear (v. 10).[26]

2. Discipleship as a learning process
The story of the blind man in 8:22-26 and the story of blind Bartimaeus in 10:46-52 function as the frame of the central section on discipleship. We are probably to read into the final statement "he followed him (i.e. Jesus) on the way" (10:52) a

confirming indication that this whole section was intended to speak to the evangelist's readers, who were themselves "*on the way*" in their lives of discipleship.[27]

The call to discipleship is a call to open oneself to a model of learning. This model is based on simply "being with Jesus" (Mark 3:14), accompanying him, experiencing his authority, receiving his teaching and sharing his way to the cross.[28] In that sense "the story of Jesus is also to be the story of his followers."[29] His way was flowed into their way. And their way has become the way of discipleship.[30]

The title that heads Mark's Gospel seems to fit this aspect of being on the way.[31] Mark's work as a whole is entitled "the beginning of the good news..."(1:1). His whole story – from Galilee to Jerusalem and back again – is the "beginning" of proclamation, the beginning of the church's "way", which is begun and shaped by the way of Jesus. This entire journey motif gives an inherently missionary character to Mark's Gospel. The Christian message is described as a way, as a mobile, dynamic transmission of God's Word that sweeps through the heart of Judaism. It is just a beginning.

3. Mission from the empty tomb
Unlike the other Synoptics, Mark has no final commission from Jesus to the disciples. Yet it is worthwhile to consider whether there is another kind of missionary mandate, namely the sending from the empty tomb, 16:1-8.[32]

Mark 16:1-8 is sometimes called the "empty tomb pericope". This, however, is misleading. The point is that the gospel proclamation issues from the gaping mouth of the tomb with all the authority and power of the divine Word. The angel does not say in Mark, as he says in Matthew: "He is not here; for he has been raised..." (Matt 28:6), but vice versa: "He has been raised; he is not here" (Mark 16:6). Mark does not begin with an empty tomb to be explained by a resurrection. The viewpoint is not apologetical, but kerygmatic. The account does not turn on the enigma of the disappearance of a corpse; it turns on the angelic proclamation of a divine message.[33]

For some interpreters, the story ends in total failure. The disciples are scattered. It is argued that the women did not execute the angel's command, because cowardly fear incapacitated them. The disciples therefore never heard the message, never met the risen Lord, and were never made apostles. Mark's narrative totally discredits the disciples.[34] This interpretation overlooks the ambiguous character of the women's silence in 16:8. It is a typical response to an act of divine power: They are struck with awe.[35] The very existence of the Gospel of Mark proves that the power of the Word of God cannot be fettered by human weakness. The contrast between v. 6 and v. 8 is the contrast between the divine power and the human weakness.

The point at which the Gospel ends has implications for a study of Mark's perspective on mission. Without a post-resurrection commission, the continuing significance of Jesus' pre-resurrection commissions is highlighted.[36] Jesus initially calls his disciples in order that he might make them fishers of men (1:17). Early in his ministry he moves them out to begin their mission (6:7-13).

The abrupt ending of the Gospel seems to be intentional; it is Mark's device to get the readers involved in the story. It has been an invitation to discipleship and to mission. They are called to be part of the unfinished, ongoing story of Christ's mission on earth. Mark has no resurrection appearance like the other Gospels, but he has an invitation to meet the living Lord, as they have met and followed him in his earthly ministry, on the way.

III. Hermeneutical perspectives

1. A corrective to a triumphant mission
A comparison between the "longer ending" of Mark and the original Mark without this ending leads to the questions: Are the driving out of demons and gift of healing (16:16-18) regular features of mission and evangelism? And what is the significance of the passion narrative and the passion christology for mission?

In the New Testament as a whole there are some tensions as regards the issue of mission and healing. While the Marcan tradition considers the performers of "signs and wonders" to be a threat to the church, the Book of Acts assigns to them a positive role in the Christian mission; see ch. 4 of the present study. M. Arias has the following comment on the problem with the added promises in the "longer ending": "If this promise is as universal as it sounds ("these signs will accompany *those who believe*"), most of us, and millions of evangelists and witnesses throughout Christian history, are disqualified as evangelists, as truly evangelized, or as true believers, because we lack the apparently promised miraculous evidence."[37]

In our time Christian mission is sometimes presented in triumphant terms, in which Christian soldiers march ever onward and God's kingdom swiftly spreads from shore to shore. Mark's perspective on mission can serve as a corrective to an unrealistic optimism. The witness of believers may occur in a world that is indifferent or even openly hostile, and the proclamation of the gospel may take place in the context of difficulty and persecution. "Instead of offering more effective or successful methods, Mark points to the way of the cross, the path of self-sacrifice and humble service."[38] The followers of Jesus are called to service, to suffering, and to sacrifice, not to power, prestige and position (cf. Mark 10:35-45).

2. An open-ended story – an unfinished mission
Another point of hermeneutical interest is the abrupt ending of the original Gospel. Some scholars argue that the negative example of the women in 16:8 itself serves as an apostolic commission. Mark calls on his audience to obey God and "go and tell" by narrating the disobedience of the women and their refusal "to go and tell".[39] In other words, the narrative characters are afraid to finish the story; the readers must therefore do so themselves, regardless of the consequences. "If the women

won't take the charge, then the audience must. They become the recipients of the angel's charge."[40]

However, as noted previously, this interpretation overlooks the ambiguous character of the silence in 16:8. But the question still is: does this story have anything to say to our world, and if so, do we have "ears to hear" it? C. Myers makes a comparison with the novel *The Neverending Story* (1983) by M. Ende.[41] The boy Bastian "jumps into" the narrative, giving it a new beginning. After many adventures in which he learns more deeply about his true self, Bastian returns to his own real world, a transformed person.

In similar fashion, Mark's narrative of discipleship can continue only if we realize, like Bastian, that we are in fact characters in the very story we thought we were reading. Mark, like Ende's novel, puts the "future" of the narrative in the hands of the reader. And he can do so precisely because he believes that the story and its subject are not "dead past" but "living present". But how do we "jump into" the gospel and make it our own? Mark's reader crisis cannot be resolved through a mere leap of imagination, but only by "taking up the cross" and following Christ. The new story is one in which we are no longer only readers but also agents.[42]

In which way, then, can Mark's story be ours? If we would identify with any of the characters in Mark's story, it can legitimately be only that of the rich man (10:17-22) and the scribe (12:32-34). To illustrate the first option: like the former, we (in the West) are preoccupied with the religious prospect of "eternal life" – and are summoned instead to discipleship. Jesus' call comes to us too as a specific challenge to turn from our privilege and restore justice to the poor. And this is precisely what the rich man found too hard to do.[43] We are failing like the first disciples. Yet, though "betrayal" is not lightly viewed, there is an equally strong counter-discourse of "pardon". Because Jesus "goes before" us (16:7), a new start can always be made on the discipleship adventure.[44]

3. Mission from the periphery

What does it mean for today's mission that the starting point of Jesus' kingdom ministry is located in the Galilean periphery? I shall point to three different ways of answering this question.

The first example comes from O. Costas – an Americo-Hispanic scholar with deep roots in the radical evangelical tradition. According to Costas Mark's "Galilean accent" has three implications for contextual evangelization.[45]

First, Mark's Galilean model implies that contextual evangelization should have a socio-historical foundation based on the periphery. When the gospel makes "somebody" out of the "nobodies" of society, when it restores the self-worth of the marginalized, then it is truly good news of a new order of life.

Second, evangelization does not only have a public message but also takes place amid the multitudes. The Galilean multitudes can be found everywhere. There is not a neighbourhood, town, city, state, nation, or continent that does not have a Galilee. One must always look for the powerless, the marginalized, and the voiceless to discover the concrete reality of Galilee.

Third, there is the global scope of evangelization: that is communicating the gospel from the periphery of the nations. Some make the mistake of starting in Jerusalem rather than in Galilee and end up frustrated or co-opted by the ruling "powers and principalities". They gear the message to a select few rather than the harassed multitudes and find themselves left with a historically harmless church, a private gospel, and a plastic Jesus. Instead a prophetic, liberating and holistic mission must ask, *Where* is our base, *who* is our target audience, and *what* is the scope of our evangelistic task.[46]

A similar approach to Mark's "Galilean accent" can be found in the Korean *minjung* theology. The exegete Ahn Byung Mu sees the Korean term *minjung* ("people") as analogous to Mark's "crowd" (*ochlos*).[47] The *minjung* are outside the sphere of the dominant Jewish groups; this includes the poor, the tax collector, the impure. Mark advances an ideology of "receptivity": the leper, the sinner, the woman, the child are all to be received unconditionally as subjects of the kingdom. Jesus teaches his disciples to live among them and look at life from their perspective.[48]

The third example comes from B. K. Blount – a Biblical scholar and black American. Blount compares the situation in today's black church to the situation in which the Gospel arose. Using a socio-linguistic approach to the texts he argues that Mark's message has a particular meaning for the African-American Christians. "The message is, Go preach! That is not to say, Go talk from a lofty pulpit in a well-attended and even better-funded megachurch. It is to say, instead, Go break down the boundaries that oppress African-Americans and divide African-Americans from each other and African-Americans from other Americans".[49]

The basic starting point for these interpretations is Mark's emphasis on the inclusive character of God's kingdom. From this follows an inclusive view of the community.[50] Furthermore it is presupposed that Mark wants the story of God's kingdom to do something in the lives of his readers. They are invited to continue the boundary-breaking kingdom that Jesus has initiated. The readers are challenged to finish Mark's story – each in their concrete situation.

Notes

1   Cf. Georgi 1986, 164ff.; Theissen 1975.
2   Arias & Johnson 1992, 37.
3   Klaiber 1997, 41-42.
4   Senior & Stuhlmueller 1983, 214.
5   Cf. Pesch 1980, 59-60; Kelber 1974, 67-85.
6   The way image reflects Mark's dual eschatology that the Kingdom has both come and not come; cf. Via 1985, 186.
7   Cf. Senior & Stuhlmueller 1983, 216.
8   Cf. Månsus 1993, 154-156.
9   Cf. Kappen 1977, 123.
10 Cf. Kappen 1977, 124.

11   Cf. Arias & Johnson 1992, 40. See also Nolan 1977, 70.

12   Cf. Blount 1998, 8.

13   The Kingdom of God is not just proclaimed in verbal form. G. M. Soares-Prabhu 1982, 247, argues that words and deeds go hand in hand in the kingdom ministry of Jesus, and one would be quite unimaginable without the other: "Words without deeds to "fulfill" them would have been as empty as deeds without words to expound their meaning...There is no true word that is not at the same time a praxis. Thus, to speak a true word is to transform the world."

14   Cf. van Canghe 1972.

15   On the historical background of Galilee see Freyne 1980.

16   Cf. Costas 1989, 55-56.

17   Legrand 1990, 53.

18   Kelber 1974, 62-63.

19   Kelber 1974, 51-52.

20   Senior & Stuhlmueller 1983, 218.

21   So, for instance, Weeden 1971; Kelber 1985.

22   So, for instance, Best 1986; Hurtado 1996, 17-18.

23   The Twelve are to be intimately associated with Jesus, not only by *being* with him, but also in *doing* what he himself does; cf. Moloney 1991, 139.

24   Cf. Verhey 1984, 75.

25   Williams 1998, 137. See also Blount 1998; Nissen 1980, 279.

26   Cf. Hurtado 1996, 16.

27   Cf. Hays 1997, 81: "Within this central unit Jesus presses forward his pedagogical project of reshaping the disciples' understanding of his mission and of theirs".

28   Cf. Klaiber 1997, 49.

29   Donahue 1978, 378-379.

30   Cf. Pesch 1980, 60.

31   Cf. Senior & Stuhlmueller 1983, 216.

32   Doohan 1986, 130, states: "The episode of the empty tomb... forms Mark's final commission".

33   Cf. Legrand 1990, 76.

34   See Weeden 1971, 48-50.

35   Moreover, the silence of the women can be explained by the messianic secret. So, for instance, Radermakers 1974, 418.

36   Cf. Williams 1998, 148.

37   Arias & Johnson 1992, 36.

38   Williams 1998, 150.

39   So, for instance Boomershine 1981; Tolbert 1989, 288-299. Objections to this view may be found in Williams 1998, 148.

40   Blount 1998, 196.

41   Myers 1988, 449.

42   Hays 1997, 91, in a similar way explains the strange ending of Mark's Gospel by saying that it is "a Gospel of uninterpreted gestures and suggestive silence." The author continues, "Precisely for that reason, it summons readers to supply the ending by taking up the cross and completing the interpretation in their own lives of discipleship. The Gospel of Mark cannot be "understood" from outside; it can be read rightly only through following Jesus in

self-involving, self-sacrificial service".

43 Myers 1988, 450.

44 Cf. Myers 1988, 420.

45 Costas 1989, 61-90. Notice that Costas uses the term "evangelization" almost in the same way as I am using the term "mission".

46 Costas 1989. 69-70.

47 Ahn 1981, 136-151.

48 Cf. Myers 1988, 440. For a similar accentuation of the contrast between centre and periphery see Koyama 1980.

49 Blount 1998, 10.

50 On the inclusiveness of the Marcan community see also Via 1985, 86; Kee 1995, 66f.; cf. Nissen 1994, 228-231.

4.

The liberating ministry of Jesus and the Acts of the Spirit: The mission perspectives of Luke-Acts

Introduction

Luke differs from the other evangelists at one essential point: he not only wrote a Gospel, but also the Book of Acts. This factor is important for the theme of mission.

The existence of two books from the same author raises a number of questions: How is the story of Jesus related to the story of the church? To what extent is Jesus a model for the church? Where do we see a continuation and a discontinuation between the two books? And how is the gospel communicated to a non-Jewish audience?

It has often been argued that Luke's salvation history consists of three distinct epochs: (1) the epoch of Israel, including John the Baptist; (2) the epoch of Jesus' ministry which is seen as the middle period of salvation; and (3) the epoch of the church inaugurated by the day of Pentecost. In his famous work, H. Conzelmann has characterized the second period as "Die Mitte der Zeit". Furthermore, he maintains that the Holy Spirit in Luke's writings was "no longer the eschatological gift, but the substitute in the meantime for the possession of ultimate salvation."[1]

There are good grounds for believing that this reconstruction is correct by insisting that the church lived in an era which differed in crucial respects from the period of Jesus' earthly ministry. But it is misleading to argue that Luke regarded the church's mission in the power of the Spirit as a substitute for eschatological expectation. Imminent eschatology and salvation history are by no means contradictory or mutually exclusive understandings.[2] The Holy Spirit is prominent not only in Acts but also in the Gospel. Therefore, it is more correct to say that Luke unites the time of Jesus and the time of the church in one era of the Spirit. The two times are certainly not identical but neither can they be divorced from each other.[3]

Certain issues are of specific importance in Luke's theology of mission, e.g. the ministry of the Holy Spirit, the centrality of repentance and forgiveness, the good news to the poor, and the encounter between gospel and culture. These and other issues will be discussed in this chapter, which has three parts: the first deals with the basic mission perspectives in the Gospel of Luke, the second dwells mainly on the understanding of the Holy Spirit in the two writings; the third part focuses on the mission discourses in Acts.

I. The proclamation of the Jubilee – the Gospel of Luke

1. The "Great Commission"

Two passages are of specific importance for mission in Luke's Gospel. The first one is his version of the "Great Commission" in 24:44-49:

> "Then he said to them, 'These are my words that I spoke to you while I was still with you – that everything written about me in the law of Moses, the prophets, and the psalms must be fulfilled'. Then he opened their minds to understand the scriptures, and he said to them, 'Thus it is written, that the Messiah is to suffer and to rise from the dead on the third day, and that repentance and forgiveness of sins is to be proclaimed in his name to all nations, beginning from Jerusalem. Your are witnesses of these things. And see, I am sending upon you what my Father promised; so stay here in the city until you are clothed with power from on high'."

In this passage six important aspects of mission are underlined: (1) The *basis* of mission: the death and the resurrection of Jesus. (2) The *fulfilment of the Scriptures*: the disciples are reminded that the life and death of Jesus must be seen in the light of the Scriptures. (3) The *content* of mission: this is summarized as *repentance* and *forgiveness*. (4) The *purpose* of mission: it is to begin "from Jerusalem" but is intended for "*all nations*". (5) The disciples are called to be *witnesses*. (6) Mission will be accomplished in the power of the *Holy Spirit* (cf. v. 49).

These aspects are "the fibers of Luke's mission theology" which run throughout the Gospel and Acts, binding this two-volume work together.[4] Some of these aspects will be considered later on in this chapter. First we shall pay attention to the specific relationship between Scripture and mission.

It should be noticed that *a re-reading of the Scriptures* was to be the source of mission. This is already the case with the Emmaus story (24:13-35). The appearance of Jesus to the disciples on the way to Emmaus is actually a session on hermeneutics, opening the Scriptures, which in turn opened their eyes and gave them a new message to share.[5] In the same way, the passage of the last commission records that Jesus opened the minds of the disciples to understand the Scriptures. As Arias notes, "the living Christ was present in the early community as the hermeneut for a new reading of the Scriptures, from the context of their total experience of Jesus, his ministry, his death, and his resurrection."[6]

2. Jesus' proclamation in the synagogue of Nazareth

The second major passage to be considered is Jesus' proclamation in the synagogue at Nazareth in Luke 4:16-30. In Luke's Gospel this story plays almost the same role as the Great Commission in Matthew's Gospel. This is seen from its content and its place at the outset of Jesus' ministry. The passage is not only the inaugural event launching Jesus' ministry, but also a programmatic introduction of Jesus and a prefiguration of events to follow.[7]

In addition, this passage shows – in the same way as the missionary mandate in Luke 24 – that the re-reading of the Scripture plays a significant role for the mission. At the beginning Jesus reads a portion of the prophet Isaiah:

"The Spirit of the Lord is upon me, because he has anointed me to bring good news to the poor. He has sent me to proclaim release to the captives and recovering of sight to the blind, to let the oppressed go free, to proclaim the year of the Lord's favour" (vv. 18-19).

In these and in the following verses we have a number of issues which are of great importance for the understanding of mission: (1) The year of the Lord's favour; (2) good news to the poor; (3) liberation and forgiveness; (4) the setting aside of vengeance; (5) rejection by Israel, and (6) God's work among the Gentiles (the role of the Holy Spirit).

In this section some of these issues will be commented upon briefly – while others will be postponed to later sections.

The first issue is the understanding of "the good news to the poor".[8] It is remarkable that many interpreters understand this text in a spiritual sense. The terms "poor", "captives", "blind" and "oppressed" have been seen as "categories" which designate those who are victims of inward repressions, neuroses or other spiritual ills due to misdirection and failure of life's energies and purposes.

Luke's way of treating the Old Testament is significant. It is noteworthy that he omits one sentence from Isa 61:1 ("to bind up the brokenhearted"). Instead he inserts a sentence from Isa 58:6 ("to let the oppressed go free"). This rearrangement of the material is probably due to the fact that Luke wanted to avoid the possible spiritualization of the words from Isa 61.[9]

Moreover, the "poor" (Greek *ptochos*) is often a collective term for all the disadvantaged. This emerges from the way in which Luke, when he gives a list of people who suffer, either puts the poor at the head of the list (cf. 4:18; 6:20; 14:13; 14:21) or at the end, as a climax (as in 7:22). All who experience misery are, in some very real sense, the poor. This is particularly true of those who are sick. Lazarus, the exemplary poor person in Luke, is both poor and sick. Primarily, then, poverty is a social category in Luke, although it certainly has other undertones as well.[10]

Good news to the poor is closely interrelated to the other issues: the vengeance superseded, God's working among Gentiles and the rejection by Israel. A striking change of mood takes place. Surprisingly, the audience becomes hostile to Jesus at the end of the story (vv. 29-30). The people of Nazareth refuse to believe Jesus' claim and reject him. Jesus then challenges the congregation's "ethics of election".[11] He challenges their provincialism by reminding his hearers of Elijah and Elisha who performed miracles for the pagans although many compatriots were in need.

An additional explanation is that Jesus consciously omitted the last part of Isa 61:2 with the reference to the "day of vengeance of our God". The fact that Jesus only read the portion on grace and not the one on vengeance is of great importance, because in his days the preaching of the synagogue used to put the whole emphasis precisely on these latter words.

The way Jesus stresses grace rather than vengeance reminds us of the answer he gave to John the Baptist in Luke 7:22-23 (cf. Matt 11:2-6). In his final remark Jesus said: "And blessed is anyone who takes no offense at me" (7:23). This means: "Blessed is everyone who does not take offense at the fact that the era of salvation differs from what he has expected, that God's compassion on the poor and outcast has superseded divine vengeance!"[12] This is another way of saying that the new age is for all human beings. The mission of Jesus is inclusive.[13]

3. The Jubilee as a new beginning

The references to Isa 61 and Isa 58 make it clear that the sermon of Jesus is to be understood within the context of the Jubilee year. That was a year of re-creation of a just society, based on the right of every Israelite to a secure living on his land.[14]

The concept of the Jubilee is known from a number of Old Testament legislative texts, e.g. Lev 25; Deutr 15:1-18, and prophetic texts, e.g. Jer 34:8-22; Isa 61:1-2 and Neh 5:1-13.

Throughout the history of Israel the traditions associated with the Jubilee appear to affirm two things:[15] The first is that God is sovereign over Israel, both in actual fact and in eschatological hope. The second is that the structures of economic and social life must embody the people's affirmation of God's sovereignty. In other words, God's reign and man's liberation go hand in hand.

The Jubilee was God's revolution, a new beginning in history to correct the accumulated injustices of appropriation of the families' lands. The Jubilee was intended to be a periodic restructuring of social relationships to provide freedom and the means of life for each generation. It was an act of grace from God (release, forgiveness, new beginnings) calling forth an appropriate act of grace from people to people (cancellation of debts, emancipation of the slaves). It was holistic forgiveness – at the personal and at the social level, keeping together the spiritual and material aspects of life.[16]

The concept of the Jubilee indeed permeates Luke's Gospel. Salvation "*today*" (4:21; cf. 19:9) and *fulfilment* are key words that set the tone in the inaugural sermon of Jesus. The following aspects of the Jubilee theme are expanded in Luke's Gospel as a whole.

a. *Good news to the poor.* In our society poverty is primarily an economic category, but in Luke's Gospel – as in the rest of the New Testament – this concept is more comprehensive.[17] The different aspects of poverty can be categorized as follows: (a) those suffering economic disadvantage, (b) the physically and mentally ill, handicapped, captives, widows and others; (c) a broad group of marginalized persons: tax collectors, sinners, prostitutes and others. All these persons are excluded from social and religious life. They are poor because they are deprived of what is essential for living, both daily bread and dignity.

More than any other evangelist Luke emphasizes Jesus' association with marginalized people: this includes the unclean lepers (e.g. 17:11-19), the tax collectors (e.g. 15:1-2), the Samaritans (e.g. 17:16-19) and the women (e.g. 7:11-17).

A common feature in Luke's stories is the appearance of the "other": the woman, the poor person, the stranger who suddenly takes centre stage. These persons come into this world not as mere recipients of gifts from the elites, but as those upon whom the future of the world is dependent. A "sinful woman", a tax collector, and an outsider represent the signs of "the economy of the Kingdom".[18] This is a "decentering of perspective" and a reversal of the world as it is presently known and legitimized. The poor are seen as "agents of the dawning Kingdom".[19]

b. *Liberation and healing.* In his answer to John the Baptist Jesus points to his acts of healing (7:22-23); this is an allusion to Isaiah's jubilary visions and promises (e.g. 61:1-2; 35:5-6). The gospel was not only to be heard but it was to be seen in action: "Go and tell John what you have seen and heard".

That the year of the Jubilee includes healing is also seen in other passages. This is especially clear in the story of the crippled woman who was healed on a sabbath day (13:10-17). Jesus defended his action by saying "And ought not this woman, a daughter of Abraham whom Satan bound for eighteen long years, be set free from this bondage on the sabbath day?" (v. 16). To "release" or to "liberate" is necessary for human life. Consequently it is the missionary priority.[20]

c. *Jubilee as enactment of forgiveness.* S. Ringe has argued that the forgiving of the public woman in 7:36-50 should be interpreted in light of the Jubilee idea.[21] The story makes explicit what is implicit elsewhere, namely, that in each case Jesus' relationship with the outcasts is to be understood as an enactment of the "forgiveness" or "release". The bonds that are broken with Jesus' advent are the bonds that deprive people of a place in their society. Such stories echo the Jubilee images of "return" to God found in Lev 25 as well as those in Isa 61 that point to liberation from captivity and celebration of God's eschatological reign, now recognized as present in Jesus.

The climax of Jesus' ministry is his intercession for those who were crucifying or rejecting him. "Father, forgive them; for they do not know what they are doing" (23:34). Also important are his words to the robber: "Today you will be with me in Paradise" (23:43). The gospel of Jesus is the Amnesty Gospel (M. Arias).

The Septuagint translates the Hebrew words for "Jubilee" with the word *aphesis*, which is also the Greek word for "forgiveness" in the New Testament. The same word is used not only in Luke 4:18 but also in Luke 24:47 which makes it probable that the jubilary motif is present in the "Great Commission".

d. *Rectification and new beginning.* God is the rectifier of the history. In Magnificat (1:46-55) he is described as the one who "has brought down the powerful from their thrones, and lifted up the lowly". He "has filled the hungry with good things, and sent the rich away empty" (1:52-53).

The rectification is a strong motif in the story of Zacchaeus (19:1-10). The significance of this story becomes even clearer if we compare with the story of the ruler meeting Jesus (18:18-30). In both cases, rich persons are challenged by Jesus. The ruler is called to leave everything and give it to the poor. But he gives up. The rich tax collector, however, acts according to the gospel. In 18:18-30 it is emphasized that it is impossible for a rich person to take the first step. And yet, that what is impossible for men is possible for God (18:27). And in the case of Zacchaeus *the impossible becomes possible*.[22] He is offered a new beginning.

4. Good news to the rich?

Luke has often been characterized as "evangelist of the poor".[23] It is true that he emphasizes the concern for the poor. Nevertheless, it might be more appropriate to characterize him as an evangelist of the rich.[24]

Luke has many stories about the wealthy, and most of them show how difficult it is for the rich to be saved, e.g. the rich fool in 12:16-21 and the rich man in 16:19-31. Those who are economically well off are often spiritually poor. They are self-sufficient and blind to the need of the poor.[25]

This is not to say that rich Christians are without hope. Luke "wants the rich and respected to be reconciled to the message and way of life of Jesus and the disciples; he wants to motivate them to a conversion that is in keeping with the social message of Jesus".[26] One such possible response is exemplified by Zacchaeus (19:1-10). He will repay those he has exploited and give half of his possessions to the poor. He is, in fact, the only rich person in the Gospel about whom it is explicitly told that he chose another lifestyle. If the rich repent and give up their possessions, the bad news will turn into good news. This is Luke's message to rich Christians of his own day.

5. Towards a sharing of common resources

Rectification and new beginning are some characteristic marks of the story of Zacchaeus. The same can probably be said of the parable of the unjust steward (16:1-7).

This parable has often been a puzzle for interpreters, perhaps because we tend to read it from the perspective of the haves rather than the have-nots. But some of the difficulties with this story can be solved if we realize that it contains a Jubilee teaching.

Even more disturbing than the parable are the additions made in vv. 8ff. How should we understand v. 9 where Jesus advises his disciples "to make friends by means of dishonest wealth"? These words are another way of saying "practice the jubilee which I am announcing. By liberating others from their debts to you, liberate yourself from the bonds which keep you from being ready for the kingdom of God".[27] Or as A Paoli has expressed it, "the profound motive of my existence must be 'to make friends *by means of* unrighteous mammon' and not to make mammon my friend, without being concerned whether this friendship is making enemies for me."[28]

The unjust steward expressed a solidary, sharing relationship which was totally different from the exploitation and inequality in power implied in a relationship between lender and debtor. To "make friends" by "unrighteous mammon", therefore, was the opposite of enslaving people in need. To "make friends" by giving to those in need had a liberating effect. It meant to put people on the same footing.[29]

The best example of a new sharing of resources is the community at Jerusalem, which will be described in the second part.

II. Holy Spirit, mission and community

1. The universal scope of salvation

The overall outline of the two books is geographical. In the Gospel, the ministry of Jesus unfolds in three stages: Galilee (4:14-9:50), his journey from Galilee to Jerusalem (9:51-19:40), and finally the events in Jerusalem (19:41-24:53). Thus the line goes *from Galilee to Jerusalem.*

In Acts, the mission likewise evolves in three phases. The main theme is the spread of the gospel *from Jerusalem to the "end of the earth"*, cf. 1:8: "You will be my witnesses in Jerusalem, in all Judaea and Samaria and to the ends of the earth". The author follows this as an outline for his book of Acts: chs. 1-7 describe the spread of the gospel in Jerusalem. Chs. 8-9 describe its spread in Judaea and Samaria, and the rest of the book is about the Christian mission to the whole world. It concludes with Paul's arrival in Rome.

However, this geographical outline is interrupted by a *theological* motif. Even if the Gospel has only one explicit reference to Gentile mission, namely in the mission command (24:47), the universal scope of the salvation is underlined from the beginning. The first two chapters point to Jesus as the Saviour not only for the Jews but also for the Gentiles. He is characterized as "a light for revelation to the Gentiles and for glory to your people Israel" (2:32).

As mentioned previously the universal scope of salvation is also expressed in the inaugural sermon of Jesus in Luke 4:16-30. Here we recognize a pattern which is repeated in the Acts, especially in the second half. Paul preaches first to the Jews in the synagogues, but when rejected turns to the Gentiles, e.g. Acts 13:44-52.

A similar transition from those who are first invited to new groups is reflected in the parable of the banquet, Luke 14:16-24.[30] The invited guests offer contrived excuses so the host opens the banquet to "the poor, the crippled, the blind, and the lame" (14:21). When places still remain open, the servants are sent out to the "roads and lanes" (14:23) until the hall is full.

When interpreting this parable one should distinguish between a pre-Lucan form and Luke's use of this parable. In the pre-Lucan form both groups of non-privileged probably refer to various marginalized groups within Israel – groups for whom Jesus cared. In the Lucan usage the second group of non-privileged seems to be a metaphorical expression for the Gentiles. However, in both cases there is an insistence on the universal scope of salvation. The will of God for a celebration cannot be stopped by those who reject the invitation.[31] The festival hall is to be full of guests. This is an expression of God's universal will for salvation. The right to be included in the community of God's people is not defined by one's heritage or status but only by response to God's universal invitation.

2. The boundary-breaking role of the Holy Spirit

The Holy Spirit has a crucial function in Luke's writings. It is the real agent of mission in the Acts of the Apostles, which might well be entitled "the Acts of the Spirit". The role of the Spirit, however, is also evident in the Gospel. It is the "power of the Spirit" that accompanies Jesus to Galilee as he begins his mission (Luke 4:14; cf. v.18). The radiation of that mission beyond the boundaries of Palestine is already signaled in the second part of the Nazareth incident (4:23-30). In this story we see a relation between God's universal will to save and the liberating ministry of Jesus.

For Luke, the outpouring of the Spirit demarcates the beginning of a new age. This is expressed already in the infancy narratives. The great characters are all filled with the Spirit (Luke 1:15.41.67; 2:25.36). They are promised that God will redeem his people and liberate those who are exploited. In the life of Jesus, God's Spirit begins to fulfill that promise: those in pain are liberated, the poor are cared for, the outcasts and rejected are brought home.[32]

This liberating ministry continues after Easter. On the day of the *Pentecost* the first disciples are filled with the Holy Spirit (Acts 2:1-13). In his sermon Peter explains what has happened by referring to the prophecy of Joel:

> "In the last days it will be, God declares, that I will pour out my Spirit upon all flesh, and your sons and your daughters shall prophesy, and your young men shall see visions, and your old men shall dream dreams. Even upon my slaves, both men and women, in those days I will pour out my Spirit, and they shall prophesy" (Acts 2:17-18).

This passage makes the point that participation in the blessings which God is pouring out on the human race is open to all human beings ("all flesh"), regardless of age, sexual, or social distinctions.[33] Even those on the lowest rungs of society's ladder will speak prophetically in this dawning of the new age. The Spirit begins to break down divisions, and will not become accommodated to the established structures of authority.[34]

The Spirit's role in widening the horizon of the mission is carried through in the rest of Acts. To mention just a few examples: Philip's encounter with the Ethiopian eunuch is made possible through the agency of the Spirit (8:29.39). The same applies to Peter's encounter with Cornelius (10:1-11:18). In a similar way, Paul's mission is guided by the Spirit. He and his fellow-worker Barnabas are "set apart ...for the work to which I have called them" (13:2). Paul is prevented from going to Asia in order that he might take the decisive step of entering Macedonia (16:6-10). The decision to go to Jerusalem is also inspired by the Spirit (19:21; 20:22).

The conversion of Cornelius is of special importance since it indicates a breakthrough to Gentile mission (10:1-11:18). The acceptance of this Gentile into the Christian fellowship is confirmed by a *second Pentecost*: now the Spirit is poured out even on a Gentile and his family (10:44-48). In his report to the community in Jerusalem, Peter explains that it was the Spirit who told him to go to Cornelius, "making no distinctions" (11:12). This new insight arose not because Peter had studied the Scripture, but because God himself was acting. It was the *impartial God* who drew Peter the Jew and Cornelius the Gentile together (10:34).

3. The function of meals and households in Luke's mission
Another important component in Luke's mission theology is the table fellowship. It indicates his inclusive vision of God's people.

Luke gives particular attention to Jesus' table fellowships with marginalized persons. Jesus eats with tax collectors and sinners (Luke 5:30; 15:1-2). Thus he threatens the sanctity of the Jewish society as the people of God, breaking taboos by including unclean people, outsiders in the meal fellowship. Jesus is threatening the very character of the group by opening it up to outsiders.[35] The parable of the great banquet (14:16-24) combines an open, boundary-breaking invitation with the rejection of the invitation by the "insiders".

These meals preview the mission experience of the community in Acts: the Jewish-Christian community will struggle to accept table fellowship with Gentiles, and the outcome of that struggle becomes decisive for the universal mission. The key issue in the Cornelius story of Acts 10-11 is that of table fellowship with a Gentile.

In this connection we should also notice that *house churches* play a significant role in Acts. The house functions in Acts as a place of evangelism and growth.[36] An example is the businesswoman, Lydia, who together with her household is baptized. This prosperous seller of a luxury item now invites Paul as a guest to her home (16:11-15). In a similar way the Roman jailer and his whole family are baptized. The jailer brings Paul and Silas "into the house and set food before them; and he and his entire household rejoiced that he had become a believer in God" (16:34). These and other stories show that group commitments rather than individual decisions were standard in the growth of the church. A pattern is now set for proclaiming the gospel across geographical, cultural, ethnic, social, economic and sexual boundaries.[37]

In Luke's view, the house church represents a providential place of opportunity.[38] Thus, in the closing verses of Acts, he shows that despite Paul's confinement to a rented house, his missionary work proceeds with great success: "He lived there two whole years at his own expense, and welcomed all who came to him, proclaiming the kingdom of God and teaching about the Lord Jesus Christ with all boldness and without hindrance" (28:30-31). The phrase "with all boldness and without hindrance" suggests a conviction on Luke's part that house churches will henceforth be the most promising of all social institutions for the proclamation of the gospel.

By way of summary we can say that meals are an invitation to a new community.[39] Salvation means acceptance, community and new life. Hospitality is an essential part of Luke's understanding of mission. "By virtue of their lived faith members of the house church congregations quite naturally "invite" their neighbours to travel God's way with them".[40]

4. The Holy Spirit and the community of ownership
Table fellowship plays a significant role for the first Christians in Jerusalem (Acts 2:42.46). This fellowship is characterized by some other features as well.

First, it was a community of common ownership. The first Christians gave until all needs were met – those who had too much gave up their surplus and treated nothing as their own, 4:34. And they gave according to their ability (cf. 11:29). All this is accomplished in the power of the Spirit.[41]

Second, as noted previously this sharing of common resources can be seen as an expression of the idea of the Jubilee.[42] The basic characteristic of this church was the close relationship between the unity in heart and soul (4:32a), the sharing of goods (4:32c) and the witness to the resurrection (4:33). As pointed out by de Santa Ana, this common ownership of goods "reflects at the material level the kind of spiritual communion which should prevail in the Church".[43]

Third, this sharing of possessions is based on a strong sense of the imminence of the Kingdom of God. The prototype of their lifestyle has to be found in the teaching of Jesus on a care-free attitude. The nearness of the Kingdom of God has liberated human beings from every kind of bondage.

Fourth, the inner life of the church is connected to its outer life. The Christians were finding "favour with all people". The impact was so positive and attractive that daily there were more converts and the number of the community membership was increasing. In other words, the transformed economic relationship among these Christians is closely related to "the phenomenal evangelistic outreach".[44] M. Arias has characterized this attractive quality of life as "centripetal mission or evangelization by hospitality".[45]

Luke's description of the first Christians gives rise to some crucial questions. One of these is, to what degree his way of describing them is influenced by his theological interests. In other words, are the passages of Acts 2:41-47 and 4:32-37 based on historical facts? In form criticism both texts are usually labelled as "summaries", that is, stories which generalize and idealize some single incidents with a definitive purpose. Does this mean that these passages are purely idealized pictures of the Jerusalem community without any basis in history?

It is not easy to give a clear answer to this question.[46] Probably there is a historical core behind these "summaries". This is not to deny that Luke's portrait of the church is idealized. In fact, he insisted on an equalization of ownership within the community.

An additional question is: did Luke consider the community in Jerusalem as a model to be imitated? Or was his theological thinking marked by a delay in the coming of the parousia so that his own audience were perhaps unable to adopt the pattern of the first believers? As far as I can see, Luke's portrait of the primitive community at Jerusalem served as a model for his own readership. The situation is not unlike that of 1 Cor 11:17-34. In both these passages we have a conflict between "eschatological egalitarianism" (the social utopia)[47] and sinful division within the community.

For Luke it makes a radical difference whether people are controlled by the Holy Spirit or by money.[48] Various passages in Acts indicate this difference. It is perhaps seen most clearly in Acts 8:4-25 where Luke points to the contrast between the money-making magus (Simon) and the apostle. The magus makes money by trafficking in the supernatural. The apostle has no money; he is poor, but makes many rich. Thus, possession of the Spirit of God is accompanied by the readiness to give away money – and the gift of the Spirit itself – freely. The apostle does not act by virtue of some independent power that he possesses and controls (his own power or piety; cf. 3:12 and 14:14f.) but only in continual dependence on the power of God which is in some way released and applied through prayer.

5. Spirit, baptism and miracles
The activity of the Spirit is considered to be an extraordinary and obviously supernatural phenomenon. This fact provokes a number of difficult questions, e.g.: is there a specific "Spirit-baptism" to be distinguished from "water-baptism"?[49] What is the significance of speaking in tongues? What is the role of the miracles in the spreading of the gospel? These are historical questions, but they have a hermeneutical relevance as well.

a. *The relation between Spirit and baptism.* There are nine explicit references to baptism:[50] 2:38 (the Pentecost); 8:12-17 (the Samaritans); 8:36ff. (the Ethiopian eunuch); 9:18 (Saulus); 10:44-48 (Cornelius); 16:15 (Lydia); 16:33 (the jailer); 18:8 (Crispus and the Corinthians); 19:1-6 (the disciples in Ephesus). Only four of these passages contain a reference to the Holy Spirit. In 2:38 the gift of the Spirit is given *in* baptism; in 8:12-17 it is given *after* baptism. The same seems to be the case in 19:1-6. Finally in 10:44-48 the Spirit is given *before* baptism.

The Pentecostal movement usually considers baptism in the Spirit to be a second (pentecostal) experience distinct from and subsequent to conversion. Moreover, the Book of Acts is usually seen as supporting this understanding. However, the stories in this book do not provide any clear picture. It seems impossible to say what is "normal", although many interpreters would refer to 2:38[51] – the only passage in Acts which directly relates to each other the three most important elements in the conversion-initiation: repentance, water-baptism and the gift of the Spirit. In the last analysis the only thing that matters in deciding whether a man is Christian or not is whether he has received the Spirit or not.[52]

b. *Speaking in tongues* is a phenomenon which has often been overestimated. In Acts there are only a few references to "speaking in tongues", namely 10:46 and 19:6 and probably also 2:1-4. In each case Luke is obviously describing men caught up out of themselves, that is, in ecstasy. The Pentecost in Acts 2 has to be recognized as an ecstatic experience which at least included elements of audition (sound like a strong wind), vision (tongues like fire) and automatic speech (glossolalia). However, interpreters differ as where to put the emphasis. It is debatable whether we have here a miracle of speech or a miracle of hearing.[53]

It is not clear if Luke refers to the same phenomenon as Paul describes in 1 Cor 14. Nor can we say whether Luke considered his description of the ecstasy of the first Christians to be normative for the life in the communities of his own time. As noted above there are historical as well as ideal elements in his picture of the first community. But there is no indication that ecstasy should be constitutive for the ideal Christian community.

c. *"Wonders and signs"*. Luke's treatment of miracle is another point of dispute. The Book of Acts has no less than 25 stories of miracles. In nine cases they are labelled "wonders and signs". This phrase has a positive value. Elsewhere in the New Testament the phrase is often used in a negative sense (e.g. John 4:48; Mark 13:22). And yet Luke boasts of the "wonders and signs" as acts which demonstrated God's hand in the mission of the church.

Luke seems to consider the miracles of the early Christian mission as more spectacular than those of any rivals – "*great* signs and wonders", "*extraordinary* miracles" (8:13; 19:11). To be sure, Luke has a tendency to a "theology of glory" or triumphalism which stands in contrast to other parts of the New Testament.[54] In the Gospel of Mark the publicity and the propagandist value of miracles is disparaged and a faith based on miracle is usually treated with reservation and disapproval (e.g. Mark 8:11ff.; cf. John 4:48). Paul in a similar way insists on the cross as a correction to a "theology of glory" (1 Cor 1:18-25).

On the other hand the contrast between Luke and Paul should not be over-emphasized. Even if "wonders and signs" are characteristics of the church's mission according to Acts, the first Christians are not spared suffering and persecution (Acts 8:1ff.; 12:1ff.). There is also a certain restraint in the miracles he records, and he sharply contrasts the miraculous progress of the gospel with magic (8:18-24; 13:6-12; 19:13-20).

The miracles are significant in that they point to the Pentecost as the arrival of a new age.[55] This new age manifests itself in powerful acts. It is an indication that salvation is not just for the soul but also for the body. Salvation means a restoration of life – a redemption of our bodies (cf. Rom 8:23).

III. Mission and dialogue in Acts

1. The missionary speeches

The Book of Acts has a number of speeches among which the so-called "missionary speeches" are of special interest.[56] The most important discourses are Peter's sermon at Pentecost in Acts 2:14-36 and three sermons by Paul. In what follows I shall draw attention particularly to Paul's discourses because of their different content and approaches.

In *Antioch of Pisidia* Paul speaks to a *Jewish* audience (13:13-43), in *Lystra* his audience is *Pagans* (14:5-20), and in *Athens* he addresses *Greek philosophers* (17:22-31). Each of these speeches has the form of a monologue; nevertheless the content is dialogical. They can be characterized as "including dialogues", that is, Paul pays regard to the questions, viewpoints and experiences of his listeners.[57]

At Antioch Paul enters the synagogue and proclaims the gospel for the Jews. The approach is one of scriptural exposition. Paul points to the *history of Israel*, and his basic argument is that Jesus is Messiah. In Lystra he addresses the Pagans. First he comments on the confusion which has arisen because they want to identify himself and Barnabas as Hermes and Zeus. Then he points to *God's creation*: God sends rain from heaven and crops in their seasons. At the Areopagus Paul's proclamation is marked by the fact that those who listened belonged to the elite in *Greek culture*.

If Paul had spoken about the history of Israel in Lystra, it would have been meaningless to the audience. It would also have been a mistake to speak of fertility and the growth of the earth in Athens, or about the unknown God in Antioch. There is no agreement among scholars on the extent to which these missionary speeches reflect the actual proclamation of the first Christians. Some would argue that they in fact say something about the concrete proclamation. Others maintain that the speeches reflect Luke's concept of Paul. Yet, even in this case there is a remarkable similarity between the approach of the speeches and his reflections in 1 Cor 9:19-23.

More important than this disagreement is the theological and hermeneutical aspect of these speeches. Paul is portrayed as engaging in three different tactics in order to get his message about Jesus through persuasively and appropriately to three different audiences. The proclamation of the gospel has to be formed according to the context in which the hearers are living.[58] In this sense one should not speak of an "objective" (or neutral) gospel which has the same form irrespective of time and place. If the message altogether is to reach the audience at all, it must be communicated in a dialogical form.

An additional note on the relation between Jews and Gentiles is in order. To be sure, the turn to the Gentiles follows upon the rejection by Israel but it is not wholly explained by this. The "salvation of all flesh" is intended by God from the beginning.[59] The baptism of the Ethiopian, the conversion of Cornelius, and the mandate of Paul to go to the Gentiles are clearly the result of an explicit divine initiative, regardless of the response of the Jews. The speeches in Acts 14:15-17 and 17:23-31 affirm that the offer of salvation to the Gentiles is not a mere crust from the table of Israel but is part of God's saving care for all peoples already expressed in creation.

2. Paul's speech at the Areopagus – failure or success?

The speech at Areopagus is one of the most famous missionary texts in the New Testament. It is therefore natural to go more in detail with this text.

The speech is sometimes characterized as a failure. It is argued that Paul arrived in Athens from Beroea, almost unintentionally, and while he was waiting for his co-workers he spent his time walking around in the city. He then became provoked by seeing the city full of idols (17:16). Therefore he "argued" in the synagogue and the market place. By doing so he caught the attention of the Greek philosophers, who brought him to the Areopagus. Paul held a speech in which he attacked their superstition and he attempted by means of intellectual arguments to persuade them of the truth but without success.

This is the reason why he used a different approach when he came to Corinth: "I did not come proclaiming the mystery of God to you in lofty words or wisdom. For I decided to know nothing among you except Jesus Christ and him crucified" (1 Cor 2:1-2). According to this interpretation Paul has replaced the rational argumentative proclamation (the dialogue) by a different form which is based on the irrational and illogical, i.e. the cross of Jesus Christ. This reconstruction of the events is actually a very dubious one for the following reasons.

In the first place, it is a very disputable methodology to resort indifferently to Acts and to the letters for the purpose of reconstructing Paul's state of soul.[60] There is no doubt that the cross is central to Paul's proclamation of the gospel. But it is by no way clear that Acts 17 should be interpreted in the light of 1 Corinthians. It is much more obvious to argue that the words of 1 Cor 2:1-2 have nothing to do with Paul's experience in Athens. It is more likely that Paul was dealing specifically with the gnosticizing tendencies of the Corinthians.

Secondly, it is not evident that Luke in Acts 17 is describing a failure in mission. If so, why should he use his space to do this? On the contrary, at the end of the chapter it is said that "some of them joined him and became believers, including Dionysius the Areopagite and a woman named Damaris, and others with them" (17:34). What missionary in these circumstances would have regarded it a defeat to have achieved so much in a single sermon?

Thirdly, rather than being a failure this speech in Luke's view has to be seen as a model for the Christian approach to intellectual representatives of the pagan religiosity. The speech gives an example of dialogue in the primitive church, cf. the use of *dialegomai* in v. 17. Here the Lucan Paul is setting a pattern. As E. Haenchen says, "Luke would not have described this particular event if he had not seen in it an altogether special meaning: actually, a sort of program for mission."[61]

3. The context of the Areopagus speech

Acts 17:16-21 sets the stage for the speech at the Areopagus. Luke's way of narrating indicates that we now are in the heart of Greek culture.[62] He borrows the style of a travel guide and describes the cultural landscape composed of various Greek philosophical schools, the intellectual climate of affected dilettantism and curiosity (17:18.21). He leads us on a tour of the religious landmarks of the city (17:16). This lengthy prologue helps us to see the significance of the speech at Athens: the encounter of the gospel with the Greek culture.

It is said that Paul's spirit "was deeply distressed to see that the city was full of idols" (17:16) so that he argued in the synagogue and in the marketplace with those he encountered (17:17). The verb "argue" is the English translation of the Greek *dialegomai* which is also used in some other passages in Acts (e.g. 17:2; 18:4.19; 19:9-10). This word has the force of "to argue", "to reason", "to contend", that is, the missionary activity of Paul is described as one of dialogue.

A controversy arose when some Epicureans and Stoics heard Paul preaching "Jesus and the resurrection". The conclusion of some listeners was that Paul "seems to be a proclaimer of foreign divinities" (v. 18).[63] Therefore, the philosophers brought Paul to the Areopagus and demanded that he explain his new teaching.

There is a puzzling contrast in attitude between Paul's strong reaction in v. 16 and the much more conciliatory one in v. 22: "I see how extremely religious you are in every way". This comparison reveals the ambiguous character of religion. The reactions attributed to Paul show a variety of possibilities.[64] One is the emotional disgust typical of a minority as a "sect" – the characterization of the images as "idols" (17:16) implies a negative judgment. It reflects a Jewish judgment on Greek piety that is a minority viewpoint vis-à-vis the dominant culture of Athens. Another is the attempt to find some positive elements in discussion with members of the majority.

4. The content of the speech: points of contact, continuity, critique and contradiction
It is this second possibility which is adopted by Paul in his speech, which has three parts:[65] (1) points of contact (vv. 22-23), (2) continuity and criticism (vv. 24-29); (3) contradiction (vv. 30-31). The first two parts have many similarities to the approach of Hellenistic Judaism to the Greek culture and philosophy.[66]

a. Points of contact
Paul's address begins with highest praise for the Athenians: by every criterion they are very religious people (17:22). Of course, this is the *captatio benevolentiae* of the rhetorical address, but it is more than this. As Paul was passing through the city, observing their sacred places and objects, he saw an altar with the inscription "To an unknown god". Such an altar was built in honour of unknown gods in order to prevent the gods from being angry if they did not receive any adoration. This is an expression of a radical polytheism.

It is, however, interesting that Paul interprets the inscription in a different way: behind this polytheism is a hidden longing for the one, true God. Thus, he makes the decision to begin where the listeners are in their own religious quest.

Paul finds a point of contact in the concept of God, but for him there is a great distance between this "*neutral*" God (v. 23) and the Christian proclamation of a *personal* God (vv. 24-31). Therefore, in the end of v. 23 he can declare his intention: "What therefore you worship as unknown, this I proclaim to you" (cf. John 4:22).

b. Continuity and critique

Paul's declaration of his intentions leads to a series of statements about God, about God's character (vv. 24-25) and God's dealings with humanity (vv. 26-28).

The unknown God acknowledged by the Athenians was in fact "the God who made the world and everything in it" (v. 24). The following statements (vv. 24b-25a) inform the audience that God is the Lord of the created order and is not capable of being domesticated by humans. He "does not live in shrines made by human hands" resounds the declaration in 7:48. Moreover, the proclamation that God is Lord echoes the statement of Peter in 10:36. In turn, v. 25b speaks of how God gives life, breath, and all things, so that one hears echoes of Paul's declaration at Lystra concerning God's generosity (14:17).

Several of these statements may reflect Isaiah, e.g. the critique of locating God in shrines made by man. The same applies to the attempt of depicting him in sculptures made from gold, silver or stone (v. 29). However, it should be added that these ideas about God correspond to a large degree with philosophical ideas in Stoicism.[67]

In vv. 26-28 the focus shifts slightly from God's character to the way in which he interacts with human beings. Many of the ideas expressed in these verses resemble what has been said in other speeches in Acts, e.g. the idea that God is near to every man echoes Peter's statement in 10:35.

The appropriate human response to God's ordering of the world is to seek to know him, while recognizing that God is the one in whom all human beings exist. This insight is confirmed by quotations, not from the Jewish scriptures but from pagan poets who affirm that God is the locus and origin of all human life (v. 28). Quoting from the verse, "We too are his offspring" from one of the Greek poets, Paul speaks of himself and his audience as children of the one God: "in him we live and move and have our being".

In this part of his speech Paul is pictured as establishing as broad a common ground as possible with his listeners, regardless of their religious background.[68] Faced with a non-Jewish audience Paul was obliged to adopt a new method. He became theocentric in his approach.[69] But he does not stop at that. There is also something specific Christian in his message, which is evident from the last part of his speech.

c. Contradiction

The crucial shift in Paul's argument comes in the last two verses. A contrast is made between two times (v. 30): the times of ignorance and the time to repent.[70] And there is a reference to the eschatological judgment and the resurrection of Jesus (v. 31; cf. v. 18). In these verses the author insists on three points:

1. All people are in need of repentance.

2. The world will be judged in righteousness by Jesus.

3. The credibility of this claim is underlined in the fact that God has raised him from the dead.

By these elements the speech is given a specifically *Christian* content. The audience reacted differently. When they heard of the resurrection of the dead, some mocked, others were polite, but declined. But some listeners joined the new faith. As noted previously this does not mean that the author is negative to the method used in this speech. Rather he gives expression to the fact that the proclamation of Christ's bodily resurrection was the great stumbling block for the Greeks.

5. Dialogue in Ephesus
We have seen that the Greek word *dialegomai* is used in several passages. One of these is Acts 19:8-10 which is of particular interest. Luke records that Paul

> "... entered the synagogue, and for three months spoke out boldly and argued persuasively about the kingdom of God. When some stubbornly refused to believe and spoke evil of the Way before the congregation, he left them, taking the disciples with him, and argued daily in the lecture hall of Tyrannus. This continued for two years, so that all the residents of Asia, both Jews and Greeks, heard the word of the Lord."

According to this passage Paul is spending two years and three months in the activity described as being in dialogue ("arguing"). The location of Paul's dialogue is noteworthy.[71] First it takes place in the synagogue. He is there until he is forced by other people to leave. The second location is called "the lecture hall of Tyrannus" – the word translated as "lecture hall" in the NRSV is the Greek word *schole;* cf. our word "school". Paul has moved into the physical environment of the Greek philosophers!

The text also reveals something of the subject matter of the dialogue. In the synagogue it turns apparently on the meaning of the Kingdom of God, which is the key issue in Jesus' proclamation. It must have been about the shape of God's kingly rule on earth. How are the human facts of suffering and impotence to be related to the rule of God in the light of the death on the cross of the Righteous Servant? These are questions which are still of great relevance in the dialogue with Jews and even Muslims.

The text does not inform us about the content of the dialogue in the hall of Tyrannus. But it is recorded that the talks continued for two years "so that all the residents of Asia, both Jews and Greeks, heard the word of the Lord." Taken literally Luke is exaggerating. But perhaps he just wanted to underline that Ephesus was the "city of dialogue", that is, the place for the encounter between the gospel and Greek philosophy and various religious movements.[72] The role of Ephesus as a place of dialogue is supported by the fact that other New Testament writings which focus on the encounter between Christianity and Greek thinking seem to be related to this city. 1 Corinthians is written from this place. Its cultural milieu is reflected in the letters to the Colossians and the Ephesians. And the Johannine tradition is often associated with Ephesus.

It would be misleading to suggest that "dialogue" was the only form of mission in which Paul was engaged.[73] Actually there were at least three other forms.[74]

Firstly, there was a kind of intra-faith dialogue with some disciples of Jesus who knew only the baptism of John (Acts 19:1-7).

Secondly we have the story of an unsuccessful attempt by some Jewish exorcists in Ephesus to cast out a demon through invoking of Jesus' name (19:11-20). When they themselves fall prey to the demon's power, many new believers, who are still practising magic arts burn their books, said to be valued at fifty thousand pieces of silver. Luke concludes this story by noting, "So the word of the Lord grew mightily and prevailed" (v. 20). This story shows that religion is always ambiguous. When it is invaded by demonic forces, dialogue is not the appropriate stance. Then it is replaced by confrontation.

Thirdly, mission can also have the form of unmasking an ideology. Acts 19:21-41 is a story about a conflict between Paul and the cult of the goddess Artemis. The guild of silversmiths whose prosperity depended upon the production and sale of little shrines devoted to this goddess felt threatened by Paul's preaching. Thus, the worship of Artemis both supported and was supported by the economics of big business. Luke's readers on the other hand need to know that their common life may well challenge the economic status quos of their pagan neighbours. Some will experience this challenge as a welcome and be led toward faith, but others will try to persecute the church.[75]

IV. Hermeneutical perspectives

In this concluding section it is impossible to discuss the hermeneutical implications of all the issues which have been touched upon in the preceding pages. I have selected a few topics which I consider to be of special interest in today's mission, e.g. the relation between the poor and the sinners, the problem of selective Bible reading, the theme of the Jubilee, the Holy Spirit in mission and the content and method of dialogue.[76]

1. Good news to the poor – and to sinners

It has often been discussed whether the central message of Luke is the forgiveness of sins or social justice. This is a discussion not only among biblical scholars but also among missiologists. Thus the "evangelicals" have asked the "ecumenicals" the question, "Do you weep for the *lost*?". However, the counter-question from the "ecumenicals" is, "Do you weep for the *poor*?"[77]

In Luke's Gospel this is not an either-or. Jesus is presented both as "the friend of sinners" and as the spokesman for the poor. D. Bosch is therefore right in describing Luke's mission as "practising forgiveness and solidarity with the poor."[78] The great majority of those who are considered "lost" are also those who are poor in the material sense of the word.

T. D. Hanks, a Latin American liberation theologian, has commented on the discussion as follows: "Some Christians wish to preach a gospel of socio-political liberation to the poor, whereas others want to offer forgiveness of sins to the rich.

But Jesus does not offer us the luxury of two gospels, one for the rich and one for the poor... Luke 4:18-19 forbids us to remove the socio-political dimension from the gospel, *and* Luke 24:46-47 forbids us to limit the gospel to a purely horizontal level by ignoring forgiveness of sins."[79]

The Jubilee addresses the whole human situation in terms of oppression and liberation. It is a paradigm both of human need and of God's good news in Jesus Christ. To proclaim repentance and forgiveness is not merely the ministry of absolution, but the announcement of total liberation of any form of oppression, in the power of the Spirit. Luke, then, sees salvation as a liberation *from* all kinds of bondage and as a liberation *to* a new life in Christ.

In recent years the "evangelicals" and the "ecumenicals" have come closer to each other. Nevertheless it is still so that evangelicals frequently accuse the ecumenical movement of a selective use of Scripture. The high profile of some biblical portions in ecumenical theology, e.g. Luke 4:16-30 in liberation theology, lends credence to this allegation. On the other hand, many say that evangelicals are equally selective. This may be seen in the prominence of the Matthean "Great Commission", Matt 28:19-20, in evangelical missionary circles.

Both "evangelicals" and "ecumenicals" have to ask the question: how do we read, quote and use the Bible? Both movements are in constant danger of using the Bible simply to confirm what they have been saying all the time, and hence the richness and depth of the whole Bible does not come to life. In many ways Christians in the South read the Bible in a less biassed way because as poor, suffering and oppressed (or at least very close to them) they are in a better position than Christians of the North (and West) to hear and understand all implications of the good news. "The Bible which we Westerners had read so comfortably all these years, spiritualising away the many passages about the poor, had been freshly expounded to us in a fierce judgement upon us".[80]

2. Towards a prophetic-critique hermeneutics

At this point it might be helpful to see how Luke challenges our inherent tendency to read the biblical texts selectively.

Luke presents Jesus as reading the Scripture in a way which is quite different from that of his contemporaries, e.g. the Dead Sea community. This is clear from an analysis of Luke 4:16-30. Among Jesus' contemporaries there was a tendency to interpret the Old Testament in a manner which was favourable to themselves. In the terminology coined by J. A. Sanders, this would be a "*constitutive*" reading of the text. In a constitutive reading the blessings and promises of Scripture are seen as flowing towards the group itself whereas every possible curse applies to the out-group or enemy. An *in-group exegesis* means that a community fails to contemporize Old Testament traditions as challenges to the in-group. Instead the traditions are understood as confirming the belief of the group itself.[81]

An alternative way of reading the Old Testament can be described as *prophetic-critique hermeneutics*. This approach, which challenges the in-group is employed by Jesus himself. In a prophetic reading the emphasis is on God's freedom to bless whom God wills in the way that God wills. Thus, the townspeople of Nazareth are described as being provoked to rage at hearing the prophetic message which lets them know that they do not hold a place of privilege in the fulfilment of the promises of God depicted by the prophet Isaiah.[82]

If Sanders is correct, the concept of Jubilee in Isa 61 was understood by Jesus' audience as referring to blessings promised particularly to Israel at the time of God's eschatological reign. The prophetic reading challenged that assumption of privilege, but left the socially revolutionary implications of the Jubilee imagery intact. In that way, the text of promise was turned into a threat: the poor to whom the good news would come and the captives who would be set free might be any of God's children.[83]

Probably there were two motives for Luke in recording the sermon of Jesus in ch. 4 – as well as the parable of the Great Banquet in Luke 14:16-24.[84] Firstly, he wished to stress the proclamation of the good news for all the dispossessed. Secondly, he wanted to say that these stories contained a *call* to the Christian congregations to be open ones. Christians of the second and third generation could easily become closed groups practising "in-group exegesis".[85] In other words, Luke wanted to prevent Christians from subverting Jesus' prophetic critique of the in-group into a constitutive axiom.

Today, we are challenged in the same way not to adopt a constitutive reading of the biblical texts. Instead we must consider what the prophetic criticism means in a situation which is quite different from that of biblical text(s).

3. The Year of the Jubilee and the debt crisis

The Lucan paradigm for mission is proclaiming the Jubilee. What is the implication of the Jubilee for today's mission? We must re-read the biblical texts (Isa 61 and Luke 4) and interpret them in a global context.[86] The biblical Jubilee calls for international justice.[87]

Though, in its original context, it was concerned with a particular people – the people of Israel – in its eschatological perspective it is concerned with humanity as a whole (cf. Isa 61:1ff; Luke 4:18-19; 7:22). Out of a theo-centric faith emerges a view of man which places all human beings on an equal basis. The land and all its resources belong to God (Lev 25:23; Ps 24:1). Every man in this world has a fundamental right to enjoy the resources of this earth; to deprive him of this god-given privilege is a serious sin.[88]

In this connection I want to draw attention to two points mentioned in the document "Rika och fattiga" ("The Rich and the Poor") published by the Swedish Lutheran bishops.[89] The first point is that the relation between poor and rich should be seen *from the perspective of the poor*. The poor have a privilege of interpretation.[90]

The second point is the close link between *the economic debt of the poor and the moral debt of the rich*. If the basic rights of the poor (to a decent life) are neglected, a moral guilt on the part of the rich will arise. In other words, the relationship between the rich and the poor is not just an economic problem. It has to be seen within the context of guilt and blame.[91]

The one who meets us as herald of the Jubilee of God's reign does so in the particular historical, social, and economic circumstances of his time, just as we are responsible and responding to the same message in the midst of our own historical situation. Each generation must take responsibility for responding to God's decree of liberty, and for doing justice, in its own circumstances and for its children.[92]

4. The Holy Spirit in mission

It is not an overstatement to say: "The intimate linking of pneumatology and mission is Luke's distinctive contribution to the early Church's missionary paradigm".[93] The story of Peter's encounter with Cornelius is especially significant in the light which it throws on the sovereign work of the Spirit in mission. W. Hollenweger has pointed out that this is the story not only of the conversion of Cornelius but also of the conversion of Peter and the church.[94]

Peter realizes that a power greater than his own has broken down the fence which protected devout Jews from the uncleanness of the heathen world. He can do nothing but humbly accept the fact and receive these uncircumcised pagans by baptism into the fellowship of the church (10:47-48).

Mission changes not only the world but also the church. L. Newbigin notes that is not as though the church opened its gates to admit a new person into its company, and then closed them again, remaining unchanged except for the addition of a new member. Mission is not just church extension. It is something more costly and more revolutionary. It is the action of the Holy Spirit who in sovereign freedom both convicts the world and leads the church toward the fullness of the truth which it has not yet grasped (cf. John 16:8-15). "Mission is not essentially an action by which the church puts forth its own power and wisdom to conquer the world around it; it is rather, an action of God, putting forth the power of his Spirit to bring the universal work of Christ for the salvation of the world nearer to its completion."[95]

Mission is a risky endeavour. Its outcome is unpredictable. "The Cornelius story shows that it is not easy for God to teach the Church that He does not practice partiality. To many of us the signs are strong that He has many ways of working in his world."[96]

5. The message and method in dialogue

In recent years the question has been raised: Can the Acts of the Apostles serve as a model for our relationship with people of other faiths? To answer that question we must look at the context in which the mission took place.

Many passages in Acts are centred on the internal debate between Jews and (Jewish) Christians. Most of those who listened to the witness of the apostles were familiar with the expectations about the Messiah and what it meant to speak of Jesus as Christ. This material would be relevant also in a modern dialogue between Christians and Jews.

It will be wrong to assume that all this can be translated across other cultures and ages and the same methodology used when we relate to Hindus, Buddhists, Muslims etc. However, Acts 17:17-34 and Acts 19:8-10 describe dialogues with persons who belong to a non-Jewish faith. Paul was aware that neither the message nor the method he used in relating to those with a Jewish background was adequate with this situation.[97]

Two aspects of the dialogues in the Acts call for our attention. The *first* aspect relates to the *location* of the dialogue. According to Acts 19:8-10 Paul was arguing and pleading with the Jews in the synagogue for the first three months. Then he moved into the "lecture hall of Tyrannus", which is the physical environment of the Greek philosophers. In Acts 17 he was in dialogue in a similar way with people on the market place of Athens.

These examples indicate that the dialogue does not take place on Paul's own terms and in a neutral environment. The agenda and terms of reference of the conversations are set by the other parties to the dialogue.[98] This is different from our own usual forms of activity. We tend to invite people to come into our structures where they will be able to listen to monologues of proclamation in an environment where we are totally at home. In Paul's approach depicted in Acts dialogue becomes a venture – almost in the same way as the meeting of Peter and Cornelius.

It seems probable that Paul used more than one mission strategy. "Paul could switch from Jewish to Greek methods of reasoning, and from the synagogue to a lecture hall".[99] He spent three months in the synagogue engaging the Jews in rabbinic dialogue. And when he spent two years in the lecture hall of Tyrannus he might have used what the Greek called the "Socratic" method.

The *second* note relates to the specific *approach* and *content* of the Areopagus speech. The strategy of this address is remarkable.[100] The choice of Stoic principles as a point of entry and the quotation of familiar Greek writers virtually guarantees attention and a sympathetic hearing – at least initially. The degree of overlap between the concepts of this popular philosophy and what the author regards as the basic Christian worldview is striking, and serves the reader as a demonstration of what can be done in approaching with the gospel those who have no familiarity with the teachings of the Jewish scriptures.

This deals with some issues which have great importance in Greek philosophy, including in particular the quest for the ultimate reality: How should we as human beings relate to the world, to the *logos* and to the divine essence?

It has been noted that in the encounter between the gospel and Greece, Greek thought grows in breadth and depth, but Christian thought takes on new dimensions as well. The gospel no longer responds only to the expectations of Israel's prophets. Now it is thrust into the heart of a cosmological and metaphysical search. Continuity with Israel is now fitted into the larger continuity of the history of the nations. The gospel finds new echos in this larger context: it encounters the fundamental question of Being and the One, and takes on a universal value, for the West immediately, and for other metaphysical civilizations, such as India, indirectly.[101]

This raises the question if the Greek religious and philosophical traditions can be seen as a preparation to the gospel almost in the same way as the Old Testament. This would correspond to the view which sees the world religions as preparations for Christ. If this approach is adopted, one must ask in which manner Christ can be seen as the fulfilment of the longings and aspirations of mankind (especially adherents of non-Christian religions), and in which way he is a correction to that aspiration.

There is one essential element in the Areopagus speech which is incompatible with Stoic expectations – the resurrection of Jesus as a historical event. What is the implication of this for the dialogue with people of other faiths?

Notes

1 Conzelmann 1964, 95. The German original "Die Mitte der Zeit" was first published in 1953.
2 Cf. Dunn 1977, 348-349; Marshall 1970, 121. 129; Nissen 1984, 92, note 12; Soards 1994, 189.
3 Cf. Bosch 1991, 87.
4 Senior & Stuhlmueller 1983, 259.
5 McAfee Brown 1984, 21-32, has shown that Luke 24:13-35 reflects a new form of knowledge. Cf. Nissen 1989, 274-275.
6 Arias & Johnson 1992, 58-59.
7 Cf. Ringe 1985, 42.
8 For a more detailed analysis see Nissen 1984, 74-78.
9 See, for instance, Soares-Prabhu 1978, 204-205.
10 Cf. Albertz 1983, 199; Pobee 1987, 20; Bosch 1991, 99.
11 Nissen 1984, 75.
12 Bosch 1980a, 56; cf. Jeremias 1971, 200; Ford 1983, 81-83.
13 Kee 1995, 187-207, rightly underlines the inclusive strategy of Luke-Acts.
14 Cf. Sloan 1977.
15 For a more detailed analysis see Ringe 1985, 16-32.
16 Cf. Arias & Johnson 1992, 62.
17 Cf. Liebschner 1979; Nissen 1984, 12-13.
18 Cf. Moxnes 1988, 168.
19 Nissen 1984, 171-173.
20 Cf. Arias & Johnson 1992, 69.
21 Ringe 1985, 66-71.
22 Nissen 1984, 82.
23 So, for instance, Degenhardt 1965.
24 E.g. Schottroff & Stegemann 1986.
25 Cf. Nissen 1984, 90-91.
26 Schottroff & Stegemann 1986, 91.
27 Yoder 1972, 73.
28 Paoli 1973, 147.
29 Cf. Moxnes 1988, 142-143.
30 Cf. Senior & Stuhlmueller 1983, 264-265.
31 Cf. Sandnes 1981, 123-134.
32 Cf. Senior & Stuhlmueller 1983, 269.
33 Covenant renewal is thus depicted as worldwide in scope and as potentially universal in its inclusiveness; cf. Kee 1990, 31.
34 Cf. Seim 1995, 52.

35   Cf. Moxnes 1986-1987, 161-162.
36   Cf. Matson 1996, 187.
37   Cf. Kee 1990, 63.
38   Cf. Koenig 1985, 107.
39   Notice that many of the Lucan meal scenes combine repentance and hospitality, cf. Sandnes 1994.
40   Koenig 1985, 106.
41   Cf. Flender 1967, 166: "The Church is the place where the exalted one manifests his presence and where the Holy Spirit creates anew."
42   The term "all things in common" (2:44 and 4:32) is inspired by the Old Testament idea of the sabbatical release, cf. the allusion to Deut. 15:4. It also has parallels to the Greek idea of friendship.
43   Santa Ana 1977, 40.
44   Sider 1977, 99.
45   Arias 1982.
46   For a more detailed discussion see among others Nissen 1984, 85-90.
47   Notice also the addition made to the Lucan version of the institution of the Lord's Supper: "take this and *divide it among yourselves*" (Luke 22:17).
48   Cf. Barrett 1979, 291-292.
49   Dunn 1970, 90: "There are few problems so puzzling in NT theology as that posed by Acts in its treatment of conversion-initiation. The relation between the gift of the Spirit and water-baptism is particularly confusing."
50   See Hartman 1994, 89.
51   Cf. Kjær-Hansen 1995, 71.
52   Cf. Dunn 1970, 93.
53   For a discussion of this problem see Dunn 1975, 148-152.
54   For a comparison between Luke and other New Testament authors see Dunn 1977, 174-202.
55   Cf. Synnes 1994.
56   For the identification of the missionary discourses see among others Wilckens 1974.
57   Cf. Hammar 1975, 57-59.
58   Dunn 1977, 12, notes that "*kerygma in the NT probably includes the idea of proclamation at a particular time and place. That is to say, kerygma is always situational to some degree - to some degree conditioned by the circumstances which the proclamation called forth*" (author's italics).
59   Cf. Senior & Stuhlmueller 1983, 271.
60   Cf. Legrand 1990, 109.
61   Haenchen 1971, 530.
62   Cf. Legrand 1990, 109.
63   It should be noted that Socrates was tried and sentenced to death for similar charges; cf. Haenchen 1971, 527.
64   Cf. Moxnes 1995, 123.
65   Cf. Schneider 1981, 173-178. Dupont 1979 in a similar way divides the speech into three parts: vv. 22b-23, vv. 24-29, vv. 30-31. He contends that the structure serves the argument of the speech against idolatry. By contrast Soards 1994, 96, divides into two parts: vv. 22b-28 and vv. 29-31.
66   Wilckens 1974, 100, is probably right in arguing that the speech in its present form reflects Luke's theology, but it follows a traditional pattern for mission within primitive Hellenistic Christianity which again is influenced by Hellenistic Judaism.
67   Cf. Moxnes 1995, 123.

68 Cf. Kee 1990, 64.
69 Cf. Ariarajah 1985, 45 .
70 The necessity of repentance is an important theme in many speeches, e.g. Acts 2:38.
71 Cf. Cracknell 1986, 27.
72 Cf. Cracknell 1986, 28.
73 According to Larkin 1998, 183, Luke's assessment of non-Christian religions is negative. Although God has left a witness to people in every culture that a beneficent creator God exists (14:15-17; 17:24-28), the beliefs and practices of non-Christian religions reveal that they are the product of blind ignorance (17:23) and foolish rebellion (14:14-15; 17:25-29). Luke also links, though tangentially, the demonic and non-Christian religions (e.g. 26:18; 16:16-18; 19:13-16).
74 Cf. Cracknell 1986, 28-29.
75 Cf. Koenig 1985, 113.
76 Other issues which are not discussed in this section include the importance of household mission and the relation between proclamation and healing.
77 Cf. Bosch 1980b, 33.
78 Bosch 1991, 84-122. Bosch considers Luke's understanding of salvation as encompassing the total person (*aphesis* as both forgiveness and release/liberation); see p. 107. By contrast, according to Larkin 1998, 179, it is spiritual salvation that is Luke's focus throughout Acts.
79 Hanks 1983, 112.
80 Cf. Verstraelen 1980, 46. The quotation is from S. Barrington-Ward, "In Search of a Whole Gospel", in *CMS News-letter*, no. 436, October 1980.
81 Sanders 1975.
82 Cf. my analysis of Luke 4:16-30 in I.2.
83 Cf. Ringe 1985, 44.
84 Cf. Nissen 1984, 77.
85 According to Ringe 1985, 45, Luke appears to have interpreted the account with a "constitutive" hermeneutic concerning the privileged position of the church in receiving the promised blessings. Nevertheless he has sustained and developed the ethical implications of the Jubilee images themselves.
86 This applies not only to Luke 4, but to other texts as well, e.g. Luke 16:1-8. On the hermeneutical consequences of this text see Ukpong 1996, 208: "This parable challenges Christians to be committed to work towards the *reversal* of oppressive structures of contemporary economic systems, and to take life crises as challenges to rise to new heights in response to the demands of the kingdom".
87 See also Ucko 1997.
88 Robinson 1978, 363-379.
89 "Rika och fattiga" 1993, 33-34.
90 Rika och fattiga, 34. Liberation theologians speak of "the epistemological privilege of the poor". This expression is used to underline the fact that the way the poor view the world is closer to the reality of the world than the way the rich view it. Cf. Stam 1979, 122-141.
91 For further reflections on this relationship see Nissen 1984, 161.
92 Cf. Ringe 1985, 93.98.
93 Bosch 1991, 114; cf. Larkin 1998, 181.
94 W. Hollenweger 1979. For a critique of Hollenweger's view see Klaiber 1997, 82-83. The author argues that Peter learns something in this story, namely the impartiality of God (10:34-35) but this he does not learn "in dialogue with persons of another faith" (Hollenweger 1973, 10), rather through a series of visions which God granted him and Cornelius.

95 Newbigin 1978, 66.
96 Stendahl 1977a, 124-125.
97 Cf. Ariarajah 1985, 46.
98 Cf. Cracknell 1986, 27.
99 Bakke 1987, 82.
100 Cf. Kee 1990, 65.
101 Cf. Legrand 1990, 110.

5.

Sent into the world:
Mission and incarnation in the Fourth Gospel

Introduction

The relation of the Fourth Gospel to mission remains a disputed subject among scholars. This dispute is closely related to the question for whom and for what purpose the Gospel was written. Was it addressed to those already converted in order to strengthen their faith in Jesus? Or was it addressed to non-believers in order to win them over to faith in Jesus? In the first case the Gospel would serve as a community document, in the second it would be more of a missionary document. The disagreement has arisen mainly from the discussion of one particular text, John 20:31.[1]

More recently, it has been argued that the Gospel of John is not a mission document but an "in-house" product, mostly polemic and sectarian, from an isolated Christian community quite uninterested in mission to the outside world.[2] In this interpretation the main focus is on ecclesiology – especially the relation between the community and the world – not on mission in the sense of winning new believers.[3]

However, in the Gospel of John mission is not just to be subsumed to ecclesiology; it has its weight of its own. "The Christological focus of the Fourth Gospel is the key to understanding its theology of mission, as it is for every other aspect of John's message".[4] This point is underlined by the so-called "Sendungschristologie".[5] Furthermore, the work of Jesus and his disciples is characterized as a mission to the world (17:18; cf. 20:21 and 4:31-38).

The disagreement as to the understanding of mission in John depends to some extent on the way in which "mission" is defined. Mission is usually defined as "sending" or "going out" to non-believers. Even though this aspect is important for John, his concept of mission cannot be limited to it alone. Johannine mission is dual in character. It is both sending and gathering. Both aspects are held together by the concept of incarnation.

I. Mission as sending

In the twofold character of mission that follows we shall deal first with the aspect of sending.

1. The sending of the Son

J. McPolin has provided a helpful schematization of four types of sending that occur in the Fourth Gospel:[6] (1) John the Baptist is sent by God to testify about Jesus (1:6-8; 3:28); (2) Jesus himself is sent by the Father to testify about the Father and do his work (4:34; 17:4 etc.); (3) the Paraclete is sent by both Father and Son to give testimonies about Jesus; (4) and, finally, the disciples are sent by Jesus to do as he did (20:21; 17:18).

These missions are interrelated. All four are accomplished in the arena of the "world", and ultimately, have the salvation of the world as their goal. All involve a personal relation between the sender and the sent. All revolve around Jesus: John announces his coming, the Paraclete confirms his presence, the disciples proclaim his Word to the world. But the endpoint of this Gospel's missiology is not Jesus but the Father. The Father, alone, is *not* sent. He is the origin and the goal of all the testimony of the Gospel; cf. John 1:1-18 and 17:20-23.

The Gospel is about Jesus, but Jesus is about God. "John was concerned to confront his readers through Jesus with God".[7] Johannine christology is perfectly transparent in the sense that Jesus does not attract attention to himself but points to the Father whom he constantly reveals. The Father is the centre of the Gospel; Jesus is "only" a medium, in other words "the way". As revealer of God he lets all the light pass through him to the Father.[8]

While the sending of John the Baptist is of lesser interest for the mission of the Fourth Gospel, the three other sendings are of central importance.

One of the most important designations of Jesus is the "one sent".[9] Christ's identity is defined as the envoy of God, sent into the world on a specific mission.[10] As the "one sent", Jesus seeks to accomplish the Father's work and will. In the cardinal passage of 3:16-18 it is underlined that Christ is God's messenger who comes to accomplish a distinct and unique mission. The purpose of this sending is summed up in the statement that "God did not send the son into the world to condemn the world but in order that the world might be saved through him" (3:17).

The *motivation* of mission is *God's love for the world* (3:16). "The message of the gospel of John is that the Son of God assumed human flesh to give his life and in this way express fully the Father's love for all humanity".[11] As a consequence, John's portrait of Christ is decisively formed by the concept of love. This is emphasized by different sayings of Jesus, for instance, 10:11; 15:13 and 17:19.

The content of these sayings is love, in which Jesus reveals the real nature of God's essence. His love has its climax in the sacrifice and devotion for others. That is why his death as self-giving is the most supreme expression of God's being. The passion narrative in general is an illustration of the words in 3:16;[12] God's love is manifested in sending forth his son to the world and sacrificing him on the cross (3:14-16). As a grain of wheat that dies in order to produce new grains for others, so does Jesus manifest the divine love by suffering and dying for others (12:24-25). In fact Jesus' whole life is a lying down his life for others.

The *purpose*, then, of Christ's mission is *the giving of life*. This is underlined throughout the Gospel, for example 3:16; 5:24-25; 6:57; 10:10; 11:25-26; 17:2; 20:31. Jesus came that we should have life, and that abundantly (10:10).[13] In John it is all about life, the processes of life.[14] From the beginning was the Word, the Logos, and it was life, and the life was the light of humanity (1:1 and 4). And so John speaks of the Spirit giving birth to a new life of divine quality. New birth is seen as re-enforcing and re-vitalizing life on the model of the creation itself, that is when God breathed breath/spirit into earthly clay.

2. The sending of the disciples

What is specific to John is that the Father's sending of the Son serves both as the *model* and the *ground* for the Son's sending of the disciples (20:21). Both sendings, Christ's and the believers's, are to the world. Jesus came "to save" the world, not to judge it (3:16-17) and the disciples are sent into the world (17:18) "so that the world may believe" (17:21).

Three times in John's Gospel Jesus explicitly commissions these disciples as his "sent ones" (4:38; 17:18; 20:21). Let us look at these texts in reversed order.

(a) *The mission command (20:19-23)*. The good news of the incarnation becomes the good news of the resurrection.[15] We hear in this passage that the living Christ came and stood among the disciples. The Lord was "coming" in the resurrection as in the incarnation. That coming was not a brief visit from the eternal world. The Word came to stay, "to dwell among us" (cf. 1:14).

The coming of the living Christ is the presupposition for the Great Commission: "As the Father has sent me, so I send you" (20:21). Mission means to be sent. The entire Gospel is about sending and being sent. "The disciples rejoiced when they saw the Lord" (20:20). The resurrection was an experience of "seeing" God's presence through Christ in their midst, in their place, and in their circumstances. The good news of the incarnation – "he pitched his tent and dwelt among us" (1:14; NRSV: "became flesh and lived among us") – became now the good news of the resurrection: "Jesus came and stood among them".

We should notice that the task of forgiving or retaining sins is given to the disciples by the risen Jesus in the context of their being sent as he was sent, and is oriented, not to community members only, but to "anyone" (20:21-23).

It seems that the mission of the disciples is, like that of Jesus, to "take away the sins of the world," to draw people from darkness into light (1:29; 12:46). Like Jesus the disciples are sent into the world with the revelation of God, and like him, they meet with rejection. The function of the Fourth Gospel, then, is to enable the community to step back from its situation of rejection, to reflect upon it in the light of the fate of Jesus, and to be sent out again with its faith renewed.[16]

(b) *Sent into the world (17:18)*. While the Great Commission in 20:21 is silent as to the concrete goal of mission, the second passage indicates that the disciples are sent into the world: "As you have sent me into the world, so I have sent them into the world" (17:18). John 17 is usually entitled the "Priestly Prayer of Jesus". However, the word "priest" does not appear in the text, while the verb "send" (Greek: *apostellein*) occurs seven times. Legrand is therefore right in calling the text "the great missionary prayer".[17]

According to 17:18 mission is to the world which again shows its incarnational character. However, there is a tension in the incarnation: The disciples are *sent into* the world, but they *are not of* the world (cf. 17:16). Yet, the foundational verse for mission in the Gospel of John is 3:16.

In John the "world" has three different meanings. First it can denote the created world, the universe (e.g. 1:4); second, it refers to the human world – people (e.g. 17:18); finally, it can signify the worldly system that opposes God's will (e.g. 15:20). In this third aspect the world is "human society as it is structured in opposition to Christ and to the followers of Christ".[18]

In short, the world is human society as such, as it is organized and maintained for the good of some but the harm of others and to the detriment of the love of God. "So, for John, evil does not lie in creation but in the human response to creation and to the Creator. Not that what is human is evil as such: the Logos is and remains the light of the human race, and Jesus appears as the fulfilment (even if also the transcendence) of many human hopes".[19]

(c) *Reaping and harvesting (4:31-38)*. The third passage in which Jesus gives a direct commission to mission is at the end of the story of his conversion with the Samaritan woman, 4:31-38. Here the mission of the disciples is characterized as reaping and harvesting what has been sown by others (vv. 35-38).

Who are these "others" in whose labours the disciples are going to enter (v. 38)? It has been suggested that the "others" were the prophets in the Old Testament or John the Baptist and his disciples or Jesus associating the Father with himself in the work (v. 34). The last suggestion is the most attractive, since in the Johannine theological perspective any mission is preceded by the missions of the Father, the Son and the Paraclete. Therefore the disciples' mission is none other than harvesting what has been sown.

In v. 36 mission is presented as "receiving (wages)" and "gathering (fruit)". This concept of "gathering" plays a significant role in other Johannine passages. As the good shepherd Jesus has to gather the "other sheep" into one "sheepfold" (10:16). He also has "to gather into one the dispersed children of God" (11:52). "I, when I am lifted up from the earth, I will draw all people to myself" (12:32).

Almost all these passages associate "gathering" with the death of Jesus. This is confirmed by 12:24 which is a key word in Johannine mission. Jesus' saying about the grain of wheat means that from his death will come the new people of God, the union of God's scattered children, the gathering of the flock (12:24.32; 11:51f.; 10:16ff.; 17:21). For John that Jesus "bears fruit" is mission, as is the fact that he "gathers in fruit", "receives wages" (4:36).[20]

3. The sending of the Spirit
In John's Gospel the Holy Spirit is of central importance for mission. This is clear from the last commission and from the farewell discourses. According to 20:22 the risen Christ "breathed" on the disciples and gave them the gift of the Spirit. In the farewell discourses the Spirit is called the Paraclete, a term which has a range of meanings: Helper, Comforter, Advocate, Intercessor, or Mediator.

The Spirit sent by the Father does for the post-Easter community what Jesus did for his disciples. Thus the Paraclete is "with" the disciples (14:16), "teaches" and "guides" them (14:26; 16:13), reveals the Father's message to them (16:13) and enters into a prophetic confrontation with the unbelieving world (16:8-11).

The Paraclete does not simply replace the presence of the risen Christ in the community but *intensifies* it. D. Senior points out that this intensification is linked to the church's missionary experience. The Paraclete sent from the Father by Jesus will "bear witness" to Jesus just as the disciples, too, will "bear witness" (15:26-27). The Paraclete confronts the power of evil in the world, just as Jesus had done and just as the community must do (16:8-11; 17:14-18). The "greater works" (14:12) done by the community and its more penetrating understanding of Jesus' teaching are also tied to the community's mission experience.[21] Taking the gospel from Palestine to the "end of the earth" and reinterpreting the teaching of Jesus for the Hellenistic world were bold steps for the post-Easter missionary church. Luke sees this creative development – a development far beyond the horizons of Jesus' own ministry – as guided throughout by the power of the Holy Spirit. Could it not be that John works out of a similar conviction?[22]

The Synoptics attribute the power of the missionary preaching and testimony before hostile powers to the presence of the Holy Spirit in the community. When the disciples are dragged before the authorities, they need not worry in advance about what to say, for it will be given them by the Spirit, "for it is not you who speak but the Holy Spirit" (Mark 13:11 and par.). This understanding of the Spirit is taken up in the Johannine farewell discourses where the Spirit is described as Jesus' and the disciples' "Counsellor" who will arm the disciples as Jesus' witnesses and convict the world as regards its true situation (15:26ff.; 16:7-14).[23]

The Spirit should not be conceived of as a comfort for the already comfortable, or as belonging primarily to the realm of warm religious experience of grace and forgiveness. It seems an indispensable function of the Spirit to make our witness for Christ and the kingdom of justice and peace on earth bold enough to confront and rattle the powers that be.[24]

This is probably the reason why the Paraclete is called the "*Spirit of truth*" (15:25; 16:13); this again is parallel to what Jesus says about himself in 8:32. There is no consolation without truth. However, people often act as if consolation is fostered precisely by avoiding the truth. Confused with easy optimism, consolation is reduced to the level of deceitful, false or hypocritical talk.[25] But in relation to the world, the mission of the Spirit is to convince, to admonish, to illuminate, and to judge (16:7-11).

The function of the Spirit in relation to the disciples is most clearly described in 16:12-15. In this passage John indicates the dialectic between the present Spirit and the original gospel: The spirit "will guide you into all the truth", which is balanced by "he will not speak on his own" (16:13). Again, "he will declare to you the things that are to come" (16:13), which is balanced by "he will glory me, because he will take what is mine and declare it to you" (16:14). The dialectic of the Johannine concept of revelation is summed up in the word *anangellein*. For it can have the force of "*re*-announce", "*re*-proclaim", but in 16:13 as in 4:25 it must include some idea of new information, new revelation, even if new revelation is drawn out of the old way of reinterpretation.[26]

This means that "the teaching function of the Spirit for John is *not* limited to recalling the *ipsissima verba* of the historical Jesus. But neither does the inspiring Spirit create wholly new revelation or portray a Jesus who is not in substantial continuity with the once incarnate Jesus. There is *both freedom and control* – liberty to reinterpret and remould the original kerygma, but also the original kerygma remains as check and restraint."[27]

4. Mission and mutual love

As is clear from the introduction some interpreters find that the Johannine community is an introverted sect without missionary interest. Thus, W. A. Meeks argues that the otherworldly, exalted Christ is directly related to the communal experience of the Christians for whom the book was written. His conclusion is that the "book defines and vindicates the existence of a community that evidently sees itself as unique, alien from its world under attack, misunderstood. It could hardly be regarded as a missionary tract".[28]

It is often argued that John has limited the love command. The love of one another (13:34) has replaced the love of neighbours and enemies. This limitation corresponds to a characteristic Johannine limitation of the scope of God's concern: it is for the disciples, not for the world (cf. 14:22-24; 17:9).[29]

However, despite the inner-directedness of the Johannine love language, the community never became an isolated sect – like that at Qumran. The foundation of the fellowship in the divine commission to continue the witness of the Son kept it oriented towards the world. Evangelization is still the primary task of the community.[30]

As noted previously, love is the motivating force of the missionary endeavour (3:16; 10:17-18), even when such love results in death for oneself (12:24-26; 15:12-17). "The life of love in the community of disciples becomes the trademark and the credential of the missionary community: 'If *you* have love for one another, then *everyone* will know that you are my disciples' (13:35)".[31]

The disciples gives witness to the world in so far as they love each other (13:34f.). This love is at its greatest when they give their life for their friends (15:13), for in doing so they demonstrate that they are not "of this world", that is, their life is defined not by the destructive powers of hate and death but by the life-giving power of God revealed in Jesus. As Jesus has loved them until the last second of his life, so the disciples are to love one another. In and through their love for each other they are called to give public witness to the life-giving power of God's love in Jesus. By this *praxis of agape* all people will know that they are Jesus' disciples.[32]

The Johannine form of mission has a structural similarity with the Old Testament "centripetal" concept of mission. It is "mission by attraction".[33] Fellowship is, simultaneously, the means, the end and the result of mission, "that they may all be one" (17:21). No less than this is the Johannine vision of universal mission.

II. Christ as God's universal invitation

1. "Come and see"

"What are you searching for?" (John 1:38)[34] These are the first words of Jesus in the Fourth Gospel. They indicate a theme of great importance for the author. Throughout the Gospel people are searching for something. It seems as if they are searching for fellowship with God and other persons, for the meaning of life, for a place to belong.

What is the answer to their search? In 1:35-51 we have essential notes of the call of discipleship: "seeking" (v. 38a), "finding" (v. 38b), "coming and seeing" (v. 39), "remaining with Jesus" (v. 39b), "missionary sharing" (vv. 40-42) are among them.[35] Each of these characteristics are worth considering.

In John the term *seeking* is often used to designate the deep desire that characterizes religiously significant attitudes and actions. Throughout the Gospel such themes as "seeking glory", "seeking to kill", "seeking the will of the one who sent me", and "seeking the truth" emphasize the theological importance of the term by marking the ultimate motivations of various character.[36]

Finding: John refers several times to "where Jesus is and remains". The ultimate purpose of the work of Jesus is to reveal to the disciples this "where" of his living and to take the disciples there with him. "...where I am, there will my servant be also" (12:26; cf. 14:2-3).

Coming and seeing: both are terms indicating faith. "Coming to Jesus" is the same as "believing in Jesus" (6:35). Both terms indicate the experimental dimension of faith.

Remaining: At the invitaton of Jesus the disciples came and saw where he was staying, and they remained with him (v. 39). The term "remain" is often used in John. Its theological importance is particularly evident in 15:1-17. This term designates the intimate union that expresses itself in a way of life lived in love (15:9 and 15:17).

Missionary sharing: In John discipleship implies missionary sharing of the experience of Jesus. Already John the Baptist witnesses to his experience of Jesus (1:34), leading his disciples to the same experience (1:35-42). Later the Samaritan woman shares her experience of the prophet with the people of the town (4:29). In a similar way, Mary Magdalene is asked to share her experience of the risen Lord with others (20:17).

To sum up, then, the invitation of Jesus to "come and see" seems to mean: 'Here is the fulfilment of your dreams and longings'. This is not to say that all the disciples had great expectations. Nathanael for one was sceptical. Nevertheless Philip said: "Come and see!"(1:46). So Nathanael follows the invitation and does indeed see greater things: the heaven is opened (1:51). Here – in the person of Jesus – is the meeting point of eternity and time. In Jesus the divine reality is revealed in the world of human beings. Jesus is the centre: this centre is the bestowal of meaning from which all other meanings derive.[37]

In this context we should also note John's intention to express the universality of Jesus, namely the listing of christological titles. This is especially clear in the section on Jesus and his first disciples (1:35-51). Here John presents Jesus successively as Lamb of God, rabbi, Messiah, the prophet announced by Moses, Son of God, King of Israel and – outside the structural framework – the Son of Man. In other parts of the Gospel this listing of titles is continued (Logos, Lord, Saviour).

The intention of this characteristic of John is to incorporate deliberately into the understanding of John whatever christological labels are current in the church. In so doing the author seeks to express the universality of Jesus and to assert implicitly that the reality of Jesus transcends any such labelling which explains the addition of the unconnected Son-of-Man saying in John 1:51.[38]

2. The Prologue

John's language has a distinctive and strong universalist character. This is clearly seen from the Prologue. In the first part (vv. 1-10) he describes the divine-human encounter in general terms using designations like Logos, God, all things, life, light, shines, darkness, world etc. Then follows a transition passage (vv.11-13). In the latter part (vv. 14-18) the author uses specific Christian terms, such as the only begotten Son, Father, grace, truth, Jesus Christ and glory.[39]

John's use of Logos is one example of the universal scope. Scholars have sought the origins of Logos in many different places, e.g. Hermetic and Gnostic literature, Stoicism, Philo, the creative Word in the Old Testament, the Wisdom literature. The value of this research is that, by way of comparison or contrast, it brings out the manifold aspects of the Johannine thought. Jesus is seen as a fulfilment of all this but in a specific way. As Kysar puts it: "Yes, Christ is all of this – Stoic Logos,

Old Testament Word, and Jewish Wisdom – rolled into one person. And that is the thrust of the prologue, I believe: Logos for the Christian is a *person*. The Logos is not an abstract philosophical concept. It is not a category of religious experience. Nor is it speculative religious mythology. It is a person, infleshed, living, historical person".[40]

The light and darkness motif is another example of the universal scope. These images are engaging for readers because the interplay between light and darkness is a fundamental feature of human existence. In the latter part of the Prologue (vv. 14-18) attention shifts to the significance of the incarnate Word for those who believe. Instead of speaking of "all things" and "the world", the text says that "the Word became flesh and "lived among us" and that "*we* have seen his glory", voicing the confession of the community of faith (1:14). The imagery changes to reflect this focus. Instead of cosmic images like light and darkness, the text alludes to Israel's particular history by speaking of the glory that filled the tabernacle, of the "grace and truth" that God announced at Mount Sinai, and of the law given through Moses.[41]

Thus, the opening lines of the Prologue deal with the relationship of the Word of God to all humanity, using images that would have had wide appeal. The images used in the first part of the Prologue are focused enough to be meaningful yet broad and evocative enough to engage a broad spectrum of readers. Yet readers would also have heard something new and perhaps disturbing, for enlightenment does not come through instruction in the Mosaic law or training in philosophy but through faith in Jesus.[42]

The Prologue sets the tone for the rest of the Gospel.[43] It is the conceptual "centre" of the Gospel from which all of its other dimensions radiate. The central affirmations are made in v. 1 and v. 14.[44] Jesus is the Word with God from the beginning, and so intimately bonded with God that the Word can be called "God" (vv. 1-2). The revealing Word begins a progressive penetration of the human sphere. All created reality is made in and through the Word; all created reality finds "life" and "light" through it (him), vv. 3-5. This Word is so embedded in the human sphere that it becomes "flesh" and lives in the midst of the community (v. 14).

This Logos christology makes sense as a means of describing God's working in all human lives. On the other hand the Fourth Gospel also affirms that religion as a human phenomenon is deeply ambiguous: "The light shines in the darkness, and the darkness did not overcome it" (1:5).[45]

3. Inclusive and exclusive aspects of Johannine christology
There is a rich store of symbols in John such as light, door, way, shepherd, wine, water, bread etc. Most of these symbols are universal and related to the ordinary life situations of man.

Of special importance is the "I am" sayings. Here the divine name is linked to such predicates as "bread", "truth", "life" or "way". These predicates are symbols of the human quest for God. The hungers and longings signify the long search for the face of God, a search depicted in Wisdom literature precisely in such forms. John implies by such declarations as "I am the bread of life" (6:35) and "I am the light of the world" (8:12) that in Jesus, God's manifest presence and the groping of humanity for God meet.[46]

The Johannine symbols stand on the boundary between various Jewish and Hellenistic modes of speech. They evoke associations from various quarters and transform them to convey a distinctive message. They are given a specifically christological referent, so that they point in their own ways to Jesus, the Messiah and Son of God who came down from heaven to be crucified: he is *the* light, *the* bread, *the* wine. The various images direct attention to the cross, the distinctive lens through which all symbols should be viewed.[47]

In a highly suggestive article G.W. MacRae proposes that John deliberately incorporated this variety of symbols, traditions, and perspectives into his Gospel in order to emphasize the universality of Jesus. According to MacRae, for John no single conceptual mode, Jewish, Greek, or Gnostic was adequate to grasp the meaning of Jesus, who fulfilled them all without being fully captured by any one of them. The bewildering variety of Johannine "backgrounds" would thus have a positive value for interpretation.[48]

The tendency to move from the more particular to the universal was itself a phenomenon which could be seen in many religious systems of that time. But for John's community it is not due simply to the impact of a more cosmopolitan culture. The universalism of the message flowed from the universal significance of Christ himself. Jesus revealed God, and only faith in this Jesus was adequate. John intends us to see that Jesus Christ is the fulfilment of the expectations of mankind. But he "wishes to imply that as long as one tries to grasp Jesus as a Jew or a Greek, as a Gnostic or a traditional Christian would, he both succeeds and fails, for Jesus is the fulfilment of these expectations, but he is caught up in none of them. Only the great act of self-giving love which engenders love within the Christian community can reach him".[49]

The christology of the Fourth Gospel is marked by a peculiar combination of inclusive and exclusive aspects. "In certain passages Jesus not only provides a place, but he also becomes the *entrance* to that place or even *the place* itself. In the Fourth Gospel we can speak of a "hospitality Christology".[50] In such all-encompassing christology Jesus is the temple for the true worship of the Father. He is the new holy place. Yet at the same time the exclusiveness and uniqueness of Christ is maintained. He is the exclusive revealer: no one has ever seen God except the One and Only Son (1:18). He is the only way to the Father (14:6).

4. Mission as dialogue and witness

John's Gospel differs from the Synoptics in that it portrays the entire history as a cosmic mission. The Synoptic tradition uses the metaphor of the kingdom as the keynote of Jesus' mission. The mission of the Johannine Jesus is not only to fulfill the hope of Israel for God's rule but to reveal the face of the unseen God to all humanity (1:18) – a humanity which is searching for God.

Three passages are of particular importance because this search is performed by persons coming from various religious traditions. In ch. 3 Jesus is approached by Nicodemus, a representative of the *Jewish* leaders. In ch. 4 he meets a representative of the *Samaritans*. And in ch. 12 some *Greeks* desire to see Jesus.[51] In the first two passages mission takes the form of a dialogue.[52] These stories are both of historical and hermeneutical interests.

a. On rebirth (Jesus and Nicodemus)

The first story is a conversation between Jesus and Nicodemus (3:1-21).[53] Nicodemus is described as the thoughtful seeker for truth. On the one hand he symbolizes "man as he is" in need of an entirely new origin for his salvation and yet unable to see the possibility of it.[54] On the other hand he is a communal symbolic figure. He represents those Jews who have some sympathy for Jesus but who nevertheless hesitate to join him.[55]

Two things are characteristic for religious seekers. First, they are living "*at night*". The term "night" seems to have a double meaning. It has a literal aspect denoting the fearfulness and insecurity of Nicodemus. And it has a symbolic aspect denoting his lack of understanding. The discourse in John 3 is held together by an inclusion. It begins with Nicodemus coming to Jesus at night, it ends on the theme that people have to leave the darkness and come to light (vv. 19-21) – probably a reference to 1:5. The note that Nicodemus comes "at night" is repeated in 19:39. This suggests that he does not walk in light. "Nicodemus appears as a man of inadequate faith and inadequate courage, and as such represents a *group* that the author wishes to characterize in this way".[56]

Secondly, a religious seeker will often be content with a "*teacher*". In v. 2 Nicodemus addresses Jesus as follows: "Rabbi, we know that you are a teacher who has come from God". A teacher is a person who helps us to a better understanding of our existence.

Nicodemus' opening statement looks like an ascertainment but it is more than this; it is a quest for salvation. The following dialogue indicates that Jesus takes him seriously in his honest search for the truth. Yet, Nicodemus is corrected at decisive points.

The dialogue focuses on the meaning of a begetting from on high. This is also seen from the context. Here we must look at the structure of 3:1-21.[57] This passage can naturally be divided in two parts. First it is argued that begetting from above through the Spirit is *necessary* for the entrance into the Kingdom of God – natural birth is insufficient (vv. 2-8). In vv. 2-3 the *fact* of begetting is described, and in vv. 4-8 the *how* of the begetting is illustrated.

In the second part of this passage the point is that the begetting is made possible *only* when the Son has ascended to the Father, and it is offered only to those who believe in Jesus (vv. 9-21). This is another way of saying that begetting through the Spirit can come about only as a result of Jesus' crucifixion, resurrection and ascension.[58]

According to John 3 participation in God's new order is not possible through ancestry and circumcision; it is made possible only through the Spirit. In v. 8 John uses an analogy which involves a play on words. Both in Aramaic and Greek the same word means "spirit", "breath" and "wind". And who can control the wind or say whence it comes or whither it goes? The breath of life is sovereign and supremely free. Spirit moves among us as wind, entirely free of human control.

Somehow we know whence and how people become Jews. Perhaps we also know what impels people to "join" the Christians. But the wind (= the Spirit) blows where it chooses. In John's understanding the wind (or spirit) is the wind blowing from Jesus who is called the Logos, in the beginning with God and Himself God (1:1-2). It is life which breaks a path where it chooses.[59]

From the analogy between wind and spirit we can learn the following: The wind is a reality. But you cannot see it except in its effects. The same is true of the Spirit. It is a reality, but its nature cannot be perceived except in its effects. In John's Gospel these effects are clearly seen in the new way of life of the community. Born of the Spirit, the disciples are free like the wind. They are not dependent on other's ideas, criticism and approval. At the same time they are moved by the Spirit to love each other. This is their new identity.

In John 3 we have an example of the longings and aspirations uttered by a representative from one of the religious traditions (Judaism). However, the concept of rebirth itself conveys such a longing. It is the longing for a totally new being, a longing to transcend oneself. In New Testament times many people were dreaming of such things. Indeed this dream seems to be as old as the human race.[60] In the Hermetic literature rebirth means a process of divinization. In his new being the reborn is in fact the All in all made up of all powers, cf. Corpus Hermeticum, the tractate "On Rebirth" (XIII,2). Some trends within modern psychotherapy and within new religious movements point in the same direction.[61]

This idea of divinization is not found in John 3. By contrast, the main emphasis is on the element of discontinuity. Rebirth means a radical transformation and it is *not* something that can be attained through human efforts.

Thus, there is a novelty in John's thought when compared with Judaism as well as Hellenism. The Jewish religion, which Nicodemus represents, is inadequate; it cannot move forward continuously into the Kingdom of God. A moment of *discontinuity*, comparable with physical birth, is essential. Man as such, even the Jew, is not by nature able to enter the Kingdom of God. John differs also from Judaism by saying that the Kingdom has already been manifested in the person and work of Jesus. The language of rebirth borrowed from Hellenism helps John to express his realized eschatology: Eternity is now!

But John also differs from Hellenism by insisting on the incarnation and the historical character of Jesus Christ in vv. 14-16. He does not just take over the concept of rebirth, but he incorporates it into his proclamation of Christ without subscribing to the idea of divinization.

Furthermore, it has often been argued that v. 13 reflects the redeemer-myth in Gnosticism.[62] But the similarity to Hellenistic ideas should not be overemphasized since the author at the most crucial points differs from the redeemer-myth. He insists that Jesus is a *historical* person. The description of Jesus as the "one who descended from Heaven, the Son of Man" refers to the incarnation. The crucial point in v. 13 is the same as in 14:6 and 1:51: *No one* has ascended into heaven but the Son of Man. Christ *alone* is the link between God and men (cf. 1:51). There is no access to God independent of him (14:6).

This understanding of v. 13 is supported by the fact that v. 16 refers to Jesus as "the only begotten" Son of God. The importance of these words can be seen by a comparison. The famous Hindu Swami Vivekananda has argued that there is no "only begotten" son of God. There is a plurality of avatars, there are many "sons of God". God has incarnated himself a number of times. This is a pivotal point in the encounter of Eastern spirituality and Western narrow-mindedness. Christians maintain that the "Lord can manifest himself only once; there lies the whole mistake".[63] Vivekananda's position resembles that of early Gnosticism, but it differs substantially from that of John. In his understanding the uniqueness of Jesus Christ is beyond question.

b. On living water (Jesus and the Samaritan woman)

The second story is the conversation between Jesus and the Samaritan woman in John 4:1-42. As in John 3 this story is both of historical and hermeneutical interest. The historical background might be the origin of the Samaritan mission.[64] But at the same time the story functions as a Johannine paradigm for mission.[65]

Within the literary unit of John 2-4 the Samaritan woman is clearly contrasted with Nicodemus. As he comes to Jesus at night and disappears into the shadow, confused by Jesus' self-revelation, she encounters Jesus at high noon, accepts his self-revelation, and brings others to him by her testimony.[66]

John 4 is clearly a mission story (cf. 4:34-38). When the townspeople come to Jesus, they do so because of the "woman's testimony" (v. 39), and they finally confess him to be "the Saviour of the world" (v. 42).

The dialogical character of the encounter between Jesus and the Samaritan woman is obvious.[67] But Jesus intention is not therapeutic. The dialogue is not of the Socratic type either that is, an epistemological and pedagogical dialogue. Instead it is a soteriological dialogue: Dialogue with Christ brings two characteristics of all authentic dialogue to maximum itensity. The first characteristic is confrontation. The second one is change. The partners change each other and only the end of their confrontation shows where their dialogue has led.

The story has two dimensions, closely related and of equal importance: the social and the religious.

As regards the *social dimension* the woman is an example of those people who are rejected by this world. She was an inferior person, an outcast. She had several odds against her.[68] First, she was a woman – a fact which had many implications in the society of her time. Then she was a Samaritan which meant that Jews considered her to be ritually impure and not to be associated with. This impurity is implied in the wording of v. 9.[69] Finally, in her own society she was expelled because of the way she had lived. She was a sinner.

It is precisely with such a person Jesus talked about the great existential questions: the living water and the place for the true worship.

Jesus breaks down all three barriers which made the woman to an outcast.[70] He brought the message of love which is boundary-breaking. In the course of this conversation different things are revealed to the woman. She realizes who she is – "Come and see a man who told me everything I have ever done!" (v. 29). She is given a new life, a radically new beginning. At the same time she recognizes that Jesus is Messiah. This is the only time in the Gospel of John that Jesus says that he is Messiah (v. 26). And this he tells to a woman who has the wrong faith.

Here we touch upon the second aspect of the story: the *spiritual dimension*. The dialogue between Jesus and the Samaritan woman has the character of faith meeting faith. It concentrates on two issues.

The first part of the dialogue deals with *the living water* (vv. 6-15). Here we are led from the daily problems with supply of water and food to something more deep and more comprehensive.[71] This is not to say that the needs of everyday life are without importance. Jesus is the living water, the water of life – in the same way as he is the bread of life (6:35). This means that he is the one who gives both things: water in the literal sense and water as an expression of the Spirit. He is both the creator of life and the renewer of life. The living water is the renewal which the gospel brings into the daily life.

The second part of the dialogue deals with the question of *the place for the true worship* (vv. 16-26). The woman asks whether it is on this mountain (Garizim) or in Jerusalem where we should worship. Jesus answers that worship has nothing to do with geography. Worship is not bound to a particular place. God is Spirit, and those who worship him should do so in spirit and truth. "Spirit and truth" are not to be understood as conceptions which can be acquired and owned once for all. Spirit and truth cannot be achieved through philosophical and religious speculations.

"Spirit and truth" means that God is a living person who has revealed himself in Christ. To worship God in spirit and truth is to worship him in Christ, to be caught by him. We are not going to know God by seeking him at particular geographical localities. The only way to know God is that he reveals himself for us – irrespective of who we are and irrespective of where we worship.

For the Samaritan woman the situation at the well became worship when Jesus revealed himself to her (v. 26). In this way any daily situation can become a worship. And any daily situation in a similar way can become a witness and mission. When the woman had heard the self-revelation of Jesus she left her jar at the well. She ran into the town to tell people what had happened. "Come and see... He cannot be Messiah, can he?" (v. 29).

Following the witness of the woman the townspeople came to the well and many of the Samaritans "believed in him because of the woman's testimony" (v. 39). The wording of the Greek text is parallel to John 17:20. Here Jesus prays for his disciples. The evangelist tells us that he prayed not just for them, "but also for those who will believe in me through their word". This woman is the first and only person in Jesus' public life through whose word of witness a group of people are brought "to come and see" and "to believe in him". The pattern in the two texts is the same: someone is brought to Jesus through the word of another but comes to believe in him definitively because of Jesus' own word. In a sense, there are "no second-generation disciples" in John, because all are bound to Jesus by his own word. Thus, the role of the Samaritan woman in the coming to the faith of the townspeople is precisely that assigned to his disciples by Jesus himself on the night before he died.[72]

In summary, John 4 is a Johannine paradigm for mission. In this paradigm Jesus' method is fundamentally dialogical, following the questions and issues raised by the Samaritan woman and pursuing his revelation purpose to the very end. The climax of the dialogue is Jesus' self-revelation in 4:26, but the movement of the entire dialogue centres on the woman and her needs (vv. 10.13-14).

The whole dialogue which was for Jesus the medium for revelation and proclamation, becomes for the woman a journey of self-discovery. The astonishing thing is that in the end she becomes a missionary. "Because of her sex, nationality and deplorable history (9.17-18.27), the woman represents the lowest grade of humanity to whom Jesus' mission of salvation could be directed. If such a woman, then, can be deemed worthy of Jesus' self-revelation, then nobody can be excluded from his saving mission".[73]

III. Hermeneutical perspectives

A number of hermeneutical perspectives in John have already been noticed at the preceding pages. In this final section some of these perspectives will be developed, and others will be added.

1. A trinitarian perspective
One of the most important aspects of Johannine mission is its emphasis on the theological or even trinitarian aspect of mission. John's Gospel is one of the strongest biblical supports for the understanding of mission as *missio Dei* that is the movement of God to man, in creation, in incarnation and redemption, a movement involving Father, Son and Holy Spirit.[74]

John's Gospel in many ways prepares for the intrinsic bond between trinity, incarnation and mission. This is also noted by the orthodox theologian G. Mar

Osthathios. He highlights the importance of the incarnate Logos. Furthermore he states that "the Father created the world through the Logos in the movement of the Spirit, the Son redeemed the universe, incarnate by the tabernacling of the Spirit as the agent of the Father and the same Father will consummate the salvation of the world through the Holy Spirit, sent by the Son from the Father as the Paraclete. This is the meaning of *Perichoresis*."[75]

According to Mar Osthathios mission is the ontological nature of God which is love (*agape*). Hence God is Himself Love or Mission. It is the outreach of this love that prompted God to create all things visible and invisible and also prompted Him to send His only begotten Son for the salvation of the world and to send the Holy Spirit for the consummation of salvation.[76]

Two aspects of this understanding of mission should be noticed. First it can be seen as an alternative to two other models of mission: on the one hand the christocentric exclusivism; on the other hand the pluralist theology of religion.[77]

Secondly, it helps us to see the social dimensions of the doctrine of Trinity.[78] The distinction of the persons is essential for communion within the Godhead, just as relationships are essential for personhood. The mystery of this divine communion is indicated in 1 John in the words: "God is love; those who dwell in love are dwelling in God, and God in them" (4:16).

This social dimension of the idea of the three-in-oneness of God is important in John. W. Klaiber aptly speaks of John's hermeneutic as a "hermeneutic of the Spirit and of Love". The love of the disciples among themselves and their unity lets the world recognize that the Father has sent Jesus into the world as the bearer of his love (John 13:34; 17:23).[79]

2. In dialogue with various religious traditions

Recent scholarship seems to agree that the Johannine community was in dialogue or contention with a wide spectrum of groups and ideologies in the first century.[80] The Gospel is not only the end product of a succession of encounters with other groups and viewpoints that have influenced John's theology, but in its finished form it may well represent an attempt to communicate with a variety of dialogue partners.

One of the most interesting dialogue partners is Gnosticism. Many would argue that influences from some kind of very syncretistic (or gnosticizing) Judaism have to be assumed if the character of the Gospel of John is to be explained and understood. This, however, raises the question: if a movement or tendency towards Gnosticism can be seen within and through the syncretistic "mix" of the period, is John part of that movement? And if an affirmative answer is at all appropriate, did the Fourth Gospel *increase* the gnosticizing tendency of this trajectory, or did it *resist* it.[81]

The author seems to be quite sensitive to movements and currents of his time. This attempt of John to express his Christian experience in a language that would awaken echoes in a non-Christian world around him should always remain an inspiration and model for us to continue the same process in our own times.[82]

The question is: how far did John go along with his readers? And how far should we go in our dialogue with people of other faiths? Are there some criteria for this dialogue? J. D. G. Dunn has argued strongly that John was deliberately attempting to portray Jesus in a manner as attractive as possible to would-be (Christian) Gnostics, while at the same time marking out the limits he himself imposed on such a presentation. Two points are mentioned: (a) John affirms that the Word *became* flesh – not appeared as or "came down into" – but *became*. This is a clear assertion of the historicity and reality of incarnation. (b) The central importance of Jesus' death in John's theology. The incarnate Logos *dies*. Both of these assertions can be seen as a critique of would be (Christian) Gnostics.[83]

3. An incarnational model of mission

The Fourth Gospel is significant for the universal mission of the church because of its peculiar combination of the universality of Christ and the incarnation. John offers an incarnational model of mission.

John's presentation of Jesus as Logos is important for the dialogue with other religious traditions. As early as the second century some of the Church Fathers stated that Christ had a special function as *Logos Spermatikos*. This is to say that the Spirit of Christ, which like a grain of seed is lying behind the religious systems in the non-Christian cultures and religions, is sprouting forth, sometimes dimly and sometimes in real beauty and splendour, in poetry, rituals, holy scriptures and external arrangements (cf. Acts 17:23-28).[84]

In modern time a number of theologians have used a similar approach to non-Christian religions. This applies especially to those who are living in an Asian setting. Here Logos have been compared with Tao, Atman, Brahman and other divine principles.[85]

In fact, there seem to be good reasons for making this comparison. From the start the Gospel is cosmic and universal. The issues are all ultimate: the origin and meaning of creation, the attainment of authentic life, the search for God. These are elements common to all religious systems. But a Christian interpretation cannot remain at that. The important thing is that John moves from these universal elements to the earthly, historical Jesus. It is a movement from the universal to the particular, from eternity to history, from the impersonal to the personal. And men and women are called to follow that movement, and thereby realize that Jesus Christ is the unique revealer of the living God (1:18).

This movement to the second part of the Prologue with its specific Christian language is indispensable for any dialogue. From the hour of incarnation "we have not only the Logos as a grain of seed or as small beams of light flashing out from the religious systems, but now we have God revealed in His fulness."[86] The uniqueness of the incarnation is given in the closing sentence in 1:18. Here it is said that God the One and Only "has made him known (i.e. the Father)". "Declared him, not only by giving one side of the godhead, like an Indian *Avatara*, not only by giving the essence of an inner pattern, as the buddhists have it in their idea of the *Bhuta-ta-tha-ta* and the *Tatha-ga-ta*, but giving in a historical and personal life, in all-embracing love and power, the full expression of the heart of God".[87]

4. "I am the way"

The "I am" sayings have often been seen as the "exclusive verses" in the Bible because they present Christ as unique, as the only way to God and to salvation (cf. Acts 4:11-12). Previously I have argued that this understanding is not quite accurate. Instead they are a peculiar combination of inclusivism and exclusivism. Thus, the famous statement: "I am the way, the truth, and the life" (John 14:6) reflects a continuity with other religious traditions as well as a certain discontinuity.

It is certainly not accidental that in ch. 14, as elsewhere, John uses specific notions and terminology from the religious traditions of his contemporary world. For instance, among Jews it was customary to speak of "the way". In Jewish tradition we meet the term the "Way of the Torah", and the Qumran community designated it self as the Way. A third example is the "way" of John the Baptist.[88] The multiplicity of religious ways and paths was an issue in the New Testament period.

Today we have a similar variety of ways. The first Sura of the Koran is characterized as the way (or straight path). Hinduism knows three ways to salvation. Buddhism talks about the Eightfold Path. In Chinese tradition Tao is seen as the Way, the chief way.

These traditions from the New Testament period and from modern times indicate that such longings and aspirations of humanity are to be recognized. They reflect the universal condition of all mankind, created in and through the eternal Word of God. Here is the element of continuity.

But equally the Christian community believed then, as it must still do, that the Way of God has been most clearly discerned in the way that Jesus followed – the path of rejection and suffering, of abandonment and death. This way of Jesus is clearly discontinuous with all other religious ways.[89]

5. The role of the Holy Spirit in mission

The original meaning of the second sentence in John 1:14 is something like: "he pitched his tent and dwelt among us". The metaphor is to live in a tent rather than a stone house. This imagery gives a very dynamic understanding of mission.

This dynamic understanding of mission is underlined by the role of the Holy Spirit in John. This is most clearly seen in the passage of 16:12-15 the meaning of which can be spelled out in three points:[90]

Firstly, what can be given to and grasped by this group of first-century Jews is limited by the time and place and circumstances of their lives. It is true knowledge of the only true God and in that sense it is the full revelation of God (17:3.6). But it is not yet the fullness of all that is to be manifested.

Secondly, it will be the work of the Holy Spirit to lead this little community, limited as it now is within the narrow confines of a single time and place and culture, into "the truth as a whole" and specifically into an understanding of "the things that are to come" – the world history that is still to be enacted.

Thirdly, this does not mean, however, that they will be led beyond or away from Jesus. Jesus is the Word made flesh, the Word by which all that is came to be, and is sustained in being. Consequently all the gifts which the Father has lavished on mankind belong in fact to Jesus, and it will be the work of the Spirit to restore them to their true owner.

In short, the Paraclete will receive everything he has to say from Jesus but he will contemporize it in each period and each place. In this the Spirit will not only pass on what was received from Jesus but will ensure also the element of the contemporary and original, to face new situations meaningfully.

This function of the Holy Spirit, then, is to lead the community in *all* truth. There is the prospect here of coming into a new understanding beyond what the group has already reached. A similar dynamic understanding of the Spirit is reflected in John 3:8: The Spirit blows wherever it pleases.[91] The promise in John 16:13 is a remarkable one. We are plainly told that there is more to be learned than can be found in the recorded teachings of Jesus to his disciples during the years of his ministry (cf. 14:12). We might tend to think of the Bible as a book containing timeless truths. This, however, is not how John sees the work of the Spirit.

The sayings about the Paraclete in John 14-16 throw light on the relationship between text, Spirit and community. The community under the guidance of the Spirit is given guidance on the meaning of Scripture for new historical situations. The Spirit enables the community to perceive senses of the biblical text that had previously remained hidden.[92]

The Holy Spirit makes Christ more present, more comprehensible, more transforming. In its Spirit-prompted mission to the world, the church discovers the true meaning of the Word made flesh.[93]

Notes

1   The problem arises because there is a textual variant in the Greek of John 20:31. Some manuscripts read in the present subjunctive ("that you may go on believing"), and others read in the aorist subjunctive ("that you may begin to believe"). The relation of the tenses to the meaning and to John's purpose is complex. See, for instance, Brown 1966-1970, lxvii-lxxx; Rensberger 1989, 153.

2   See Käsemann 1966.

3   See also Kuhn 1954, 167.

4   Senior & Stuhlmueller 1983, 283. See also Popkes 1978, 64.

5   See Bühner 1977; Kuhl 1967; Comblin 1979b.

6   McPolin 1969, 113-122.

7   Barrett 1978, 97.

8   Cf. Kavunkal 1993, 121.

9   For further reflections on this theme in John, see Comblin 1979b, 1-19.

10   Forty times the motif "the one who sent me" is repeated in John's Gospel (twenty-four times with *pempein*, fifteen times with *apostellein*) with God as the sender and Jesus as the agent.

11   Erdmann 1998, 216.

12   Jervell 1978, 58-59.

13   Life abundant includes material as well as spiritual blessings, cf. Nissen 1984, 179.

14   Cf. Stendahl 1990, 28.

15   Cf. Arias & Johnson 1992, 79-82.

16   Cf. Onuki 1984, 102-115; Rensberger 1989, 144.

17   Legrand 1990, 141.

18   Winn 1981, 69. According to Barrett 1978, 426, the world in John is "the whole organized state of human society, secular and religious".

19   Rensberger 1989, 146.

20   Cf. Olsson 1974, 247.

21   Senior & Stuhlmueller 1983, 287.

22   Senior & Stuhlmueller 1983, 287-288.

23   Cf. Klaiber 1997, 100. The author notes that the presence of the Spirit means that the disciples can leave the actual work of persuasion up to God's Spirit freeing their preaching from a tense and forced demand of performance, and in so doing leading to a true *parrhesia*, confident authority trusting the effectiveness of the Spirit.

24   Cf. Stendahl 1990, 32.

25   Cf. Müller-Fahrenholz 1995, 95.

26   Dunn 1975, 352. According to Brown 1966-1970, 716, the term *anangellein* suggests that "the declaration of the things to come consists in interpreting in relation to each coming generation the contemporary significance of what Jesus had said and done".

27   Dunn 1975, 352.

28   Meeks 1972, 69.

29   See, for instance, Käsemann 1966, 101-130.

30   Cf. Perkins, 1982, 106. For a more detailed discussion of the Johannine concept of love and community see Nissen 1999.

31   Arias & Johnsen 1992, 93.

32   Cf. Fiorenza 1983, 323.

33   Popkes 1978, 67. This relation between mission and community is also emphasized by Ruiz 1987.

34   This is a direct translation of the Greek *zeteite*. NRSV has "What are you looking for".

35   See the observations by Vellanickal 1980, 134-135. Cf. Kavunkal 1993, 131-132. In a very stimulating article D'Sa 1984 argues that John 1 should be seen as a hermeneutical model for reading the entire Gospel. According to Klaiber 1997, 62, the long section of 1:19-2:11 ought to become a model of how to lead someone to Jesus.

36   Cf. Schneiders 1991, 192.

37   See Cahill 1976.

38 Cf. MacRae 1970, 19.
39 Cf. Vellanickal 1982, 150.
40 Kysar 1976, 25.
41 Koester 1995, 123-126. Koester points out that the Genesis text was well-known among Jews, Samaritans, and even some Greeks. Readers unfamiliar with the biblical tradition may have heard echoes of other cosmological teachings in the opening lines of the Gospel.
42 Cf. Koester 1995, 132.
43 Barrett 1978, 130, rightly comments on v. 1: "John intends that the whole of his gospel shall be read in the light of this verse".
44 Cf. Cahill 1976, 65; Senior & Stuhlmueller 1983, 284.
45 Cf. Cracknell 1986, 105-106.
46 The predicative "I am" sayings are to be taken as recognition-formulas in Bultmann's famous classification: 'What you understand by the bread of life and long for in it is fulfilled in me'. Bultmann 1968, 168.
47 Images with strong roots in Judaism are expanded and universalized, enabling them to evoke a broad range of associations: manna becomes bread for the world, and the light in the temple becomes the light of the world. Koester 1995, 234.
48 MacRae 1970. This counteracts to a considerable extent the sectarian danger of being closed off to other people.
49 MacRae 1970, 23.
50 Koenig 1979, 133. See also Rebell 1987, 53.
51 The Greeks who wish to see Jesus in 12:20-22 are widely and correctly interpreted as an indication of a Johannine mission to the Gentiles.
52 According to H.-J. Klauck the Johannine mission was directed towards individual persons. The Johannine community did not use fishing nets, but fish hooks. "Einzelmission und Einzelseelsorge hiess das Gebot der Stunde", Klauck 1985, 204.
53 For a more detailed analysis see Nissen 1993.
54 This interpretation is among others voiced by R. Bultmann 1968, 95.
55 See among others Rensberger 1989, 37-41.
56 Rensberger 1989, 40.
57 On the unity of John 3:1-21 see Rebell 1987, 135ff.
58 Cf. Brown 1966-1970, 136 and 145.
59 Cf. Vogel 1983, 80-81.
60 Cf. Rebell 1987, 151.
61 Various attempts have been made within new religious movements to find biblical evidence for the idea of reincarnations. One of the favourite texts is John 3. But this text is about a rebirth *in* this life as a presupposition for eternal life. For a critique of Rudolf Steiner's speculative use of the Gospel of John, including 3:5, see Nissen 1992.
62 Cf. the verbs for ascending and descending.
63 Vivekananda 1953, 270.
64 See Cullmann 1976; Brown 1979, 43-47. Cf. Schneiders 1991, 186: "The basic purpose of the Samaritan Woman story in the gospel itself is to legitimate the Samaritan mission and to establish the full equality in the community between Samaritan Christians and Jewish Christians."

65 For a more detailed analysis see Okure 1988.
66 Cf. Schneiders 1991, 187.
67 See the penetrating analysis by Chappuis 1982.
68 Cf. Russell 1982, 23-26.
69 On this aspect see Seim 1987, 68.
70 On the role of women for mission in John see Seim 1987; Schneiders 1991, 180-199; Brown 1979, 183-198; Maccini 1996.
71 The most commonplace communication may expand to become suddenly firm and substantial; cf. Chappuis 1982, 11.
72 Cf. Schneiders 1991, 192-194.
73 Okure 1988, 184.
74 Cf. Klaiber 1997, 61: "If the missiological slogan of the *missio Dei* as the foundation of all mission work applies anywhere in the New Testament, then it is to the Johannine writings."
75 Mar Osthathios 1995, 85. The concept of *perichoresis* (mutual interpenetration of the persons) can be traced back to John of Damascus. See also Raiser 1991, 95-96.
76 Mar Osthathios 1995, 87. The author argues that the genuine motivation of mission is neither the fear of hell nor the hunger for heaven, but the love of Christ that constrains every Christian to manifest the sharing love of the Holy Trinity and always do the will of God (p. 90).
77 See also chapter 9 of this study. Mar Osthathios 1995 claims that proponents for the pluralist model tend to speak of a christology "from below" whereas the trinitarian understanding presupposes a christology "from above".
78 Cf. Raiser 1991, 96.
79 Klaiber 1997, 72-74.
80 E.g. Senior & Stuhlmueller 1983, 280; Brown 1979.
81 Cf. Dunn 1977, 298.
82 Cf. Vellanickal 1982, 150-151.
83 This is also a criticism of Käsemann's thesis that the Gospel of John reflects a "naive docetism"; se Dunn 1977, 298-302.
84 Cf. Reichelt 1939, 94.
85 Examples from the Indian setting are Patro 1974, 134-138; Vellanickal 1982, 151. Another Indian contribution to the study of the Gospel of John is Sister Vandana 1981. Throughout her book she compares the stories and sayings of the Fourth Gospel with passages from the Indian religious traditions, especially the Upanishads. This is clearly an "Ashramitic" interpretation, pursuing a dialogue with traditional Hindu religiosity with emphasis on the spiritual and individual elements. Other trends in India are a sober historical criticism, and an interpretation which is put in the context of social change. For a review of the Gospel of John in India see Spindler 1980.
86 Reichelt 1939, 95.
87 Reichelt 1939, 95. The terms *tathata* or *bhutathata* mean the Absolute, conditioned by nothing, which is in itself that which is; cf. Raguin 1979, 111-112.
88 For these references see Brown 1966-1970, 629.
89 Cf. Cracknell 1986, 84-85.
90 See Newbigin 1978, 202.

91   N. R. Thelle argues that the concept of the Spirit in John 3:8 should be linked with John's Logos christology, Thelle 1991, 13-14.

92   Cf. Hays 1997, 252.

93   Cf. Senior & Stuhlmueller 1983, 288.

6.

Constrained by the love of God:
Paul's foundation and practice of mission

Introduction

Any understanding of Paul's mission has to deal with a number of questions. One of these is the nature of our *sources*. Earlier studies tended to "fuse" the Paul of the letters with the Paul of Acts.[1] In this chapter, however, I shall focus almost exclusively on his own letters. Although Acts contains much material that is unquestionably based on reliable tradition, it remains a secondary source on Paul.

The principle source to Paul's mission theology is his own correspondence. The following letters are usually regarded as authentic Pauline material: Romans, Galatians, 1 and 2 Corinthians, Philippians, 1 Thessalonians and Philemon. Two of the letters attributed to him have a specific character, Colossians and Ephesians. For this reason and because their authorship is disputed the mission theology of these letters will be taken up in a separate chapter. The Pastoral letters will not be considered. They are probably written by a disciple of Paul and deal with internal community problems rather than with mission.

Another question relates to the character of Paul's mission understanding. To what extent is it marked by his *personal* experience?

A third question is how to define the term "*mission understanding*". This term might include both theory and practice. In the first case the focus is on the theological foundation or motivation for Paul's mission. In the second case it is on his mission activity, its content and form.

In the past, many scholars have described Paul's theology as a dogmatic system without much inner relation to his missionary work. Other scholars have gone to the opposite extreme and argued that Paul's genius was that of a great missionary and religious personality. Only recently have an increasing number of scholars begun to recognize that there is something wrong in the very distinction between Paul's mission and his theology. His theology and his missionary activity were inseparable from one another.[2] It is today widely acknowledged that Paul was the first Christian theologian precisely because he was the first Christian missionary.[3]

Paul's theology and his mission do not simply relate to each other as "theory" to "practice" in the sense that his mission "flows" *from* his theology, but rather in the sense that his theology is a missionary theology.[4]

Theory and practice are thus closely related. Nevertheless, for practical reasons this chapter is divided in two major sections. The first one is about the foundation of Paul's mission – "*why* mission?" In the second part the focus will be on *how* his mission was performed.

I. The motivation for Paul's mission

1. Paul's conversion and call

The inner unity of mission and theology can be traced back to the beginnings of Paul's life as a Christian. Paul's conversion at Damascus is recorded both in Acts (9:1-19; 22:4-21; 26:9-18) and in his own letters, especially Gal 1:11-17; 1 Cor 9:1-2 and 1 Cor 15:8-10. The description in Galatians is of particular interest, since the conversion is closely related to his call for mission. "But when God who had set me apart before I was born and had called me through his grace, was pleased to reveal his Son to me, so that I might proclaim him among the Gentiles..." (vv. 15-16).

In this passage Paul describes his experience in terms of a prophetic call similar to that of Isaiah and Jeremiah. His experience is usually referred to as his conversion. However, it has been argued that it is a call rather than a conversion: "Here is not that change of "religion" that we commonly associate with the word *conversion*. Serving the one and the same God, Paul receives a new and special calling in God's service. God's Messiah asks him as a Jew to bring God's message to the Gentiles."[5]

There are good reasons for this objection to the phrase "Paul's conversion" if the term "conversion" carries connotations of a change of religion.[6] But certainly, the call of Paul resulted in a radical change of direction, a complete reorientation. The best way of describing what happened to Paul might therefore be to use the double terminology: conversion *and* call.[7]

A few points should be added on the importance of Paul's conversion and call. First, it is evident that *prior* to his conversion Paul was a zealous Jew who emphasized the observance of the law (Gal 1:13-14; cf. Phil 3:4-6).

Second, what happened to Paul at Damascus was interpreted as due to God's action. "By *the grace of God* I am what I am" (1 Cor 15:10).

Third, this conversion meant a *radical revision* in his way of life and in his world-view. From being a persecutor of the early Christian movement, Paul becomes one of its chief protagonists. From one "zealous for the traditions of the ancestors" (Gal 1:14), Paul becomes the "apostle to the Gentiles". From a blameless keeper of the law, he becomes one who completely discounts the law's value for the Gentiles.[8] "Paul's encounter with Christ compelled him to rethink everything from the ground up".[9]

Fourth, in the Damascus experience Paul came to recognize Jesus not only as raised by God, but also as exalted to a position of universal lordship. The scope of Christ's saving significance is cosmic and universal, embracing both Jews and Gentiles.[10]

From his conversion experience Paul was convinced that the God of Israel exercises his sovereignty over all creation and all people in freely choosing to call

all to salvation through Jesus Christ. This was the cornerstone of his mission theology.[11]

2. The universal scope of salvation (Romans)

The theology of Romans is closely tied to the Pauline mission with its historical and eschatological perspectives. It is in no way accidental that the letter is framed by a pair of texts that describe the way in which Paul saw his role. These texts are Rom 1:1-17 and 15:15-25.[12]

Rom 1:1-17 has often been treated as a mere "theological introduction" while Rom 15:15-25 has been acknowledged as a description of "the ministry of Paul". Actually, both texts have the same scope: never having visited Rome, Paul introduces himself to the Christians of that city, presenting himself as an "apostle" in the context of a concrete missionary project, that of carrying the gospel to Spain. Paul was on his way to Rome to win support for what he considered would be the last step of his apostolic career. His theological exposé is couched in the context of a missionary project.

The opening verses in ch. 1 gives a self-portrait of a missionary. Thus, Paul characterizes himself as a "servant of Christ Jesus". He is an "apostle", who is "set apart for the gospel of God". In Pauline usage, the words "apostle" and "gospel" are correlates, and both are missionary terms.[13] Paul also says: "I am a debtor both to Greeks and to barbarians, both to the wise and to the foolish" (Rom 1:14). What Paul owes to mankind is nothing but the gospel of Christ.

This insight is the background of the famous words in Rom 1:16-17: "For I am not ashamed of the gospel; it is a power of God for salvation to everyone who has faith, to the Jew first and also to the Greek". Two things should be noticed. First, Paul sees himself as an apostle among Jews and Gentiles, introducing his mission to the church in Rome. He wants to make clear to them how his mission fits into God's total plan and scheme.

Secondly, the word "first" reflects Paul's attempt at solving the problem of Israel's place in the history of salvation which is the main theme in Rom 9-11. However, the order 'first Jew, then Greek' does not mean a dilution of his basic conviction about the revelation of God's power to save all who believe.[14]

The viewpoint in the first eight chapters of Romans is explicitly universal. At various points, Paul links his concern for the Gentiles with basic statements about the character and purposes of God. Three passages are of particular interest. In Rom 3:29-30 the oneness of God is linked explicitly with the justification of the Gentiles. Rom 2:11 emphasizes the impartiality of God in his judgement. And in Rom 3:21-22 the righteousness of God is now revealed for all who believe without distinction. *All*, in fact, are ungodly, and *all* are called to experience God's justice in Jesus Christ. The saving death of Jesus is for *all*, Jews and Gentiles alike. Thus, "it is the 'justification of the godless', the justification by faith, that opened the road to the nations (Rom 3:27-29)."[15]

While respecting certain historical advantages of one people over the other (cf. Rom 3:1-2; 9:4-5), Paul proclaimed a gospel of "no distinction" between Jews and Gentiles in condemnation before God (Rom 1:18-3:20), "no distinction" between Jews and Gentiles in access to God (Rom 3:21-5:11), and "no distinction" between Jews and Gentiles in the one body of Christ (Rom 9:1-11:36; cf. Eph 2:11-22). These "no distinction" texts were based on Paul's belief in the universality of Christ: "For there is no distinction between Jew and Greek; the same Lord is the Lord of all and is generous to all who call on his name" (Rom 10:12; cf. Gal 3:28). It was this gospel that Paul endeavoured to express in all his missionary activities and all his pastoral responsibilities.[16].

To sum up, then, in Romans Paul uses a number of concepts which are of central importance for the foundation of mission:[17] God's grace is the foundation of mission; faith is the only fundamental demand, and this faith is based upon a gift which is called the justification.

In addition to this it should be noticed that the opening chapters have been the basis for a debate over Paul's view of *pagan religiosity*. At first glance the description in Rom 1:18-32 appears to be very negative. It is not easy to see any connection to the Paul who speaks to the Greeks in Athens (Acts 17). Paganism is seen as idolatry and apostasy, cf. 1:25: "they exchanged the truth about God for a lie and worshipped and served the creature rather than the Creator...".

It has often been argued that this attitude towards paganism is a common feature in Paul's missionary preaching. He appealed to the Gentiles to "turn to God from idols, to serve a living and true God" (1 Thess 1:9; cf. Rom 1:18-32). This accusation of idolatry was a strong motif of Judaism in its dialogue with the Gentiles, and it finds a place in Paul.[18]

However, the major reason for this evaluation of paganism is not to be found in Paul's missionary preaching. Rather, we should look at his theological argumentation. The *order* of his reasoning is not coincidental. First we have the positive statement about the justification by faith (1:16-17), then follows a negative statement about the sins of the Gentiles: *Since* God has revealed himself exclusively in Jesus Christ, any admittance to God "from below" is closed – be it the Jewish observance of the law or the Greek search for wisdom (cf. 1 Cor 1:18ff.; Rom 1:22).

This interpretation is confirmed by the fact that according to Paul the Gentiles have the possibility of knowing God (1:19-20) and of fulfilling the law (2:14; 2:26-27).[19] Paul is convinced that the God who can be met in nature is the same God who gave the law and who sent Jesus.

In other words, the revelation of God's wrath (1:18-3:20) can be understood only in the light of the revelation of God's righteousness (1:16-17; 3:21-22). Or putting it a little more forcefully, 3:21-22 is to 1:18-19 as premise is to conclusion and not the reverse.[20]

From 1:18-31 two things are clear: that God has revealed his "eternal power and divine nature" in the natural order of creation (vv. 19-20), but that mankind has wilfully and consistently ignored him. "Both assertions are crucial for Paul's argument. The revelation in creation was universally available but universally rejected."[21] If both assertions are maintained, the implication is that there is a certain basis for natural theology in Romans 1-2. This means Paul's stance towards other religions is not one of "radical exclusivism".[22]

3. Ministers of reconciliation (2 Corinthians)
The passage of 2 Cor 5:14-21 contains a number of statements which illustrate Paul's understanding of mission. To begin with the text points to the importance of the death of Christ for mission: "For the love of Christ urges us on, because we are convinced that one has died for all; therefore all have died. And he died for all, so that those who live might live no longer for themselves, but for him who died and was raised for them" (vv. 14-15).

This passage more than anything else shows the deepest level of Paul's motivation of mission. It is the overwhelming experience of God's love in Jesus Christ which compels him to preach the gospel.

The implication of the death and resurrection of Christ is the coming into existence of a new creation. V. 17 has often been translated "he is a new creation". But the words "he is" are not in the original text. Linguistic observations make it more probable that we should translate: "if anyone is in Christ, there is a new creation," (NRSV) or more smoothly, "there is a whole new world" (NEB). The accent lies not on transforming the ontology of the person but on transforming the perspective of one who has accepted Christ as his context. In this passage Paul is explaining why he does not regard Jew as Jew or Greek as Greek, but rather looks at every person in the light of the new world which begins in Christ.[23]

Paul is not describing *in this context* the personal dimension of a new birth; rather he is announcing as a kerygmatic statement *the advent of the new creation* "in Christ", the dramatic recovery of the world, (formerly alienated and dislocated), by God who has acted eschatologically in Christ, i.e. the world is placed now under his rule.[24]

In the following verses, Paul describes how this transformation of history has made him aware of his vocation to be an "ambassador for Christ" and a "minister of reconciliation":

> "All this is from God, who reconciled us to himself through Christ, and has given us the ministry of reconciliation; that is, in Christ God was reconciling the world to himself, not counting their trespasses against them, and entrusting the message of reconciliation to us. So we are ambassadors for Christ, since God is making his appeal through us..." (vv. 18-20).

In this passage I want to point to three aspects:

First, Paul describes himself and other Christians as "ambassadors" (v. 20). As an ambassador the believer represents not himself but another. His ministry is not his own, but has been given to him (5:18). His message is not his own, but has been entrusted to him (5:19). Thus it is God, not Paul, who is at work in his ministry (5:20); it is God's voice that is heard in Paul's proclamation. As bearer of the message of reconciliation, Paul attempts to draw persons to God, not to himself.[25]

Second, two important things are said about the reconciliation; it is God who has acted to reconcile men and women to himself, and this reconciliation is effected through the mediation of Christ. Here we should notice also the similarity between Rom 5:1-11 and 2 Cor 5:18-21. The two passages show that "reconciliation" is but an alternative way of expressing the reality of what has occurred in "justification".[26] This is established not only by the parallelism of the expressions in Rom 5:9-10, but particularly by 2 Cor 5:19 where reconciliation is described as God's "not counting their trespasses against them".

This is not to deny that the two terms "justification" and "reconciliation" have their distinct nuances. One might ask why Paul in Romans moves from the justification in ch. 1-4 to a new vocabulary in ch. 5. According to R. P. Martin part of the reason is that Paul expressed dissatisfaction with the forensic-cultic idiom that limited soteriology to covenant-renewal for the Jewish nation and sought to universalize the scope of Christ's saving deed to include the Gentiles on the basis of faith, not covenantal nomism. Therefore, Martin suggests that "reconciliation" is the way Paul formulated his gospel in communicating it to the Gentiles. It relates to a universal human need, namely forgiveness and personal relationship; and it encompasses within its scope both personal and cosmic dimensions.[27]

Third, the message of reconciliation is for the whole world.[28] In vv. 18-20 the language is both personal ("reconciled *us* ") and universal ("the world "). It is often argued that in v. 19 we have a pre-Pauline doxological formula which is a piece of cosmic soteriology. There is, however, some debate among interpreters where to put the emphasis. If Paul is using pre-Pauline doxological formulas in v. 19, then one might see some dissonance with his own thought: In the pre-Pauline tradition the reconciliation of the world is understood as *universal* and *accomplished*, while Paul interprets it as *proleptic* and *subject to faith*.

Thus R. Bultmann defines the ministry of reconciliation as "an eschatological occurrence" that takes place in the proclamation of the Word.[29] E. Käsemann has argued for a similar approach to 2 Cor 5 and to other New Testament reconciliation texts (e.g. Col 1:15-20; Eph 2:16).[30] The two interpreters approach these passages with a key to their understanding: a basic dialectic which opposes the Word to nature and to the historical order of men's life. Other interpreters argue that this is an anthropological limitation of the texts. There need not be a conflict between the universal and the personal reconciliation.[31]

4. Firmness and flexibility (1 Corinthians)[32]

Both in Romans (1:14) and ind 2 Corinthians (5:14) Paul expresses a deep awareness of his obligation to preach the gospel to the Gentiles. The same is true of 1 Corinthians. In ch. 9 he states that he has a charge laid upon him: he is compelled to preach. "For an obligation is laid on me and woe to me if I do not proclaim the gospel" (1 Cor 9:16). Constrained by the love of God, having a "necessity" (NRSV: "obligation") resting upon him he *became* a Jew to the Jews, a Gentile to the Gentiles etc. and *all this for the sake of the gospel*, 1 Cor 9:19-23.

1 Cor 9:19-23 can be seen as "Paul's classical formulation of the maxim which characterized his whole missionary approach."[33] This passage clearly implies that he allowed circumstances and situations to determine the statement of his kerygma to a considerable degree.[34] His mission is marked by a great adaptability to men of different cultures. The question, then, is, what does such an adaptability mean? Does Paul accommodate himself without reservations? Does he change his gospel at different places? If not, what is the basis of his adaptability?

The basis of Paul's adaptability is evidenced by the structure of the text under consideration:

v.19: For though I *am free* with respect to all, I have *made* myself *a slave* to all, so that I might *win* more of them.

v.20: To the Jews I became as a Jew, in order to *win* Jews.

To those under the law I became as one under the law (though I myself am not under the law) so that I might *win* those under the law.

v.21: To those outside the law I became as one outside the law (though I am not free from God's law but am *under Christ's law*) so that I might *win* those outside the law.

v.22: To the weak I became weak, so that I might *win* the weak.

I have become *all things to all people*, that I might by all means save some.

v.23: *I do it all for the sake of the gospel*, so that I may share in its blessings.

The text proves that Paul was both a man of flexibility and a man of freedom. The flexibility is expressed especially in vv. 20-21a and v. 22a. Here Paul indicates that he understood his mission as a dialogue: To the Jews he became as a Jew, to the Gentiles as a Gentile. The way of dialogue means meeting the other persons on their own terms and really attending to what they say, believe and feel. Mission is distorted if it is presented as happening only by monologue, by one-way-proclamation.[35]

In contrast, dialogue begins where people are, and this is precisely what Paul has done according to 1 Cor 9:19-23. He had "an astonishing elasticity of mind, and a flexibility in dealing with situations requiring delicate and ingenious treatment which appears much greater than usually supposed".[36]

This flexibility is rescued from being unprincipled by its basis and its goal. The basis is given in the opening and concluding statements (v. 19 and vv. 22b-23) and in the middle of the text ("Christ's law," v. 21b). The goal is indicated by the insistence on "winning" people. Let me comment briefly on each of these items in reversed order.

a. The basic principles

(1) To "win" people. As can be seen from the arrangement above, the word "win" occurs no less than five times in the text. Hence it is quite clear that Paul's goal is the successful prosecution of the apostolic task he has been given by the risen Christ – to gain Jews and Greeks for the good news. Only if he does this can he himself have a share in it (v. 23). Paul's principle then is to accommodate himself to any condition of men if that will assist in their reception of the good news.[37]

At this point it might be useful to add a few words on the understanding of the word "win". We Westerners have often used this word in a misleading sense. We have talked about "winning souls for Christ", "overcoming the powers of this age", and "establishing Jesus' lordship" as if his lordship meant an expansion of territory. However, in the central part of the New Testament the lordship of Christ means something quite different. Here Jesus becomes Lord by emptying himself by being a servant and slave (cf. Phil 2:6-11).[38]

(2) Freedom and "slavery". It is interesting to see that in the opening and closing sentences Paul describes the relationship between freedom and "slavery" in a way that reminds us of Christ as described in Phil 2. Although Paul was a free man, he had made himself every man's "slave" (or "servant"). When he introduced this motif in his self-understanding as apostle, he wanted to emphasize the two relations which are closely connected. On the one hand, the relation between Christ and the apostle, and on the other hand, the relation between the apostle and "all people". The paradoxical notion of authority in Paul – being the apostle as well as

"slave"/"servant" of men – is a reflection of Christ's own authority (Phil 2:6-11; cf. also Mark 10:45). In other words, in v. 19 and vv. 22b-23, Paul wants to underline that the basic norm for his adaptability is given by *the model of Christ*.[39]

(3) "The Law of Christ". This leads us to another basic principle described as "Christ's law" (v. 21b). In spite of the wording ("law"), this principle should not be understood as a legal and fixed pattern which Paul meticulously follows. Rather Paul thinks of the love-commandment. For him, love is a *dynamic* concept. In Rom 13:8 it is called the fulfilment of the law. The same idea is found in Gal 6:2 when he writes: "Bear one another's burdens and in this way you will fulfill the law of Christ".

Thus, when Paul spoke of "the law of Christ", this should not be misinterpreted as though he regarded traditions about Jesus as a series of laws which had to be obeyed whatever the circumstances. Rather, it was a series of principles which had to be applied in the light of the circumstances under the guidance of the Spirit.[40] "The Law of Christ" is "the law of love" which becomes the authority for Paul's missionary adaptation.

b. The flexibility
It is on the basis of these principles that Paul shows his flexibility in relation to three different groups.

(1) To the Jews. There is much evidence to show that Paul, when among Jews, behaved as a Jew both socially and religiously. This feature is particularly stressed in Acts. Paul begins his missionary preaching in the synagogue; only after a formal rejection by the Jews does he turn to the Gentiles (e.g. Acts 19:8-10). He agrees to the circumcision of Timothy (16:3) and he takes vows according to Jewish custom (21:23).

But did Paul preach a Jewish gospel? As far as the basic "core" of the gospel is concerned, he did not make any compromise with it. In the letter to the Galatians he speaks of no less than *three* gospels. First, there is his own gospel – the gospel for the Gentiles, "for the uncircumcised" (Gal 2:7). Second, there is the gospel for the Jews, "for the circumcised" (2:7) represented by the "pillar apostles". Paul recognizes this version of the gospel as a legitimate form of the Christian proclamation, appropriate to the Jews.

So long as the proponents of each of these two gospels recognized the validity of the other and did not seek to impose their own gospel on those who held the other, Paul was content. But evidently some people had a legalistic view and opposed Paul's law-free Gentile mission. Their's is the "other gospel" which Paul attacks in fierce language in Gal 1:6-9. This third gospel seems to be a perversion of the genuine gospel.[41]

(2) To those outside the law. In his approach to the Gentiles Paul defended the law-free gospel. Faith in Christ could not and must not be made dependent on the observance of certain traditions. Therefore, if inherited traditions hindered the liberty of Christ and the worship of God, they should be abandoned.

One of the best known examples of Paul's dialogue with the Greeks is his speech on the Areopagus (Acts 17:22-31). This speech reflects the acknowledgement of the possibility of "natural religion" whereby the true God can be detected in the order and beauty of his creation (see also Rom 2:14-15).

(3) To the weak. The third group consists of the weak, that is, a group *within* the Corinthian church (cf. 1 Cor 8). With them Paul identifies completely; note the absence of any "as" in "I became weak". Paul consistently emphasizes that his apostolate is characterised by "weakness" (cf. 2 Cor 11:30; 12:9).

This means that the word "win" does not have exactly the same meaning in v. 22, where Paul has Christians in mind, as it does in vv. 20-21, where he is thinking of non-Christians. But the difference should not be exaggerated because Paul never thinks of conversion as an end in itself. Each individual has to be continually "re-won" for Christ. Growth in Christ is essentially a series of new and deeper conversions.[42]

While Paul's relation to the Jews and to the Gentiles in vv. 20-21 is an expression of his *missionary* concern, his relation to the weak reflects his *pastoral* concern. What is important, however, is that for Paul the two concerns are held together, whereas many Christians today tend to hold them apart.

By a way of summary we may say that the passage of 1 Cor 9:19-23 indicates two important dimensions of Paul's mission:[43] on the one side these verses say something about Paul's sense of responsibility: the gospel of Jesus Christ is intended for all, without distinction, and he himself is under an inescapable obligation to try to "win" as many as possible. On the other side these verses are indicative of his missionary methods. Paul's manner of preaching the gospel is one of flexibility, sensitivity, and empathy and for him, mission means neither the Hellenization of Jews nor the Judaization of Greeks.

c. Cross and culture

Paul's adaptability to different people means that he is deeply sensitive to the religio-cultural values of people and communities. But it does not mean a total assimilation into a culture or the loss of the Christian identity. For Paul, Christian identity was determined by the cross, and the cross will inevitably mean a rejection of some cultural elements and the purification of others.

Paul's preaching of the cross is most clearly expressed in the opening chapters of 1 Corinthians: "For Jews demand signs and Greeks desire wisdom, but we proclaim Christ crucified, a stumbling block to Jews and foolishness to Gentiles, but to those who are called, both Jews and Greeks, Christ the power of God and the wisdom of God" (1 Cor 1:22-24).

In these verses Paul criticizes the shortcomings of two different cultures. The Jewish demand for signs and the Greek quest for wisdom are two different expressions of man-in-the-world, man alienated from God and manifesting his rebellion in anthropocentric existence. Religious egocentricity will inevitably find Christ crucified a *scandal*, for in the cross God does the opposite of what he is expected to do; the intellectual egocentricity of wisdom-seeking Gentiles finds the same theme, *folly*, because incarnation, crystallized in crucifixion, means not that man has speculated his way up to God but that God has come down to man where man is.[44]

It should be noticed that according to Paul, men ("the world") had the possibility of knowing God "through wisdom", but since this possibility was forfeited (1 Cor 1:21; cf. Rom 1:21), God has decided to communicate with men in a completely new way: the cross.

II. Paul's missionary strategy and his communities

1. Different forms of mission in early Christianity

In early Christianity two major forms of mission can be discerned: on the one hand a mission which is organized, on the other hand a mission which is more spontaneous. This last form has often been neglected by modern interpreters. However, in the first decades Christianity was spread in the Mediterranean world not only because of great missionaries but also because of "anonymous" Christians (merchants, slaves, artisans etc.) who travelled.[45] Furthermore, Christians were also aware that their mode of life was an essential factor in mission.[46]

One may discern three main types of mission forms in early Christianity:[47]

(1) The wandering preachers who were active in Palestine before and after Easter, cf. the so-called Saying-Source; the decisive figures in the Jesus movement (in the years A.D. 30-70) were travelling apostles, prophets, and disciples characterized by homelessness, lack of family, and the relinquishing of all wealth, possessions and security.[48] They preached the nearness of the Kingdom of God and they healed the sick and expelled the demons (Matt 10:7-8).[49]

(2) Judaizing Christian missionaries who went into already existing Christian churches in order to "correct" what they regarded as false interpretation of the gospel (cf. the problem in 2 Corinthians and Galatians).

(3)   The Antiochene church which sent out missionaries to found new churches predominantly among Gentiles (cf. Acts 13:1-3; 14:26-28).[50] This mission form has been characterized by H. Ollrog as "*Zentrumsmission*", that is, mission in certain strategic centres.[51]

2. Paul's missionary strategy

How does Paul's mission fit into these models for mission? From the Acts we may get the impression that he was almost exclusively an itinerant preacher. However, Paul was not just a herald who hurried to proclaim the gospel to all nations. His ministry also had a more pastoral aspect.[52] The letters show that Paul was not content to "plant" and move on, despite some of his comments in this direction. Paul did not present himself as a mere evangelizer but as one who retained authority over these communities and who intended to help shepherd them toward the day of final salvation.

Paul's mission can best be characterized as a unique combination of the various forms of mission mentioned above. One essential aspect of Paul's mission is his involvement in "*Zentrumsmission*". There is a certain method in his selection of these centres. He preferred the district or provincial capitals such as Philippi, Thessalonica, Corinth and Ephesus, each of which stood for a whole region. These cities were the main centres as far as communication, culture, commerce, politics and religion were concerned.[53] In each of these he laid the foundation for a Christian community, clearly in the hope that, from these strategic centres, the gospel would be carried into the surrounding countryside and towns.

Another aspect of Pauline mission was his cooperation with other persons. H. Ollrog has argued that these persons were not just Paul's assistants or subordinates but truly his colleagues.[54] He distinguishes among three categories of fellow-workers: first, the most intimate circle, comprising Barnabas, Silvanus, and especially Timothy; second, the "independent co-workers", such as Priscilla and Aquila, and Titus; and third, representatives from local churches. The churches put these person at Paul's disposal for limited periods. Through them the churches themselves become co-responsible for his mission work.

3. Conflicting roles of missionaries

Still another characteristic of Paul's missionary practice is the way he combines tentmaking with his apostleship.[55] On this point he differed substantially from the second type mentioned above. This is clearly seen from 1 Cor 9, which has the form of an apology for his apostolate.[56]

In this chapter Paul is defending his apostolate against some opponents, but the exact nature of their charges is somewhat obscure. One possibility is that Paul was charged with seeking personal profit in his missionary endeavour. It is also possible that he was attacked for not daring to claim his right of support. The best explanation, however, is that the opponents taught that a Christian missionary must live as a beggar and that this was a sign of his trust in God. In other words, they build their accusations on the instructions found in the missionary charge (Matt 10:9-10 par.).

Although Paul referred to this instruction by Jesus (v. 14), he had a different understanding. He interpreted it not as a duty, but as a privilege which he did not take advantage of. He seems to represent a different type of missionary. He was a community organizer. The different ways of understanding the missionary have been elaborated by G. Theissen.[57] He considers the Hellenistic urban churches as reflecting a less radical, more middle-class society over against the wandering prophets from Palestine.

To us it seems rather strange that the Corinthians are unhappy at not having to pay for their preacher. According to Theissen the situation is created by the entrance into the Christian community of wandering preachers from Palestine who see Paul as a faithless missionary who is unwilling to put his full trust in God's providence. Theissen indicates that the conflict in Corinth is not so much between a good Paul and evil opponents, but between conflicting roles, between different understandings of the true missionary.[58]

The way Paul used the words of Jesus indicates that he did not understand it as the letter of a law. New circumstances and a new setting of life required a recontextualization of the message of Jesus. He preached the gospel free of charge and this made him independent of all men (cf. 1 Cor 9:19-23) but at the same time he became vulnerable for accusations.

The main reason why Paul maintained himself by working was that he did not want to be a hindrance to the gospel. He did not interpret the words of the Lord in a literal sense. But he did capture their essence, their spirit. The law which Paul knew was Christ as a living law in him (1 Cor 9:21), the law of the Spirit.[59]

4. In Christ – a new community

The goal of mission was the formation of a new community in Christ. The church is seen as the beachhead of the new creation, the vanguard of God's new world, and the sign of the dawning new age in the midst of the old.[60]

The Pauline *ekklesia* ("church") has often been compared to other religious and social communities in the Graeco-Roman world. Traditionally the public life of the city or nation state (*politeia*) and the household order (*oikonomia*) were the two main types of community with which people might associate themselves. However, by the first century things began to change. Many members of the society were no longer satisfied with these two institutions. Their aspirations and allegiances tended to drift away from the *oikos* and the *polis*. In increasingly greater numbers such people found their desires fulfilled in philosophical schools or even more frequently in a variety of voluntary associations that multiplied in the cities all over the world, especially in Greek centres. The novel feature of these groups was their basis in something other than the principles of *politeia* or *oikonomia*. They bound together people from different backgrounds on a different ground than that of geography and race, or natural and legal ties. Their principle was *koinonia*, i.e. a voluntary sharing or partnership.

This does not mean that every such association was open to all who wished to join. Many restricted entry to a certain nationality, family, social class or gender. Only a few appear to have opened their doors, in some respects at least, to all. The majority were established around a particular interest, vocation or commitment. These were extremely varied: political, military and sporting concerns; professional and commercial guilds, artisans and craftsmen, philosophical schools and religious brotherhoods.[61]

The Christian communities resembled the associations in many significant ways.[62] Some of the common features are: small group with intensive face-to-face interactions, membership by free decision rather than by birth, common meals and other "fraternal" activities. Both groups also depended to some extent on the beneficence of wealthier persons who acted as patrons.

However, there were also important differences between the Christian groups and the voluntary associations.[63] First of all, the Christian groups were *exclusive* and totalistic in a way that no club nor even any pagan cultic association was. Baptism meant a thoroughgoing re-socialization, in which the sect was intended to become virtually the primary group for its members. The only convincing parallel in antiquity was conversion to Judaism.

On the other hand, the Christian communities were much more *inclusive* in terms of social stratification and other social categories than were the voluntary associations. Most of the clubs tended to draw together people who were socially homogeneous.

The congregations that have come into existence as a consequence of Paul's mission find themselves in a world which was divided religiously (in Jews and Gentiles), culturally (in Greeks and barbarians), economically (in rich and poor) and socially (in free and slaves). Baptism creates a new situation. Once people have "put on Christ", there can no longer be any separation between Jews and Gentiles, between slave and free, between male and female; now all are "one in Christ Jesus" (Gal 3:27-28). As one leaves the old world and enters the new, the old hierarchical values based on the differences in people are left behind. The church creates an eschatological community where people, no matter of what background, shape, or form, are seen and accepted as equals.[64]

There is a creative tension between being exclusive and practising solidarity with others. The church is the community of people who are involved in creating new relationships among themselves and in society at large, and in doing this, they bear witness to the lordship of Christ. He is no private or individual Lord but always, as Lord of the church, also Lord of the world.[65] The church is a place for "welcoming one another to new humanity" (cf. Rom 15:7).[66]

5. The collection

An important aspect of Paul's mission strategy is his collection for the poor in Jerusalem (see 1 Cor 16:1-2; Rom 15:24-32; Gal 2:9-10 and 2 Cor 8-9). The collection is a clear example of how mission theology and mission practice are inseparable. This event must be seen within an eschatological context. Paul devoted a great deal of his energy to this act during the final years of his ministry.

Paul insisted that representatives from the various Gentile churches should accompany him to Jerusalem. The reason might be that the collection should be seen as a reinterpretation of the Old Testament concept of the pilgrimage of the nations to Zion. It is not the diaspora Jews, but representatives from all the Gentiles who will be gathered from the end of the earth and brought to Jerusalem. If this interpretation is correct, Paul blends the theme of collection with that of the eschatological pilgrimage of the nations to Jerusalem.[67]

The collection was itself a twin act of worship and hospitality.[68] The Gentiles are offering themselves to God (Rom 15:16) and they give their material gifts to their Jewish Christian brothers and sisters, cf. Rom 15:26-27: "For Macedonia and Achaia have been pleased to share their resources (*koinonia*) with the poor among the saints at Jerusalem. They were pleased to do this, and indeed they owe it to them; for if the Gentiles have come to share (*koinonein*) in their spiritual blessings, they ought also to be of service to them in material things".

For Paul the collection symbolizes the unity of the church made up of Jews and Gentiles.[69] It is a sign of partnership which involves a mutual receiving and giving.

6. The encounter between Christians and non-Christians: belief and practice

Paul's considerations in 1 Cor 9:19-23 are part of a greater context (1 Cor 8-10) where the apostle addresses the question: Is it right and proper for a Christian to eat meat which has been previously consecrated to pagan idols?

Two factions had formed within the Corinthian church on this issue. The one group – usually called the "strong" Christians – saw no problem here. They argued that there is only one God. Consequently, food consecrated to non-existent deities has no possible sacred significance for the Christian. Therefore one is free to eat anything. The other group – the "weak" Christians – felt that to eat such meat was to participate at least to some extent in idolatry, and thus to deny their exclusive oneness with Christ.

In Paul's view the question of idol meat must be subordinated to the more important issue of love. Therefore Paul refuses simply to give a "right answer". His advice differs according to the situation. At least three, perhaps four, situations can be discerned:[70]

(1) In *10:23-11:1* Paul refers to two concrete situations. First there is *the meat sold at the market* (10:25). Here Paul's answer is that you may or should eat whatever is sold and need not investigate it, for this is not a matter of conscience.

(2) Secondly, you can participate in *a (non-cultic) meal in a private home* (10:27). In this case meat may also be eaten. But if attention is drawn to the character of the food, its eating is prohibited not as in itself idolatrous, but because it places the eater in a false position and confuses the consciences of others (the pagan host, other pagan guests or other Christian guests). The situation has changed. Now it is a question of a *status confessionis* where a clear "no" to the pagan cult is required.

(3) Another situation is envisaged in *10:1-22*. Here Paul's concern is not with meat which may be *hierothyton* (10:25.27), but with *idolatria* (10:14). The focus is upon the issue whether or not Christians can participate in a pagan cult as such. Eating is an event which can be understood as a conscious action. In this way *faith* itself is at stake. The problem is not – as above – how others react, but how God reacts. Therefore, Paul's advice in 10:14-22 is a strong warning against idolatry.[71]

(4) While the situations behind 10:23-11:1 and 10:1-22 are quite evident, the same cannot be said of *8:1-13*. The problem is to decide what is meant by 8:10: "If others see you, who possess knowledge, eating in the temple of an idol..." It is sometimes argued that this eating opportunity is the same as that of 10:14-22, namely a cultic banquet following a sacrifice held in one of the temple's dining facilities, some of which have been uncovered at Corinth.

The difficulty with this interpretation is that in Paul's argument he agrees with the "strong" Christians that there is nothing wrong with eating idol meat (8:1; see also 10:25.27). It is therefore better to say that 8:1-13 aims at a situation where a meal is held in a temple restaurant but not as an occasion of worship. In that case we have here an example of *a non-cultic meal held in temple precincts*.

In order to understand why some Christians at Corinth wanted to participate in pagan meals we must ask what significance such meals had. It is often argued that they had a sacramental character. If so, it is difficult to understand why Christians would want to participate. But if these meals were predominantly *social occasions*, it is very understandable that some Corinthians would like to take part.[72] We should also remember that these Corinthians were ex-pagans with friends and relatives who had become Christians, and Paul did not forbid association with them

(1 Cor 5:10). Marriages and funerals normally involved meals in the temple precincts, and participation in such meals, at which food offered to idols was served, was a matter of family and/or social duty.[73]

To conclude, then, the "strong" Christians had no difficulties in participating in temple banquets, but this generated an intolerable pressure on the "weak" Christians which forced them to violate their consciences. Paul's advice to the readers is the same as in 10:23-11:1: You are free to maintain this form of social intercourse with pagans. But *if* your fellow-believer is hurt in his conscience, you must refrain from eating the meat. The reason is that he is a brother for whom Christ died (8:11).

Paul's own position lies between these two opposites. He neither sides totally with the strong nor with the weak. His approach to the issue of idol meat takes the form of a *compromise*. To illustrate this position we can compare with Rev 2-3.[74] In these chapters we meet some Christians ("prophets") who are said to teach fornication and eating sacrificed meat (2:14.20). What these other prophets teach is a relaxed attitude to the surrounding (pagan) culture. Their stance may be likened to that of the strong at Corinth. The author of Revelation would have despised them, but he would despise Paul's dialectical middle ground even more. It is precisely that middle ground which Revelation, with its dualistic attitude, criticizes vehemently. It is a "lukewarm" attitude (Rev 3:16).

7. Theological and christological aspects of Paul's answer

It is useful to have a closer look at Paul's relation to the strong. The argument of the strong was based on purely theistic principles (see 8:4 and 8:8). While true in themselves, such principles would lead to a distorted perspective if used in isolation from other factors. Since the new being of the Christians is constituted by love (8:2-3), every act of intelligence must be rooted in love which discerns the real situation of the other! Therefore, Paul can say as he does in 8:11: he is a brother for whom Christ died.

Paul's answer has one more aspect which deserves to be noticed. He uses a confessional formula the context of which is a confrontation with polytheistic religions of the Greek culture. The drive of Paul's argument is towards the assertion that, whatever other spiritual or demonic beings there may be, "for us" (the believers) there is only one whom we recognize as God, whom we trust and obey in a unique sense as the source of life and redemption (8:5-6).[75]

The formula in 1 Cor 8:6 has attracted much attention, and rightly so, because it ascribes to Christ the role of pre-existent Wisdom (cf. Col 1:15-20). This means that we here have traces of a cosmic Christ.

Most scholars consider v. 6 to be a baptismal acclamation, but they often fail to see its function in the context. Why does Paul cite a baptismal acclamation? Murphy-O'Connor points to three factors.[76] Firstly, it develops the idea of election suggested in 8:3. The strong are made aware that their privileged position was due, not because of their intelligence, but because of the divine love. Secondly, the baptismal acclamation reminds them that this God was not discovered by wisdom or philosophical speculation, but had revealed himself in Jesus Christ. In other words, *christology is the touchstone of authentic theism*. Thirdly, the baptism is the rite of initiation into a community, and through it the strong have become integral parts of the body of Christ. They are reminded that they belong to a community of brothers (cf. 8:11-13). The most fundamental aspect that the strong failed to take into account was the fact that they were *Christians*.

Paul's answer to the Corinthians is based on two principles. The first one goes back to the *creation*. Paul begins by pointing out that idols have no real existence. God's good gifts are not sullied by being offered to a figment of man's imagination: "there is no God but one...". Later on Paul once more refers to the creation, 10:26: "for the earth and its fullness are the Lord's". He says much the same thing to the Romans (14:14) and to the Colossians (see Col 2:21-23).

Paul's second principle goes straight to the heart of Christianity. Christianity is about loving and loving is other-centred, not self-centred, because Christian love is rooted in the *Christ event*. So having laid down the principle that all foods are good, Paul does not go on to say that a Christian may therefore eat what foods he likes. His knowledge has to be tested, and the test is: Will it help or hurt a brother for whom Christ died? Even though all things and foods are good, it is *people* that matter.[77]

III. Hermeneutical perspectives

1. The double apostolate

Paul's mission has been of much inspiration for modern missionary endeavours. Thus, in the beginning of this century R. Allen compared Pauline mission methods with modern mission methods, a comparison that did not favour the latter. Allen stressed the missionary dimension of pneumatology and the need for young churches to be independent. Mission is for Allen a spiritual matter and not just a question of method.[78] A more recent example is J. A. Grassi who has analysed Paul's great missionary plan, his concrete methods, and the Pauline church in action. According to Grassi Paul is both a herald of the word and a man of dialogue.[79]

Another example of Paul's impact on modern missiology is J. Aagaard. He points to the concept of the "double apostolate", that is Peter's apostolate and Paul's apostolate. The first one is the "pillar apostolate" (cf. Gal 2:9). This office has been fundamental to our understanding of the nature of the episcopal office in the church. Obviously, the purpose and nature of the bishop's office is modelled on this apostolate. The second one is Paul's "travelling apostolate". Paul demonstrated through his missionary travels the dynamic character of this apostolate. He visited and encouraged the members of the young churches, and founded new ones.

The purpose in underlining the two apostolates is not to separate them, but to call attention to the second one: the free, dynamic, Pauline apostolate. "This is necessary because in the Church today Paul's apostolate has gone virtually unrecognized. It is a situation where the pillar apostolate has won the day everywhere."[80]

From an exegetical point of view this insistence on the double apostolate is somewhat simplified.[81] In this model there is also the risk of over-emphasizing Paul's role as itinerant preacher. Aagaard attaches much importance to the description of Paul in the Acts.[82] Nevertheless, it is to his credit to draw our attention to a potential conflict between two kinds of mission: Church mission as gradual and continuous growth and the non-continuous and desultory type of mission. In the course of history the Petrine apostolate has been overemphasized at the expense of the Pauline apostolate, and mission as local church growth at the expense of mission through the "travelling apostolate".[83]

2. Urban mission

An additional aspect of Paul's mission need to be taken into consideration with regard to its hermeneutical relevance. His missionary endeavours were directed towards the major cities of the Roman world, and this fact has attracted much attention in recent missiology.[84] Here I shall limit my remarks to a few points.

The *first* point relates to *the necessity of translating the gospel into a new situation*. Within a decade of the crucifixion of Jesus the Christian movement had gone beyond the village culture of Palestine; the Graeco-Roman city had become its dominant environment. The movement had thus crossed the most fundamental division in the society of the Roman Empire, that between rual people and city dwellers.[85] The preoccupation with the cities was not peculiar to Paul (e.g. the foundation of the Antiochene community is not his merit). Nevertheless he contributed substantially to this transition from a rural culture to an urban culture. An important reason for this is given in 1 Cor 9: Christians should not set up obstacles to the proclamation of the good news. Adaptability is the key to any successful venture.[86] No two situations are identical in every respect.[87] Hence, customs, practices and principles that may be relevant in one situation may not be applied to another in the same way.

The *second* point is *the challenge from the Hellenistic urban culture*. Modern cities have their own "faces": They are commercial cities, administrative cities, cultural cities, "symbolic" cities etc. The same is true of the cities in Paul's time. Each city had its distinctive mark.[88] There were differences between Antioch, Ephesus, Corinth, Philippi, Thessalonica and Rome – to mention but a few of those cities which were of importance for the Christian mission.

In spite of this all major cities had some common features due to the Hellenism. In short, Hellenism is an individualistic urban culture, characterized by a cosmopolitan attitude, urbanization, rupture of tradition, individualization, homelessness and inward-directness. The city was the place where, if anywhere, change could be met and even sought out. It was the place where the empire's power was felt, and where the future began.[89] Many of these features are known from modern metropolises.

Therefore, a *third* question is how the message of the Christians could be heard by people living in a pluralistic society. In the first century there was a competition among religious groups and philosophies to offer the best answer to the question of the meaning of life. Here again there is some analogy to our contemporary situation. In the Graeco-Roman society many people were rootless and searching for new values. They longed for some form of social life wider than the family and narrower than the State. A place of belonging was offered by the many voluntary associations. They often became a "home for the homeless" – a description which might be fitting for the Christian community as well.[90] One reason why many outsiders felt a strong attraction to the Christian communities has been mentioned previously: these communities seemed to be more inclusive in terms of social stratification and other social categories than were the voluntary associations.[91]

Finally, cities have a tendency to increase *social problems*. Therefore the question is: What shape should the church take in the city? The massive presence of the poor and marginalized in the world's cities is a challenge.[92] The problem is well-known in the first century. This can be illustrated by two texts from 1 Corinthians.[93] The first is 1 Cor 1:26-31. Here we are told that the majority of the Christians were poor people. If the worldly criteria were valid, the Christians in Corinth would never have become Christians, because by those standards they were "nobodies". But the weak, the lowly, the foolish, and the despised of the present age are being lifted up. Thus the cross means a total shift in criteria. In the second text, 1 Cor 11:17-34, Paul shows that the Lord's Supper must be a special demonstration of equality and reciprocity. It is here that the new humanity freed by Christ from divisions of class, race, and sex, should be emerging most visibly from the present age. Sharing begins at the Lord's table.

The *credibility* of the Christian proclamation is closely related to the lifestyle of the community. It is in this context we must understand the famous passage of 1 Cor 12:14-27. By using the metaphor of the body of Christ Paul underlines the necessity of mutual care and mutual service. Christians are called upon to live out the new life "in Christ" in ways that are both personally and socially relevant. The church is important as prototype for the new realm of social existence which God is calling into being. Its very presence in the world, like salt and light, has a salutary effect, both in condemning evil and drawing people to Christ. It is meant to have an outreach and mission to the world – one that seeks to undercut evil and establish justice.[94]

3. The collection as a model for partnership

Pauline mission has also served as inspiration for the concept of partnership in mission.[95] Thus the collection for the poor in Jerusalem is interpreted as a model for partnership in mission.[96] As noted above, an important aspect of this collection is the unity among Jewish Christians and Gentiles Christians. This unity is strongly emphasized in the passage of 2 Cor 8-9 which contains at least four points.

First of all, the collection should be inspired by the example of Christ, cf. 2 Cor 8:9: "For you know the generous act of our Lord Jesus Christ that though he was rich, yet for our sakes he became poor, so that by his poverty you might become rich". The determinant factor is always what God has done in Christ: "It is giving that enriches, not keeping! Christ being rich, did not *cling* to his riches (Phil 2:6)."[97]

Secondly, in 2 Cor 8-9 there is a strong urge towards equalization of income. This point is underlined by the New English Bible which translates 2 Cor 8:14: "It is a question of equality." (NRSV: "a fair balance"). The Greek word for equality (*isotes*) is a key word in the whole passage. The basic idea is that of the Jubilee, the aim of which is distributive justice.[98]

The third thing to notice is that the collection should be done voluntarily (2 Cor 8:2.8; 9:7). As K. Nürnberger notes: "Considering the fact that, not to *have* makes one happy, but to give and take, i.e. *share* – is it really so incomprehensible that the Macedonians were *begging* for the *privilege* of taking part in this relief work (II Cor 8,4)?"[99] Although no orders are given about the extent of individual contribution (see however 2 Cor 9:5-6), the moral pressure on the Corinthians is nevertheless very strong.

Fourthly, it is pointed out that God will supply the needs of human beings. Reference is made to the Exodus accounts, 2 Cor 8:12-15.

It is surprising that in the arguments put forward in 2 Cor 8-9 Paul does not mention the word "money". For him the criterion for helping needy Christians is the manifestation of grace. The collection is the *result of the grace of God*. The relationship with God should be reflected in the relationship with each other. A sharing in Christ leads to a sharing with each other. This is what Paul calls "fellowship" or "community" (*koinonia*). It is a question of a community which includes both material and spiritual things. A church without this kind of community is no longer the body of Christ; it is spiritually dead.

Among rich Christians today much time and energy are spent on motivating people to give as much money as possible. It is interesting to note that this was not the problem for Paul. For him the most difficult thing about the collection seemed to be the question of how the poor in Jerusalem would receive the gifts of their fellow-Christians. Therefore he asked the Roman Christians to pray that this service "may be acceptable" in Jerusalem (Rom 15:31). In fact, the most urgent questions were how to give without humiliating and without creating dependency, and how to receive in freedom without resentment.[100]

Money can have a demonic effect. It can lead to mistrust and suspicion. Then it is not an expression of solidarity. Rather it is an instrument for domination and dependency. That was just what Paul experienced in connection with the collection. Therefore he was careful to avoid misunderstandings. The congregations should give voluntarily. They should make their own decisions as to which persons should be appointed as delegates. In short, money should be an instrument of love, not of power.

4. Integrity and openness

Inculturation and dialogue are other issues which can be discussed on the basis of the Pauline letters. Here the passage of 1 Cor 9:19-23 is of special interest. A major problem in this text – as in any dialogue – is how to maintain genuine Christian integrity while at the same time being open to people of other faiths. Integrity is usually defined as being true to oneself. How, then, can Paul be "all things to all people"? Only by finding a point of reference outside himself, the basis of genuine Christian integrity is there a commitment to the gospel: "I do it all for the sake of the gospel" (v.23).[101] Total preoccupation with Christ is the unchanging centre of Paul's life.

Total commitment to Christ might seem at first sight to involve a certain isolation from people. Not so with Paul. B. Smyth rightly remarks that he "did not, so to speak, divide his preoccupation, given a certain proportion to Christ and a certain proportion to people. His preoccupation with people was part of his preoccupation with Christ, the overflow of his preoccupation with Christ. Conversely, his preoccupation with Christ involved and included a preoccupation with people."[102] In other words, Paul is not only gospel-centred but people-centred.[103]

Some circles in early Christianity apparently thought that Paul went too far in his dialogue with the Greeks. These Christians tended to consider him as heretical. Paul on his side saw the necessity of preaching the gospel in such a way that new groups can hear its message. He tended to consider those who opposed this process to be heretics. Who then were the heretics – if any? "Putting it provocatively, one may say that the heretics in the New Testament are not those who preach the Gospel by becoming Greeks but rather the conservatives who, because they hesitate to win a new culture for the service of Christ, run the risk of being drowned by that very culture".[104]

This is not to say that we are without criteria for the inculturation and the dialogue. 1 Cor 9:19-23 (openness towards Jews and Greeks) and 1 Cor 1:18-25 (critique of Jewish and Greek culture) must be held together, if we want to get a more accurate picture of Paul's attitude towards people of other faiths. A comparison between the two passages will also show that a distinction must be made between *two kinds of stumbling blocks*:[105] (1) The stumbling block of the message of the gospel – the preaching of the cross (1 Cor 1:23; Gal 5:11). Paul does not want to make a compromise with it. (2) The messenger as a stumbling block. Paul is very particular that he should never be a hindrance between the gospel and the audience.[106]

Authentic mission has to accept this distinction. This is well formulated by P. Tillich in his "theology of culture": "But there are two kinds of "stumbling blocks":

One is genuine... There is always a genuine decision against the Gospel for those for whom it is a stumbling block. But this decision should not be dependent on the wrong stumbling block, namely, the wrong way of our communication of the Gospel – our inability to communicate. What we have to do is to overcome the wrong stumbling block in order to bring people face to face with the right stumbling block and enable them to make a genuine decision."[107]

The cross is an indispensable part of the Christian integrity. Therefore, when we attempt to understand the dialectic relationship between integrity and openness[108], we must ask the important questions: Can there be a true dialogue without preaching the word of the cross and vice versa? How can our witness to the particularity of the cross, which is so offensive and foolish to others, be shared without a show of arrogance?[109]

5. Rejection, inclusion or...?

From our viewpoint the questions raised in 1 Cor 8-10 seem strange. But in other parts of the world Christians are facing similar problems. So, for instance in Madagascar where Christians must decide whether they can participate in special forms of funeral celebration (turning the corpse). It is considered to be a social obligation, but it also has a religious meaning. It is a question of how to behave towards social norms and kinship rules. Similar problems are known from Hindu, Buddhist and Taoist contexts.

There are three ways of relating to this problem:[110]

(1) *Rejection.* Following the weak in Corinth one adopts a position characterized by *strong group boundaries.* A firm stance against idolatry is a necessary defence for the Christian community. In all areas of conflict there is a clear "no" to pagan culture and religiosity.

(2) *Inclusion.* Following the strong in Corinth one adopts a position characterized by *weak boundaries* vis-à-vis non-Christians. The basis for this position is the discovery that the Jewish-Christian monotheism has the potential of desacralizing the everyday world. Here the aim is a gradual Christianizing of the culture.

(3) *Points of contact – reinterpretation – replacement*[111]. This is a middle position. On the hand there is an emphasis on the uniqueness of salvation in Jesus Christ. Other ways to salvation are refused. This means that there is no compromise with paganism, cf. the first position. On the other hand God is conceived of as Creator. The implication of this is the accept of points of contact in the non-Christian culture. But a reinterpretation is required, and pagan symbols and rituals must be replaced by Christian concepts.

Paul's attitude in 1 Corinthians is due to the fact that he considered both the position of the strong and the weak to be extremes. Through fear the weak would have forced the community into a self-imposed ghetto. Through destructive use of freedom the strong would have committed the church to a pattern of behaviour which was indistinguishable from that of its environment. Paul wanted to avoid both consequences. If either group had prevailed, the identity and mission of the church would have been gravely compromised. However, Paul insisted that the church maintained both its identity and openness to the world.[112] And so must we when we are confronted with problems similar to those in Corinth.[113]

Notes

1   A recent example of this tendency is Patmury 1993, 147.
2   Cf. Dahl 1977, 70.
3   Cf. Hengel 1983, 53.
4   Cf. Hultgren 1985, 145.
5   See Stendahl 1977b, 7.
6   Rowland 1985, 195, argues that the Damascus event should rather be interpreted as transference of an individual from one Jewish sect to another, from the pharisaic sect to the Christian sect.
7   For a more detailed discussion see Bosch 1991, 125-129; Donaldson 1997, 3-27.
8   Cf. Senior & Stuhlmueller 1983, 167.
9   Keck 1979, 117.
10 Cf. Hahn 1965, 76-77.
11 Cf. Senior & Stuhlmueller 1983, 171.
12 For a more detailed analysis see Legrand 1990, 115-121.
13 Cf. Dahl 1977, 71 and 78.
14 Howell 1998, rightly insists on the theocentric aspect of God's righteousness. "It is the person and character of God around which the argument revolves. Not the justified man but the justifying God is on center stage. Soteriology is grounded in Christology, and Christology in Paul's doctrine of God" (p. 100; cf. p. 115).
15 Blauw 1962, 98.
16 Cf. Longenecker 1984, 36-37.
17 Cf. Olsson 1994, 66-67.
18 So, for instance, Bussmann 1971, 41.
19 Cf. Zeller 1982, 167-170.
20 Cf. Wilson 1982, 340.
21 Wilson 1982, 340.
22 For further discussion of this issue see chapter 9 of the present book.
23 Cf. Yoder 1972, 227-228. A second shortcoming of the traditional interpretation of "the new creature" as the transformed personality is that the word *ktisis* is not used elsewhere in the New Testament to designate an individual person.
24 Cf. Martin 1981, 104.

25 Cf. Crafton 1991, 97.
26 Cf. Furnish 1968, 149; Goppelt 1976, 467.
27 Martin 1981, 153.
28 For the hermeneutical importance of this see the following chapter on Colossians and Ephesians.
29 Bultmann 1951, 302.
30 In a paper presented at a "Consultation for New Testament Scholars on the Ecumenical Perspective of Their Work", held at Montreal (1963). See the reference in Wilder 1965, 210-211.
31 For a review of this discussion see Wilder 1965.
32 For a more detailed analysis see Nissen 1988.
33 Bornkamm 1966, 194.
34 Cf. Dunn 1977, 25.
35 Cf. Cracknell 1986, 29.
36 Chadwick 1954-55, 275.
37 Cf. Richardson 1979, 87.
38 See Schreiter 1981, 45; cf. Samartha 1981, 11: Christ "exercises his functions as Lord not through conquering people or ruling over them but through self-surrender and service and through accepting the burdens of others on himself".
39 Cf. Abraham 1977, 71; see also Joseph 1977.
40 Cf. Dunn 1977, 68-69.
41 Cf. Dunn 1977, 23.
42 Cf. Murphy-O'Connor 1979, 91.
43 Bosch 1991, 135, on the other hand, argues that 1 Cor 9:19-23 says more about Paul's sense of responsibility than about his missionary methods.
44 Cf. Barrett 1968, 55.
45 See the chapter on "mobility and mission" by Stambaugh & Balch 1986, 37-62. The authors state that "the early Christians spread their message through personal involvement, witness, and example, through sermons addressed to small or large groups, through letters of introduction and exhortation" (pp. 56-57).
46 Cf. Perkins 1982, 24.
47 See, among others, Zeller 1982, 179-180; Theissen 1975.
48 Theissen 1977, 14-32, argues that these wandering charismatics were supported morally and materially by sympathizers settled in local communities.
49 On the missionary charge see Nissen 1984, 44-46 and the section on "missionary discipleship" in chapter 2.
50 Perhaps the mission form of the "mother" church in Jerusalem had this character as well, cf. the relation between Jerusalem and Antioch in Gal 2:11-14. Later on Rome achieved a similar position vis-a-vis the communities in the western part of the Roman Empire.
51 Ollrog 1979.
52 Cf. Dahl 1977, 73; Senior & Stuhlmueller 1983, 185.
53 Cf. Haas 1971, 85; Bosch 1991, 130; Patmury 1993, 155.
54 Ollrog 1979, 119-125. On the structure of Paul's mission work, including the relation to his fellow-workers and his churches see also Banks 1980, esp. 152-154; 164-168.

55   See Hock 1980, 50-65.
56   For a more detailed analysis see Nissen 1984, 47-50.
57   Theissen 1975.
58   See also Scroggs 1980-81, 175.
59   Cf. Legrand 1990, 215.
60   Cf. Beker 1980, 313.
61   Cf. Banks 1980, 16-17.
62   For a more detailed comparison with other forms of community see Meeks 1983, 74-84; Tidball 1983, 76-89; Stambaugh & Balch 1986, 139-145.
63   Cf. Meeks 1983, 78-79.
64   Cf. Scroggs 1977, 44.
65   Cf. Bosch 1991, 169.
66   On this designation see Koenig 1985, 52-84.
67   Cf. Bieder 1965, 39.
68   Cf. Koenig 1985, 73-74.
69   Cf. Meyer 1986, 183-184.
70   For a similar distinction see Walter 1979, 427-428. Cf. also Willis 1985, 244-245.
71   Notice the similarity with the problem in Rom 1:18-32 and the critique of idolatry in the Old Testament.
72   Cf. Willis 1985, 48 and 63.
73   Cf. Murphy-O'Connor 1978, 554.
74   Cf. Meeks 1987, 147. For a comparison between 1 Corinthians and the Apocalypse see also Fiorenza 1985, 119-120.
75   Cf. Barrett 1968, 192.
76   Murphy-O'Connor 1978, 562-563.
77   Cf. Smyth 1980, 134-135.
78   Allen 1956. The author pleads for an unaltered application of the apostolic method, that is, for swift planting of small local churches with a minimum of administrative baggage and for immediate consecration of church leaders so that they will have self-confidence and the authority to continue the mission and pastoral care on their own.
79   Grassi 1965.
80   Aagaard 1987, 15. See also Aagaard 1983.
81   This is also acknowledged by Aagaard 1987. He states that the idea of the double apostolate need not be taken exclusively. A third model, for example, can be found in the apostolate of John which is an apostolate of love (p. 15).
82   See Aagaard 1992, 13: "Paul in his missionary approach takes dialogue for granted. Whenever he went to the synagogue, to the marketplace, to Areopagus, dialogue was his method. What alternative was there? None! He simply responded to the situation. Dialogue was a necessity."
83   Aagaard 1987, 16.
84   See, for instance, Bakke 1987, 81-84; Conn 1993. On the need of constructing a mission theology for the city see also van Engen 1996, 90-101.
85   Recently there have been an increasing number of studies that locate early Christian groups in the context of city life. The most prominent example is Meeks 1983. See also Moxnes

1995, 108-118.

86 Cf. Patmury 1993, 157.
87 The first followers of Jesus had to live as poor among the poor, cf. Matt 10:10. By doing so they would not constitute any hindrance for the proclamation of the good news. If Paul had taken over this principle directly, he would have caused a hindrance for the gospel because of *a new situation*. Cf. Nissen 1984, 49.
88 See Stambaugh & Balch 1986, 145-167.
89 Cf. Meeks 1980, 114.
90 Cf. Elliott 1981, 180-181.
91 See section II.2 of this chapter.
92 Cf. Conn 1993, 101-102.
93 Cf. Nissen 1984, 107-119; Koenig 1985, 65-71.
94 Cf. Longenecker 1984, 96.
95 For a survey of various New Testament models (e.g. the *koinonia*, the body of Christ, the eucharist, the *societas*, the collection) see Nissen 1997.
96 See, for instance, Escobar 1993, 56-66. The author finds Rom 15:11-33 illustrative of Paul's methodology and uniquely relevant to missiological reflection in Latin America.
97 Nürnberger 1978, 166.
98 Cf. Crosby 1977, 109.
99 Nürnberger 1978, 167.
100 Cf. Weber 1980, 35-36.
101 Cf. Murphy-O'Connor 1979, 91. See also Lande 1982, 7-8.
102 Smyth 1980, 106.
103 Cf. Nicholls 1977, 118.
104 von Allmen 1975, 49.
105 Cf. Joseph 1977, 79.
106 The point in 1 Cor 9:19-23 is that the missionary must be very open in his dialogue with others. He must be integrated to the point where he can command a sympathetic hearing. There must be nothing in his bearing or attitudes which would induce his prospective audience to reject him out of hand. Cf. Murphy-O'Connor 1979, 90.
107 Tillich 1959, 213.
108 Newbigin 1974, 101, has rightly noted that "the cross is in one sense an act of total identification with the world. But in another sense it is an act of radical separation. It is both things at the same time."
109 Cf. Nicholls 1977, 118.
110 Cf. Aano 1985, 61-62. The issue of Christian group boundaries has been discussed by New Testament scholars using anthropological models, e.g. Meeks 1983, 98-99; Meeks 1987, 147.
111 Cf. Paul's speech at Areopagus in Acts 17:22-31.
112 Cf. Murphy-O'Connor 1978, 573.
113 The issue of yoga is a modern example which in many ways can be seen as analogous to the issue of "idol meat".

7.

Proclamation and confrontation:
The witness to powers and authorities –
Colossians and Ephesians

Introduction

In recent years there has been much discussion of the relation between church and mission. This relation is an important dimension of the mission understanding in the New Testament. It is also central to the letters of Colossians and Ephesians. However, there is no consensus as to where to put the emphasis. Some scholars assert that these two writings are characterized by a limitation of the universal scope of mission. Thus, according to F. Hahn the point of these letters is a turning from a worldwide mission toward a world-dominating church. Here we have the beginning of a (subtle) cleft between genuine mission to the world and the pastoral needs of building up the church.[1]

A different view is proposed by D. Senior. He argues that Colossians and Ephesians do not represent the victory of a triumphant ecclesiology at the expense of a world-serving missiology. The church in these letters is not the final goal but only a means and a sign of Christ's own cosmic mission of salvation.[2] The church, then, is seen as an instrument in the proclamation of the gospel. This interpretation fits better to the way in which these two letters link together creation, salvation and church.[3]

I. Colossians

1. The situation of the Colossians

Although it is not easy to give a precise picture of the background for the letter to the Colossians, most scholars would agree that the readers lived in a syncretistic milieu.[4]

The section of 2:6-23 illustrates that this syncretism was probably a mixture of Jewish ideas, angelic worship, asceticism and Hellenistic speculations about the cosmic powers. The Colossians had come under the influence of a "philosophy" which is according to human tradition, according to the elements of the world and not according to Christ (v. 8).

"The elements of the world" (*ta stoikheia tou kosmou*) seem to be the four elements of earth, water, air and fire. The fear that their harmony might turn into disharmony and lead to earthquakes, storms and eruptions of volcanoes etc. is referred to by Ovid and Philo.[5] The teachers of this "philosophy" advocated measures for dealing with the powers. These included observing special days and taboos (2:16-18.21) perhaps circumcision as well (2:11).

It was a widespread belief in antiquity that man belonged to a cosmos that was alive, filled and swayed by all sorts of living powers. Elements like fire and water, the seasons, the sun, moon and stars, gods, demons, angels, etc. were all powers that had to be more or less controlled or subdued, be it through a mighty god (Zeus, Isis or Yahweh) or by magic. Many Jews and Christians of course shared this outlook.[6]

No wonder that some of the Colossians were fearing that they would be unable to ascend to Christ after death and were therefore purifying their souls by all kinds of abstinence from "food and drink" and observing "regulations (like) 'Do not handle, Do not taste, Do not touch'... human commands and teachings" (Col 2:20-22). It is noteworthy that the letter to the Colossians never speaks of *nomos*. Instead, it uses the noun *dogmata* and the verb *dogmatizesthai* (2:14.20) because the danger is not so much legalism but rather asceticism, which frees the soul from its contacts with the earthly temptations so that it will be pure enough to pierce through the elements to heaven.[7]

In short, the Colossians assumed that the world is a dangerous place because it was governed by invisible powers.[8] The anxieties of the readers have been described by E. Schweizer. He states that for centuries the Hellenists

> "...thought of the world as of a living and divine body, and of God as of its ruler, governing it as its head or permeating it as its soul, or surrounding it like the air in which it lives, or like the womb of a mother. Man in this Hellenistic area was not so much worried with his personal problems, his sin and his righteousness, as with the problems of this world, the meaninglessness of life, the threat of a unavoidable fate, the tyranny of the heavenly rulers, that is the star that determines every move of earthly life...".[9]

Thus, many individuals seem to have felt insecure and therefore sought for meaning, structure, stability and perhaps atonement with Tyche, or for support by powers stronger than destiny. Such support could be provided by joining to associations, participating in higher wisdom, performing certain rites or following a particular way of life.[10]

2. Liberation from the tyranny of the powers

How does the author respond to this syncretism? He does not contest the reader's view of the universe, nor does he argue that there are no principalities and powers. But he insists that they have misunderstood what Christian freedom is about, and the meaning of Christ's death and resurrection. These points are made particularly clear in two texts, 2:6-23 and 1:15-20.

The first text, Col 2:6-23, is a strong warning against syncretism. Before his reference to the reader's "philosophy" in v. 8 the author says: "As you therefore have received Christ Jesus the Lord, continue to live your lives in him" (v. 6). In this way he insists on the intimate relation between indicative and imperative, between the message of Christ and the moral action.

Moreover, Paul proclaims that in Christ alone "all the fullness (Greek: *pleroma*) of God was pleased to dwell" (1:19). "For in him the whole fullness of deity dwells bodily" (2:9). This means that Christ alone mediates between God and man, and those who are in Christ need not seek wisdom and knowledge anywhere else (cf. 2:3).

Here we touch upon a crucial point in the critique of syncretism, since the concept of "fullness" played a significant role in the reader's view of the world. They probably assumed that God is holy and unapproachable, that people are imprisoned in earthly desires and cut off from God by their bodies, and that between God and people live the angelic powers, the *pleroma*. These powers are mediators between God and people, and so it becomes necessary to placate them, which is accomplished by a rigid observance of the law (for the angels gave the law) and by rigorous asceticism.[11]

By contrast, Paul argues that the fullness is *already* present in Christ, and that it has *bodily* form. The fullness is experienced already in baptism which leads to the Christian community (2:12-13). The Colossians, therefore, have no reason to fear the principalities and powers. Christ has overcome the rebellious powers, and *liberated* the Christians (2:15).

The freedom in Christ means that the concern for special days, special taboos and the like, is outdated. As far as the influence of the "elemental spirits of the universe" is concerned, Christians are as good as dead – the powers cannot affect them any longer. "If with Christ you died to the elemental spirits of the universe, why do you live as if you still belonged to the world? Why do you submit to regulations, 'Do not handle, Do not taste, Do not touch'?" (2:20-21). Now the Christians are really *free*. They have died away from these elements/powers (2:20). They are free to use all these things as part of God's creation (cf. 2:22).

3. Reconciliation in Christ

The most famous part of the letter to the Colossians is the hymn in 1:15-20. This is also the most important contribution of the letter to a contemporary understanding of the missionary task.

The origin and content of this hymn has been subject to much discussion. It has often been argued that there was a pre-Pauline hymn underneath the present version of the text. Paul may have added a few phrases to adapt it to his purpose, e.g. the words "the church" in v. 18 and "the blood of his cross" in v. 20.

The aim of adding these two phrases was to bind Christ's cosmic role to the historical realities of the crucifixion and the Christian congregation. In doing so Paul counteracted metaphysical speculations about Christ as "head" of the universe (i.e. the body). In other words he emphasized that the reconciliation has a *historical* root.

Four aspects of the hymn are of special interest:[12]

(a) *Christ and the creation*. In Christ all things were created (vv. 15-17). He is the source, pattern, and goal of all creation, visible and invisible, whether thrones or dominions or principalities or authorities. The hymn uses "wisdom" terms to describe the relation between the exalted Christ and the creation (cf. Prov 8:22-31).[13] Similar ideas are expressed in John's prologue and in Hebrews 1.

(b) *The connection between Christ's lordship over the world and his lordship over the church*. Christ is described as "the head of the body, the church" (1:18). In Hellenistic speculations the universe was seen as a "body" with the deity of Zeus as its "head". As noted above, the author might have added the word "church" to avoid this understanding: although Christ is the Lord of the universe, his lordship should not be confused with the Greek ideas of how their gods are governing the world. While the Greeks are not separating clearly between the god and the nature, Christ' lordship is manifested *historically* and *concretely* in the community bound to him by love (cf. 1:24; 2:19).

(c) *Universal reconciliation through the death and resurrection of Jesus*. Reconciliation as renewal is described already in the earlier letters of Paul (cf. Rom 5:10-11; 2 Cor 5:17-20). But now the universal scope of Christ's reconciliation is underlined. Not only humanity but "all things" are reconciled "by the blood of his cross" (1:20). In 2:14-15 this event is described as a "victory".

(d) *Renewed nature and renewed humanity*. As noted above, it is often argued that the author of Colossians has changed the meaning of the original hymn. While the original hymn emphasized the renewal of all things, including the nature, the author emphasized the renewal of humanity.[14] This point seems to be supported by 1:21: "and *you* who were once estranged and hostile in mind...". In the following verses Paul elaborates this personal aspect of the reconciliation. He himself is the servant of this gospel (1:23). It is his task to proclaim God's word, "the mystery that has been hidden throughout ages and generations but now has been revealed to his saints" (1:25-26). The question is whether this application of the hymn means that the cosmological aspect of the reconciliation is de-emphasized.

The hymn in Col 1:15-20 is important for its focus on a *cosmic christology*. This passage is a unique combination of creation and salvation. The meaning of existence is not just the salvation of the individual. It is something more. The salvific work of Christ is described by the term reconciliation, which is a reconciliation of all things (1:20) as well as the reconciliation of mankind (1:21). God's mission encompasses all three articles of the faith: creation, salvation and the church.[15]

II. Ephesians

1. The religious background of the epistle
Almost certainly the letter to the Ephesians was originally an encyclical with copies sent to various churches in Asia Minor. Earlier, Paul (or one of his disciples) had already rejected false teachings among Christians in Colossae, a city of Asia Minor. The insights gained during that confrontation are taken up and deepened in Ephesians.

In Asia Minor of that time teachers of different religio-philosophical beliefs met and sought adherents:[16] itinerant preachers of the popular philosophy of the Stoa who showed how God is in all things; Jewish wisdom teachers with their cosmic speculations about how the world was created and how God's will was revealed through the personified Wisdom; Jewish sectarian missionaries propagating a spirituality like that of the Qumran community, teaching an ethical dualism and a spiritual warfare; early Gnostic believers emphasizing that salvation comes through knowledge, the knowledge that the Redeemer, the Perfect Man, has come to gather the souls of those who have true knowledge in order to save them out of this evil world through reuniting them with him and ascending into the highest heaven.[17]

In addition to this it has recently been pointed out that a knowledge of Hellenistic magic may very well be the most important background for understanding why the author highlights the power of God and the "powers" of evil in Ephesians. With the widespread and popular cult of the Ephesian Artemis closely linked to magical practices and beliefs, it is also argued that the first Christian communities were composed primarily of people coming from a similar background.[18]

2. All things reconciled in Christ
The author's response to this situation appears particularly clear from those passages which I have selected in what follows.

The letter to the Ephesians opens with a long meditation on the theme of election and cosmic reconciliation, 1:3-23. In this text the author sketches the cosmic scope of God's plan of salvation and its implications for the church.

Of special importance is the reference to the redemption by the means of Christ's death in v. 7, and its meaning for the whole universe. God "has made known to us the mystery of his will, according to his good pleasure that he set forth in Christ, as a plan for the fullness of time, to gather up all things in him, things in heaven and things on earth" (vv. 9-10). In this passage especially two aspects are worth noticing.

First, Eph 1:10 affirms that all of creation will be consummated in Christ (cf. Col 1:20). The author speaks of a "plan"; in Greek *oikonomia* which is derived from the word *oikos*. The whole universe is God's *oikos*, his "household". Christ is the central figure in this household. In the fullness of time all tings will be "summed up" in his person.

The Greek word used by the author is *anakephalaio*. M. Barth suggests the translation "to be comprehended under one head". This has the merit of catching the connotation of the root word *kephale*, or "head" which implies that the union spoken of involves the cosmic proportions of Christ's headship over the universe and the church.[19]

The span of this "summing up" is across the chasm of heaven and earth; it is cosmic in scope. This cosmic reconciliation is concretized in *people* (particularly Jews and Gentiles in the church; cf. 2:11-22), but it also embraces the alienated elements of the universe itself.[20]

Secondly, in this passage the author also speaks of a "*mystery*" (v. 9). This term played a significant role in the contemporary religious and philosophical atmosphere. It was often used to describe the belief that the salvation was reserved to a small group of believers. In contrast to this, the author uses this word several times in connection with a term which means "set forth" (1:9; cf. 3:3.9.10). The content of faith is secret – not because we are not allowed to know it – but because it is something, we cannot know from ourselves. It has to be revealed. And in Ephesians the whole emphasis is precisely on this point. The secrecy is to be proclaimed in public.

In Ephesians, the church is not only the recipient of revelation (1:9) but also the singular medium of revelation to the whole creation, including the cosmic powers that still oppose God's purposes (3:10; 6:10-20).[21] While 1:10 has no direct reference to the church this is the case with 1:20-23 which states that God has "put all things under his feet and has made him the head over all things for the church, which is his body, the fullness of him who fills all in all" .

Once again we notice the similarity between Ephesians and Colossians. "Fullness" is also part of the Colossian heritage of Ephesians. But here, for the only time in the New Testament, the term "fullness" is applied not simply to Christ but also to the church. This raises the question of the cosmic significance of the church.

Some scholars have argued that Ephesians expresses a tendency toward institutionalization or "early Catholicism". Thus E. Käsemann asserts that the effectiveness of the world-wide mission necessitated a total ecclesiastical consciousness. In Ephesians the "head" has a more prominent role in giving the body cohesion versus Paul, who stressed the Spirit as ruling the body. Christology lost its decisive significance and ecclesiology assumed paramount role. In fact, Käsemann contends that christology has become a function of ecclesiology in Ephesians.[22]

However, any notion of world dominion by the church is missing, but the church is equipped to do a "work of service" and to "stand against," and "resist," the attacks of evil powers (4:12; 6:13-14). The idea is lacking that one day the church will fill or replace the world. Assurance is given that Christ is filling all things (1:23; 4:10).[23] Therefore, the concern of this letter is not the expansion of the church, but the cosmic scope of Christ's lordship. Ephesians still maintains the Pauline primacy of christology. Ecclesiology is a function of christology, not the other way round.[24]

Ephesians has sometimes been used to support the idea that the church is Christ or the mystical body of the extension of Christ (especially in Catholic and Orthodox tradition). But the description of the church as the "body of Christ" and "the fullness of him who fills all in all" (1:23) do not invite to self-glory and self-promotion of the church. Rather, we find in such statements the *preliminary and missionary* character of the community, which is being filled now "with (literally, for) all the fullness of God" (3:19).[25]

3. The reconciliation of Jews and Gentiles

Another text which deserves our attention is Eph 2:11-22. Here the cosmic reconciliation is concretized in an actual historical fellowship, e.g. the church consisting of Jews and Gentiles.

The background for this passage might be described as follows:[26] The churches to whom the letter was addressed were deeply divided. Christians from among the Jews probably felt superior to Christians coming from the Gentiles in Asia Minor. At the same time Jewish Christians were excluded from the synagogues and therefore felt at home neither among Jews nor among Gentile Christians. The Gentile Christians were confused and torn apart by the many religious philosophies which had a strong influence in Asia Minor. Therefore, the author of the letter made a plea for unity.

To begin with paganism is described in a negative way which is quite different from some other passages, e.g. Acts 17. The situation of the Gentiles is hopeless. When the readers were Gentiles, they were "without Christ", "aliens from the commonwealth of Israel", "strangers to the covenants of promise", "having no hope" and "without God" (v. 12). The various phrases reveal that the situation of the Gentiles is seen in the light of Jewish privileges.

But now through Christ this alienation and isolation have been dissolved (v. 13). Those who "once were far off have been brought near" (cf. Isa 57:19). By the death of Jesus the god-less Gentiles have acquired a God. The following verses state the reason for this new situation of the readers. Reference is probably made to a hymn of peace:[27]

> "For he is our peace; in his flesh he has made both groups into one and has broken down the dividing wall, that is, the hostility between us. He has abolished the law with its commandments and ordinances, that he might create in himself one new humanity in place of the two, thus making peace, and might reconcile both groups to God in one body through the cross, thus putting to death that hostility through it" (2:14-16).

The wording of v. 14 is somewhat peculiar. Since the object is in the neuter (Greek: "making the two one") it can be interpreted in two ways. One suggestion is that the phrase has a *cosmic* meaning. H. Schlier, for instance, has suggested that the phrase is a vestige of a myth of reconciliation of heaven and earth,[28] while N. A. Dahl thinks it may reflect the myth of reunion of male and female.[29] The two explanations need not be mutually exclusive.[30]

Another and more plausible suggestion is that the phrase has a *concrete*, historical meaning. According to this interpretation the hymn reflects the fact that the Gentiles have become the heirs of the covenant of promise and part of the people of God. But the text goes further than that. It describes this "incorporation" not only as an "addition", but as a creation of a new reality, of a new body, a new person (2:15), in and by Jesus Christ, the Jewish Messiah for the Gentiles.[31]

To be sure, these statements of concrete groups (Jews and Gentiles) serve to guard against a false individualizing and spiritualizing of the idea of the body of Christ.[32] The joining of the two into "one new" whole shows that neither of the two can possess salvation, peace and life without the other. Jews need Gentiles, and Gentiles need Jews. Man needs fellow man, if he will be saved at all. In other words, the new man is created to be a social being.[33]

4. The conflict with the powers

Eph 6:10-20 is a third text which is the only place in the Pauline corpus where believers are explicitly called upon to struggle against the "principalities and powers". "For our struggle is not against enemies of blood and flesh, but against the rulers, against the authorities, against the cosmic powers of this present darkness, against the spiritual forces of evil in the heavenly places" (6:12). The question is: What is the meaning and the significance of the author's concept of "spiritual warfare".

To be sure, it is a "wrestling match" (but not war!) with the powers that be (6:12). The days are evil; the available time is short (5:16), the present time is dominated by the darkness (6:12). Satanic methods are used against the Christians (6:11; cf. 4:14). "Flaming arrows of the evil one" shower upon them (6:16).[34]

The weapons that are to be employed against these cosmic powers are not to be forged of steel by any human technology; instead, the war is to be fought with prayer (6:18) and with the renewed character of the holy community. The armour is mostly defensive:[35]

belt: truth
breastplate: justice
shoe: the gospel of peace(!)
shield: faith
helmet: salvation.

The one offensive weapon to be carried by the church is "the sword of the Spirit which is the word of God". Thus, the passage offers no sanction for conventional holy war ideology. By its peaceful existence in the world, the church community stands (6:13) as a challenge to the power of evil.

The believers are called to be evangelists. The metaphor, used in 6:15, may indicate that they are carried abroad by the gospel, rather than that they carry it. "The gospel which they hear (1:13) makes them be something which they were not before. It makes them move, go, dare, stand imperturbably. They are all commissioned and authorized by word and seal (1:13) to stand as well-equipped soldiers in the world (6:13ff.)."[36]

Such military imagery could easily mislead us. But according to Ephesians the church is not called to a crusade for attacking this or that evil or for changing the structures of society. It is first of all, called to *be* Christ's church, to stand firm and not to yield when the world's powers and principalities attack (6:10-18).[37]

5. The missionary task of the church

What, then, does Ephesians say about the church's mission in and for this world? Another text might help to answer this question, e.g. Eph 3:10: "so that through the church the wisdom of God in its rich variety might now be made known to the rulers and authorities in the heavenly places".

This passage raises the important questions: How does the church make God's wisdom known to the powers? What kind of testimony is given to the powers? It has been argued that the task of the church articulated in this passage is to preach to the powers.[38] But the author never states that the church is given this task. He merely remarks that the wisdom of God will be made known (passive voice) through the church. The church is not passive in the sense of failing to resist the influence of the powers, but in the sense that it does not act as a dispatched agent to proclaim the message of God's dominion to the powers.

Therefore a more plausible explanation is that the church visibly testifies to God's wisdom *by its very existence*[39] As H. Berkhof notes, "the very existence of the church, in which Gentiles and Jews who heretofore walked according to the *stoicheia* of the world, live together in Christ's fellowship, is itself a proclamation, a sign, a token to the Powers that their unbroken dominion has come to an end."[40]

The question of the missionary task of the church has been answered in three ways.[41] One way is to argue that in the Ephesians the "not yet" of the present world has almost totally been swallowed up in the "already" of the fulfilled hope. According to this understanding, the church has no mission except to worship God, to grow into the maturity of Christ and sit with him in heavenly places (cf. 2:6). However, the second part of the letter consists of exhortations to the Christians: They must become what they are already in the sight of God. Although Christ has already begun to fill the universe, the struggle is still on, and Christians need to grow in spiritual resistance to evil forces.

A second group of interpreters argue that in the process of building up (Eph 4:15), ever new members and new areas of the universe will be incorporated into Christ's body. The whole universe is potentially now already Christ's body and will actually become the body of Christ through the life and witness of the church. While isolated texts in Ephesians might suggest such a dynamic, expanding, and triumphal view of the church's mission (e.g. 3:10), this second interpretation hardly corresponds to the main message of the letter. The church's presence in the world is not envisaged as a crusade, but as a *diakonia*, a service. The "militant" passage in 6:10-18 does not portray a church which attacks and conquers.

According to the third interpretation what characterizes the church in Ephesians is neither a disinterested withdrawal from the world nor a conquering attitude toward the world. It is the church's worshipping and serving presence in the world which unmasks the evil powers and brings light into darkness. Ephesians gives two essential criteria for the church:[42] a) The church is *not an aim in itself.* b) The church must *not lose its essential calling.* This consists not in frantic activities to change the world. Rather, its calling is to *be* Christ's body in worship and everyday life. Its greatest service to the world is indeed to be a united church, growing up in everything into Christ, its head.

III. Hermeneutical perspectives

1. Christ as the Lord of the universe

The discussion of the relation between the original pre-Pauline hymn of Col 1:15-20 and its present shape leads to the following questions: Does it make sense to speak of a cosmic rule of Jesus Christ and of the reconciliation of all things through him? Or are his person and work related only to the salvation of mankind?

M. Barth rightly criticizes a tendency in biblical scholarship to reduce salvation to the human sphere. Christ's lordship over all created powers and things is proclaimed by many New Testament texts, including Col 1:15-17. In the Bible, nature is more than just the background of salvation. "Not only persons but also spirits, living creatures, and dead things are promised liberation (Rom 8.21); both Christians and the Church are saved not only for their own sake but as the 'first fruit of God's creation' (James 1.18)."[43]

Colossians and Ephesians are particularly important in that they emphasize Christ as the Lord of the universe.[44] The point is that Christ is not only Saviour of individuals redeeming them from sin and leading them to a pious life. "He is Lord of the whole world. He is not only the answer to specifically religious problems, for consciences tortured by sinfulness and longing for forgiveness. He is also the answer to modern Hellenistic problems in a world that had lost God and therefore its aim, its meaning, that is bound to meet its fate, that was full of fear and yet not able to evade it."[45]

In short, these two letters are important in that they contribute to a biblical cosmology which is relevant in today's religious and cultural situation. God's economy of salvation reaches out far beyond the world of Christians, even beyond the human world.

2. The importance of reconciliation

Together with 2 Corinthians the letters of Colossians and Ephesians contribute to a theology of reconciliation which is of great significance for today's mission. W. R. Burrows is right in stating that "'reconciling all in Christ' is an important paradigm or focal image for Christian mission as we move into the third Christian millennium."[46] At least the following aspects should be considered:

First, a theology of reconciliation can be discerned on three levels:[47] a christological level in which Christ is the mediator through whom God reconciles the world to God himself; an ecclesiological level, in which Christ reconciles Jew and Gentile; and a cosmic level, in which Christ reconciles all powers in heaven and earth (cf. the previous paragraph).

Second, Eph 2:14-16 is of special importance. The consequence of this passage has been underlined by H. Gollwitzer:[48] If the time of dividing wall is past, behind which God's law stood, how much more is the time of all other walls past, behind which stand only human laws. But, the consequences have not been drawn from the broken wall, instead we have misused the Christian message to sanction our own walls of nation, class and race.

Third, for Paul the justification is closely related to the question of Jewish-Gentile unity. It is by no means accidental that the Jew-Gentile pair is mentioned first in all the passages where the baptismal formula occurs (Gal 3:28; 1 Cor 12:13 and Col 3:11). In other words the reconciliation of Jews and Gentiles must be seen as *prototype* (or *model*) for the reconciliation of other groups. Gal 3:28 expresses the early Christian vision that all existential divisions are overcome in Christ. This is a theological truth even if the church and Paul himself was hesitant to the full realization and implementation thereof.[49] Applied to the contemporary scene this means that it is the task of the churches to effect reconciliation in all areas of life.[50]

3. New humanity and cultural identity

Eph 2:14-16 and other New Testament texts speak of the new man or the new humanity of the new people. The early church gave expression to this by calling the Christians the *triton genos*, the "third race" next to the existing two races of Jews and Gentiles. The idea is that "Jew" and "Gentile" are characteristics of the past which one leaves behind or at least should leave behind in order to become only Christian.

However, the author of Ephesians does not think in this way. Just as the difference between man and woman was not abolished by Christ (cf. Gal 3:28) so man does not stop being a Jew or a non-Jew when he becomes a Christian. What is put aside by Christ is not the differences but the hostility between two human groups. Christians do not replace Jews and Gentiles; rather, Israel and the nations, previously deeply divided, are joined together by Christ in his body and life.[51]

Oneness in Christ, therefore, cannot be construed to require the rejection of one's racial identity or the dissolution of one's culture in favour of some supposed monochromatic or monolithic ideal. "Rather, it has to do with the setting aside of pride and exclusivism. It is our acceptance of one another because we have been accepted by God, with such acceptance operative in every area of life."[52]

The term "third race" is open to misunderstanding.[53] This, however, is also the case with the opposite idea. We must criticize the so-called "homogenous unit" principle launched by the church-growth movement. According to this principle "men like to become Christians without crossing racial, linguistic or class barriers".[54]

Against this theory it has to be maintained that the New Testament communities were more heterogenous than a number of contemporary "successful" mission congregations.[55] However, we must also distinguish between cultural and national diversity on the one hand, and social and economic diversity on the other hand. Heterogeneity in the church might be accepted with respect to diverse races and cultures – as long as it is not combined with oppression and disrespect of the "others" – but it is certainly not right with respect to wealth and poverty.[56]

The ambiguity of cultural and national identity is illustrated by the book of Revelation. Here the world of nations, ethnic, tribal and linguistic groups is seen under a twofold perspective.[57] The nations are engaged on both sides in the final, cosmic conflict. They are associated and allied with the powers of anti-Christ. National identity can lead to national pride and self-sufficiency. But at the same time the nations at the end will bring their treasures into God's city. God shall dwell among them and they shall be his peoples (Rev 21:3). And we are made to listen to the heavenly praise of the Lamb: "...for you were slaughtered and by your blood you ransomed for God saints from every tribe and language and people and nation" (5:9).

Christ has broken down the dividing wall. This is the important message of Eph 2:14-16. What Jesus did in Palestine among Jews by creating a new fellowship[58] – is now confirmed after Easter among Jews and Gentiles outside Palestine. In Christ God has shattered the barriers that divide the human race and has created a new community. A new people of God has come into being. It is without analogy; it is a "sociological impossibility" that has nevertheless become possible.

4. Mission to "foreign" structures
It is sometimes argued that the "principalities and powers" in the New Testament letters are parallel to the "demons" in the gospels. This comparison, however, is not

quite adequate. While the demons are seen as intrinsically evil, the "powers" can have various meanings.[59] A survey of the material points to three aspects:[60]

(a) The powers can be conceived of in their general essence as part of God's creation (see Col 1:15-17; cf. Eph 1:9-10).

(b) These powers have rebelled and are fallen. They separate human beings from God's love (Rom 8:38). They fail to serve man as they should (Gal 4:2-3; cf. Eph 2:1-2).

(c) Despite the fallen condition of the powers God is still able to use them for good. The cross means Christ's victory over the powers. This can be described in two ways: as a reconciliation of all things to God (Col 1:20) or as a disarmament of the powers (Col 2:15).

The word translated "subsist" (NRSV: "hold together") in Col 1:17 has the same root as the modern word "system". The author says that in Christ everything "systematizes", everything holds together. This observation makes it natural to ask the question of a parallelism between the ancient phenomenon of "powers" and the modern phenomenon of structures.

Of course the peril of "modernizing" should be taken seriously;[61] nevertheless some of the concrete modern structures might be structurally analogous to the powers. This might include religious structures (especially the religious under-girdings of the stable societies), intellectual structures (e.g. -ologies and -isms), moral structures (codes and customs) and political structures (the tyrant, the market, the school, the courts, race and nation). The totality is overwhelming broad.[62]

Such structures are relevant in a missionary setting. This is particularly true of the economic structures created by the debt crisis. This aspect has often been neglected by Christian mission, as was made clear by the WCC Assembly in Can-berra (1991): "There is an urgent need today for a new type of mission, not into foreign lands, but into "foreign" structures. By this term we mean economic, social and political structures which do not at all conform to Christian moral standards".[63]

The conference also stated that the Spirit of truth re-establishes and restores the integrity of the human person and human communities: "As Christians and as churches we constantly experience the danger of becoming captives to the systems and structures of the world. They are the principalities and authorities, 'the cosmic forces of darkness, the spiritual forces of evil' (Eph 6:12), which induce all human beings to be tempted to do injustice to others."[64]

In which way should Christians and the church relate to these structures? Following Colossians and Ephesians the primary task of the church seems to lie in its very existence. The church is itself a proclamation of the Lordship of Christ to the powers from whose dominion the church has begun to be liberated. It does not attack the powers; this Christ has done. The church concentrates on not being seduced by them. *By her existence* she demonstrates that their rebellion has been vanquished.[65] At this point we must ask what is the reality today. Do the churches bless the existing powers in stead of depriving them of their authority and power?

5. Holy war or mission of peace?
The passage of Eph 6:10-20 has often been used as a legitimation of an aggressive mission. In recent years many theologians have criticized this interpretation, e.g. the Japanese theologian K. Koyama:

> "The crusade concept is a product of Christianity, not of Christ. The word is not in the Bible. It raises its head like a cobra in modern Christianity... 'Crusade' is a self-righteous pharisaic (holy war) military word. It does not belong to the language of the 'Prince of Peace who died on the Cross'... When did Christianity become a cheap military campaign? Who made it so? I submit that a good hundred million American dollars, a hundred years of crusading will not make Asia Christian. Christian faith does not and cannot be spread by crusading. It will spread without money, without bishops, without theologians, without plannings, if people see a crucified mind, not a crusading mind, in Christians".[66]

Although this is a reflection on the Great Commission in Matt 28:16-20 it applies to Eph 6:10-18 as well. But, as argued above, this passage offers no sanction for conventional holy war ideology. By its peaceful existence in the world the church community stands (6:13) as a challenge to the power of evil.

"Gospel witness is a word, a spoken message. It is the weakest and most impoverished kind of action. It is the weapon of a ridiculous band of people today, just as it was the weapon of the poor fishermen of Galilee".[67] This is also the weapon we must use today when we are confronted with the "principalities and powers".

Notes

1   Hahn 1965, 147.
2   Senior & Stuhlmueller 1983, 191.
3   Cf. Olsson 1994, 72. For a thorough discussion of the letter to Ephesians see also Meyer 1971.
4   For a survey of various theories about the Colossian situation see Francis 1977.
5   Cf. Schweizer 1988, 466-467.
6   Cf. Hartman 1985, 112.
7   Cf. Schweizer 1988, 464-465.

8   Cf. Keck 1976, 114.
9   Schweizer 1963, 325.
10   Cf. Hartman 1995, 36.
11   Cf. Verhey 1984, 121.
12   Cf. Senior & Stuhlmueller 1983, 196-198.
13   It is widely acknowledged that Col 1:15-20 is permeated by the so-called Wisdom christology.
14   So, for instance, Schweizer 1976, esp. 45-60; 106-109; 186-221; cf. Senior & Stuhlmueller 1983, 198: "Although Pauline thought was also concerned with the renewal of nature (cf. Romans 8), its primary focus is on the world of humanity."
15   Cf. Olsson 1994, 72. See also Kasting 1969, 138-139. Kasting states that the original cosmic soteriology is maintained even if the author added the words in vv. 17-18a.
16   Cf. Weber 1986, 67.
17   The question of Gnostic influence upon Ephesians has occupied the forefront of literature dealing with the epistle. For a survey of the discussion see Arnold 1989, 7-13.
18   Cf. Arnold 1989, 5-40.
19   Barth 1974, 1:90
20   Cf. Senior & Stuhlmueller 1983, 200.
21   Cf. Hays 1997, 62-63.
22   Käsemann 1958, 518.
23   Cf. Barth 1974, I:209. See also Meyer 1971, 33.
24   Cf. Arnold 1989, 163.
25   Barth 1959, 121.
26   Cf. Weber 1986, 66.
27   See the various commentaries to Eph 2:14-16.
28   Schlier 1958, 124.
29   Dahl 1965, 74, note 45.
30   Cf. Meeks 1977, 215. According to Meeks, the Jewish-Christian disciple of Paul writing to predominantly Gentile congregations sees their inclusion into the people of God as the primary empirical manifestation of "God's plan for the fullness of time". Thus he "historizes" the mythical language of unification which permeates the liturgy.
31   Cf. Stendahl 1977a, 124.
32   This point is stressed by P. S. Minear. See Rader 1978, 208.
33   Cf. Barth 1959, 124-125; Barth 1968, 259.
34   Cf. Barth 1959, 167-168.
35   Cf. Hays 1997, 65-66.
36   Barth 1959, 176.
37   Cf. Weber 1986, 72.
38   Wink 1984, 89. See also Barth 1974, 1:363-366.
39   Cf. Arnold 1989, 63.
40   Berkhof 1962, 41-42; cf. Yoder 1972, 150-151.
41   For this survey see Weber 1986, 74-75.
42   Cf. Weber 1986, 75.

43 Barth 1982, 167.
44 To be sure, the emphasis on the lordship of Christ also has led to Christian imperialism, especially after Christianity grew to be the official religion from the fourth century onward. Paul, of course, could not foresee such a development, and should not be blamed for it. "In his days, the lordship of Christ gave Christians freedom, not mastery" (Keck 1976, 119).
45 Schweizer 1963, 325.
46 Burrows 1998, 79
47 Cf. Schreiter 1992, 42.
48 For this reference to Gollwitzer see Rader 1978, 208.
49 Cf. Stendahl 1966, 34.
50 Cf. Barth 1968, 241-242.
51 Cf. Rader 1978, 230.
52 Longenecker 1984, 46.
53 Cf. Blaser 1972, 294ff. See also Rader 1978.
54 McGavran 1970, 198. For similar ideas see Wagner 1979.
55 Cf. Bosch 1983, 240: "Exclusive groupings of believers, whether around individual leaders for theological or other reasons (1 Cor 1:10-13) or around homogenous cultural units, are unacceptable in the Christian church."
56 For a more detailed discussion see Nissen 1984, 125f.
57 See Dahl 1974, 66.
58 The creation of a new fellowship before Easter is described by Weber 1979, 24, as follows: "Gathering together poor Galileans with a former tax collector, some probable former Jewish rebels, and including women as part of the community, a sociologically and politically impossible group had come into being."
59 Cf. Wink, 1984, 39: "*Unless the context further specifies* (and some do), *we are to take the terms for power in their utmost comprehensive sense*, understanding them to mean both heavenly *and* earthly, divine *and* human, good *and* evil powers" (italics in the original).
60 Cf. Yoder 1972, 144-146.
61 Wink 1984, 102, claims that our approach to interpretation must avoid all attempts to "modernize" insofar as this means ignoring the mythic dimension of the text and transferring it in an unmediated way into modern categories.
62 Cf. Yoder 1972, 145.
63 Signs of the Spirit 1991, 66.
64 Signs of the Spirit 1991, 73.
65 Cf. Yoder 1972, 153. In a comment on Eph 6:10-18 Berkhof 1962, 43, says that the duty of the believer "is not to bring the Powers to their knees. This is Jesus Christ's own task. He has taken care of this thus far and will continue to do so. We are responsible for the defence, just because He takes care of the offense. Ours it is to hold the Powers, their seduction and their enslavement, at a distance, "to be able to stand against the wiles of the devil" (v. 11; cf. 13)."
66 Koyama 1979, 53-54.
67 Comblin 1979a, 96.

8.

Hope and witness:
Mission in 1 Peter and the Book of Revelation

Introduction

The remainder of the New Testament consists of various books – Hebrews, the Pastorals, the Johannine letters, 1 and 2 Peter, James, Jude and Revelation – which do not contain any references to the Great Commission. Nor do they have any successful stories about the spread of the gospel or strategies of the gospel proclamation. Many scholars would therefore argue that they offer little material that bears directly on the issue of mission.

The main emphasis of these writings is on the pastoral aspects of the church. Thus James emphasizes internal congregational matters, and the Pastorals are exhortations to Christian leaders to take responsibility for the life of the communities. Emphasis is laid on the sound doctrine and on warnings against false teachings.

Yet the failure by some to find mission in these letters might be the result of a narrow definition of this term. Thus, F. Hahn states that in the Pastorals "the concentration on the life and strengthening of the churches is so strong that it is now largely impossible to speak of an understanding of the mission, in the sense in which the phrase has so far been used and was characteristic of oldest Christianity".[1]

However, even with their domestic concern, the *Pastorals* are not silent on the mission issue. Several aspects of the letter's message are worth noting and contribute, at least indirectly, to an overall New Testament theology of mission.[2] So, for instance, the universal scope of salvation is clearly stated in the confessional formula 1 Tim 3:16 ("...proclaimed among Gentiles"). And the will of God to save all people and the corresponding universal mission of Christ are strongly affirmed in 1 Tim 2:3-6.

While James, Jude and 2 Peter concentrate almost exclusively on internal problems, the missionary perspective of *Hebrews* is more evident. Two issues should be mentioned: its cosmic and universal christology (e.g. 1:1-3) and the emphasis on the people of God. There is a pointedly eschatological perspective. The followers of Christ are sojourners and pilgrims, pursuing the path toward their permanent home, heaven (11:9.13; cf. 1 Pet 1:1.17).[3]

In the following two other writings will be analysed more in detail. 1 Peter and Revelation are of special interest because they have a number of statements on the relation between Christians and the surrounding world.

I. The witness of hope – 1 Peter

1. The situation of the readers

1 Peter does not speak of a proclamation of the gospel among Gentiles. Nor does it have any conscious outreach mission strategy. It is therefore often assumed that this letter is no missionary document.

However, this definition of mission is too narrow. Mission should not be reduced to verbal gospel proclamation. It includes life witness too. According to this understanding, 1 Peter has a series of issues which are relevant to mission. The major theme is *how to live as a Christian among non-Christians*.[4] Other crucial issues are hope and the people of God. In short, this letter emphasizes Christian existence and Christian witness in relation to the surrounding world.

1 Peter orients Christian existence primarily on hope. In baptism the Christians are born again into a living hope through the resurrection of Jesus Christ from the dead (1:3). They are characterized as "exiles of the Dispersion" (1:1) or "aliens and exiles" (2:11). These are both social and theological descriptions of the letter's recipients.[5]

The *social* aspect is underlined by J. H. Elliott. In his sociological analysis of 1 Peter entitled "A Home for the Homeless", Elliott argues that incorporation within a household (*oikos*) was a universal desire in the Hellenistic Roman era. To the countless number of displaced and dispossessed strangers and aliens of this period, membership in an *oikos* meant the possibility of at least a minimal degree of social security and of a psychological sense of belonging. For the same reason the offer of a home to the homeless constituted a powerful element in the current political as well as religious missionary propaganda.[6]

In 1 Peter the "household of God" is a major ecclesiological symbol.[7] Elliott points to a close similarity between the characteristics of a sect and the community behind the letter. The Christians are to maintain the double character of a conversionist sect: an unflinching openness to the outside together with a determined internal cohesion and a distinctiveness from the outside. They must accept the suffering that inevitably follows.[8]

Alongside this social aspect there is a *theological* dimension. Because of their minority status and their different world view, the Christians are "strangers" and a dispersed people in their own land. Peter's message to his readers is that their "home" – that is their identity – is found in the "household of God" (4:17), which is the fellowship of God's people, a "spiritual house" (2:5).[9]

One should notice that God's people is not just "strangers", but "involved strangers", showing "critical solidarity" with the world, loving their enemies (cf. Matt 5:44).[10] A paradigm for this role of the Christian in society can be found in Jer 29:7. The Christians are exhorted to seek the welfare of the city.[11]

The aim of 1 Peter is neither to teach withdrawal from the structures of this world, nor to proclaim a specific order of society, but to proclaim the kingdom of

Christ.[12] In a context which is dealing with the socio-political reality Christ is not attested as the ruling one, but as the suffering and crucified one (2:21-25). It would be wrong to identify the sufferings of Christ with passivity or apathy. Emphasis is laid on welldoing, even suffering in welldoing, but this does not mean conformism, but a responsible and critical attitude to the environment (the world).[13]

2. God's household and God's people

From the perspective of society, the Christians are *paroikoi* – strangers, aliens and nonconformists. They are despicable fanatics, lowly slaves, "Christ-lackeys" etc. But in the sight of God these marginal people experience a transformation of status and dignity. Within the believing community they constitute the *oikos tou theou* (the household of God).[14]

The passage of 1 Pet 2:4-10 confirms this new status of the believers. In vv. 4-5, the link is made between Christ as "living stone" and his people, who are to be "living stones". Together they constitute a "spiritual house". Furthermore, the community is explicitly identified as a "holy priesthood", and its members are instructed to "offer spiritual sacrifices acceptable to God through Jesus Christ" (cf. Rom 12:1).

Of special interest are vv. 9-10:

> "But you are a chosen race, a royal priesthood, a holy nation, God's own people, in order that you may proclaim the mighty acts of him who called you out of darkness into his marvellous light. Once you were not people but now you are God's people; once you had not received mercy but now you have received mercy".

This passage contains a number of designations for the church all of which have their root in the Old Testament imagery of the people of God. The terminology combines regal and cultic functions.[15] "Royal priesthood" (cf. Exod 19:6) implies a joining of the kingly and priestly roles, and fits well with the more political connotations of the correlative terms in this passage "chosen race, a holy nation, God's own people." Yet the community is paradoxically called upon to be prepared to suffer, not to triumph through exercise of God-given power.

One should notice the wording of v. 9. The term "(in order) that" indicates that the designations cannot be limited to the inner Christian fellowship, but are to be considered as a service of witness for mankind.[16] So, for instance, "you are a chosen race" means that the Christian community is elected for *service* to the world.

One of the amazing things about 1 Peter is that the community's minority status and its consciousness of conversion and election do not lead to a defensive attitude.[17]

The responsibility of the Christians according to 1 Peter, is not to withdraw from the world, not to condemn it. The Christian community must offer a living witness of hope that may eventually lead the world to give glory to its God.

3. The calling to do good

The Christians are identified as "a holy nation" (2:9). This does not mean a life in isolation. On the contrary, by living holy lives, they reveal to their surrounding world God's very nature. They are called to be witnesses to the Christian hope: "But in your hearts sanctify Christ as Lord. Always be ready to make your defence to anyone who demands from you an accounting for the hope that is in you" (3:15).

The people of God who are separated from the world as God's possession must simultaneously live in the world, and for this 2:13-3:7 gives the basic guidelines, with 2:11-12 serving as introduction and 3:8-12 as a concluding summary.[18]

The author repeatedly calls for "doing good". Three reasons are given why Christians should be concerned for the welfare of their neighbours. They are to be found in the concept of the calling of God's people:[19]

Firstly, the fundamental purpose of the elect race, the royal priesthood was to *proclaim* the virtues of the One who called them out of darkness into his marvellous light (2:9-10). The subsequent verses indicate how this was to be done in terms of a compelling Christian lifestyle seen from their good works (2:11ff.).[20]

Secondly, in the face of unjust treatment the Christian household servant was also called to *follow* the example of the patiently suffering Messiah (2:21).

Thirdly, the whole church was not exhorted to repay evil with evil, or abuse with abuse, but to do exactly the opposite. They were to impart the *blessing* of doing good (3:9).

The Christians must not make an exodus from the world, nor cultivate a private spirituality by withdrawing from social obligations, nor contemplate the imminent coming of Christ with apocalyptic enthusiasms. Three examples illustrate their social duties: the relation of the Christians to the state (2:13-17), household slaves (2:18-25), and wives of non-Christian husbands (3:1-6).

The examples of slaves and wives sets a pattern of courageous witness and redemptive suffering that is the responsibility of all Christians.[21] The slaves are to carry out their service in a spirit of "reverence" (2:18). This attempt to be a good slave and a good Christian may lead to suffering. As to the wives we should notice that in Roman society a woman was usually expected to adopt the religious conviction of her husband. Therefore, Christian wives in mixed marriages were in a vulnerable situation. Nevertheless, if there are any of the husbands "who do not obey the word, they may be won over without a word by their wives' conduct" (3:1).

D. Senior rightly notes that the theology of witness developed in this letter is an important contribution to the notion of mission in the New Testament. The author does not speak of itinerant mission preaching, but he does insist that the

community members turn their interests and involvement *outside* the community.[22]
B. Olsson in a similar way notes that to be God's people, God's household on earth
– this is mission according to 1 Peter. Hence, the status, identity and self-
understanding of the Christians are of basic importance for the understanding of
mission. To be a Christian is to be in mission.[23]

II. Prophetic witness – the Book of Revelation

1. The background
The frequent references to persecution in the Book of Revelation are usually taken
to indicate that it was written during the reign of Domitian (81-96 CE), under
whom the cult of emperor worship flourished in the province of Asia. Presumably,
the Christians suffered persecution because of their refusal to participate in
veneration of the emperor. It is a point of dispute whether the persecution was a
matter of official imperial policy; it is perhaps more likely to have involved
sporadic local harassment. Furthermore, toward the end of the first century, there
were severe strains between rich and poor in Asia Minor. The Book of Revelation
seems to be shaped to some extent by those strains.[24]

The key to the structure of the book is often found in 1:19: The expression "what
is" refers to the first part 1:9-3:22, whereas "what is to take place after this"
designates the main apocalyptic part 4:1-22:5. However, it is questionable whether
this division of Revelation does justice to the author's intention since it separates
parenesis and apocalyptic vision.[25]

The claim of Revelation to be early Christian prophecy must be taken seriously.
Its main objective is not the reinterpretation of the Hebrew Scriptures nor the
calculation of the end time events, but the prophetic communication of the revelation to the seven communities in Asia Minor.[26] This means that the seven letters
are not only about the present situation of the churches, but also about their future,
and the visions in chs. 4-20 are not only a revelation of what is going to occur in
the future, but also a reference to the present situation of the churches. "The aim
of the letters to the seven churches is simultaneously to comfort the afflicted
(Smyrna, Philadelphia) and to afflict the comfortable (Sardis, Laodicea)."[27]

The Christians in Asia Minor experienced daily alienation, harassment, and
suffering. Their everyday experiences ran counter to their belief in God's might and
undermined their hope in the reign of God. It was this tension between the vision
of the Kingdom of God and the social situation that led John to write his apocalypse.[28] He seeks to encourage the Christians by creating a new plausibility structure and symbolic universe within the framework of a prophetic pastoral letter.
Apocalyptic vision and explicit parenesis have the same function. They provide the
vision of an "alternative world" in order to encourage Christians and to enhance
their staying power in the face of persecution and possible execution.[29]

2. Conflict with the surrounding culture

The seven letters in 2:1-3:22 point to different opinions among the Christians in Asia Minor as regards the attitude to the surrounding culture. Two issues in the letters are "eating food sacrificed to idols" and "immorality", almost certainly references to idolatry (2:14.20). There is a clash between two different "mission strategies": On the one hand the accommodation of the Nicolaitans; on the other hand the uncompromising attitude of the author.

The "strategy" of the Nicolaitans: In three of the letters the author explicitly polemicizes against some rival Christian prophets. Ephesus is praised because it has rejected the false prophets and shown hatred for the works of the Nicolaitans (2:6), whereas Pergamum is criticized for tolerating those who hold to the teachings of Balaam (2:14; cf. 2:15). The community in Thyatira provokes censure because it has accepted the teaching of a woman prophet named Jezebel (2:20-24).

All three terms – Nicolaitans, Balaam and Jezebel – probably designate the same group of Christian prophets who allowed their adherents to eat food that had been sacrificed to idols and to participate in pagan religious festivities. It is likely that this theological stance offered political, economic, and professional advantages to Christians who lived in the prosperous trading cities of Asia Minor, since the meat sacrificed to idols was served at meetings of trade guilds and business associations as well as at private receptions. It provided an alternative theological perspective to the "either/or" position of the author. This alternative "strategy" allowed Christian believers to participate actively in the commercial, political, and social life of their cities.

How might this prophetic group have argued theologically for such an integration into pagan society? Like the "strong" Christians in Corinth they might have reasoned that "idols are nothing" (1 Cor 8:4) and that therefore Christians could eat food sacrificed to idols. One may also participate in the imperial cult because Caesar's claim to divinity was "nothing more than a constitutional fiction to promote political loyalty to Rome".[30] On that basis accommodation is possible and, indeed, desirable given the advice of the apostles to honour the emperor (Rom 13:1-7; 1 Pet 2:17).

The "strategy" of the author: The message of John to his readers is "patient endurance", which stands in opposition to the policies and practices of the prophetic group. John will not tolerate their compromise; the conflict of the sovereignties makes it treasonous. The freedom of patient endurance is not a freedom to accommodate the claims of Domitian and so live comfortably, but a freedom from conventional standards of prosperity and power (Rev 2:9; 3:8.17), a freedom to accept poverty and powerlessness in faithful loyalty to Christ and in the expectation of his final triumph and blessing, a freedom to resist the totalitarian and religious claims of the Roman empire.[31]

The citizens of two realms, Jerusalem and Babylon, met daily in the streets of Philadelphia and Pergamum, yet they did not dwell on the same earth, although in their hearts as well as in their behaviour the forces of the two realms met in combat. The only way for Christians to understand what was happening on the streets of the cities was to listen to what the Spirit was saying through this conflict between the old and the new.[32]

The demand laid on the Christians addressed in the book is an unconditional loyalty to the one side in the vast, unseen struggle between the cosmic powers that is occurring or is imminent. There is no room for compromise – no benign acceptance of meat in an unbeliever's home, no undefiling commerce – or a "lukewarm" response. It is time for "witnessing", which can lead to death (as for Antipas, 2:13).[33]

The overall message of the seven letters is a call for sharper boundaries between the church and the world. This is also the case with other parts of the Revelation. The criticism of the surrounding culture is particularly severe in John's account of the fall of "Babylon" in ch. 18. Babylon's flaunting of wealth and power does not hide her immorality and idolatry, her oppression and murder, and, therefore, God's judgment is unveiled (18:1-8.21-24). The author calls for a spiritual exodus: "Come out of her, my people" (18:4). The exodus required is from demonic values, the pride of power (18:3.9-10) and the greed (18:3.11-19) that marked Rome's life and justified her doom.[34]

Thus, there are several counter-cultural strands in Revelation. The references to idolatry and immorality are to be understood as standing in the tradition of the Jewish concern for holiness, that distinctive pattern of life over and against the nations "it is not so among you..." (Mark 10:43). There is a challenge to the assumption that the disciple is going to be able to take part without too much discomfort in the social intercourse of the contemporary world.[35]

3. The cosmic Christ and the renewal of the creation

The prophetic witness of Revelation is based on two issues: the Christ event and the vision of a new heaven and a new earth.

Jesus Christ is not only the Lord and judge of his community (1:12-20) but he is the "King of kings and Lord of lords " (19:16). His universal kingship is based on the fact that he "had been slaughtered" (5:6) and has ransomed from every tribe and language and nation people whom he has "made to be a kingdom and priests serving our God" (5:9-10).

The cosmic christology is fundamental to the message of the book. Because the risen Christ has become the instrument of God's salvation to all the world, his "Lordship" has no peer. This theological position is the root of the conflict between the Christians and the Roman empire. Because Rome attempts to grasp a prerogative belonging only to Christ, it puts itself against God and thereby demonstrates that it is an agent of Satan.[36]

It is interesting to notice that John reverses the value of symbols of power and conquest by transforming them into images of suffering and weakness. The lamb *is* the lion. Jesus is the Messiah, but he has performed his messianic office in most extraordinary way. "John asks us to see both that Jesus rejects the role of Lion, refuses to conquer through supernatural power, and that we must now give a radical new valuation to lambs: the sufferer is the conqueror, the victim the victor."[37] The cross and not the sword, suffering and not brute power determines the meaning of history. The key to the obedience of God's people is not their effectiveness but their patience (13:10).[38]

Revelation is often interpreted as an expression of world-denial and escapism.[39] Even though John's apocalyptic language may give a first impression of world denial, that is not the case. His deepest concern is with *this* world and its ultimate destiny. The eschatology of Revelation does not inculcate passivity in its readers. Instead it calls them to an alert resistance to the seductive powers of the present age and an active obedience to a merciful God who wills to make all things new.[40] In ch. 10 there is a direct call to participate actively as a prophet rather than merely be a passive spectator. Revelation is insistent that the role of the martyr or witness is of central importance.[41]

It is not insignificant that the New Jerusalem comes down from heaven *to earth* and that the proclamation of final salvation declares that God dwells with human beings, not vice versa (21:2-3). These things occur in "a new heaven and a new earth" (21:1), but this means that "God will have redeemed and transformed the creation, not abolished it."[42] The movement of the new Jerusalem is a descent from God, not an ascent of man.[43]

Thus, we should notice that John's vision of final redemption is thoroughly creation-centred. The central purpose of the new age is heaven on earth. John's cosmic Christ and his concern for the redemption of the world lead him to his uncompromising witness theology. The consequences of such a stance might entail effective withdrawal from the social and political spheres of Graeco-Roman society – a stance completely different from that of 1 Peter. "The Christian's withdrawal from society is a prophetic act of witness to and on behalf of society. The Christians are to proclaim the good news of universal salvation to the world, and their pulpit is a heroic refusal to compromise with a system they see as aligned with the forces of sin and death."[44]

III. Hermeneutical perspectives

Common to 1 Peter and the Book of Revelation is the call for witness. In the case of 1 Peter it meant the active participation in the structures of society, in the case of Revelation it meant the active withdrawal. In what follows we shall look at some hermeneutical implications of this theology of witness.

1. Christians and the state – conformity or non-conformity?
In the first century Christians had different attitudes towards the political authorities. Some adopted a strategy of non-conformity, others a strategy of conformity.

Revelation is an example of a strategy of non-conformity. Here we have a passionate protest against the totalitarian type of political rule, especially in chs. 13 and 14. The Roman state appears as the slave of Satan. Yet, the author does not appeal to revolution in the sense of violence. We have an ethics of sufferings, but unlike 1 Peter 2 it is not combined with submission to the state. For Revelation is the gospel of hope and the basis of a religious criticism of society and power. The book implies a theology of liberation *and* a theology of martyrdom. Like the rest of the New Testament God's justice should be comprehended in the context of his cross[45].

Rom 13:1-7 is the most famous example of a strategy of conformity.[46] 1 Pet 2:13-17 has many items in common with Rom 13:1-7, but its orientation is different. Particularly in the beginning and closing verse the author is displaying a reservation which is absent in Rom 13. Thus, in v. 17 it is said: "Honour everyone. Love the family of believers. Fear God. Honour the emperor".

These four attitudes summarizes the Christian's obligation to two distinct groups – civil society with its appointed leaders and the Christian community under the rule of God[47]. A clear distinction is made: *fear* God, *honour* the emperor. Only God should be feared, the governor should merely be honoured.

The author knows that among the officials there are foolish persons (2:15), but instead of inviting the readers to violent resistance, he calls them to "do right". This term should be seen in connection with the historical and social context of 1 Peter which is different from that of Rom 13. Persecution must be taken for granted by the Christians (see 3:14.17; 4:1.12-19). And Rome is equated with Babylon (5:13).

Biblical texts have to be seen in their socio-historical contexts. They are liable to be misunderstood if taken out of context. This is particularly clear in the case of Rom 13 which has often been interpreted as expressing the metaphysical nature of the state. However, Paul's injunctions about the state are not absolute demands laid upon Christians to obey the government but conditions laid down for the Christians in Rome in the mid-fifties AD which may not have been appropriate for the Roman Christians ten years later at the height of the Neronian pogrom.[48]

This brings us to the question of correlation. The relationship between the horizons of our world and those of the text is a key factor in interpretation. Imperfect correlation is almost bound to be tendentious. If carelessly correlated to the modern situation, a text might be morally objectionable: for example, if it were used to stir up prejudice, racism or sexism, to justify violence or war or to further greed and power.[49]

By contrast, a proper correlation is dependent on "distantation", the differentiation of the worlds so that each of them is treated with integrity, but also involves the participation of the interpreter in the dynamics of the text, and the theological reflection on issues arising from it.

An example of imperfect (and comfortable) correlation is the use of Rom 13 by certain Christians in Hitler's Germany to support the Nazi regime, or the use of the text by white people in South Africa to support the apartheid regime.[50]

A corrective to such a one-sided interpretation of Rom 13 can be found in Revelation. Here we have a book which today serves as the potent resource supplying the subversive memory of the poor and oppressed. Its stark contrasts and uncompromising critique can appeal to those who find little hope in compromise with the powers-that-be and demand something more than a meek acceptance that 'the way of the world' is what God intended.[51] The author of Revelation has adopted the "perspective from below", and has expressed the experiences of those who were poor, powerless, and in constant fear of denunciation.[52]

Like the "State Theology", the theology of liberation is facing the risk of reading the biblical text naïvely: one takes from the text only what serves the interest of the reader. Biblical passages are used as "proofs" for pre-established theological attitudes.[53]

Neither Rom 13 nor Revelation consider all the circumstances of the relations of Christians to the state. Other texts should be considered as well, one of these being 1 Peter. The interesting feature about 1 Peter is its *balance between loyalty and critical distance*[54]. On the one hand the author emphasizes the eschatological situation (cf. 2:11-12). On the other we have the traditional exhortations to remain subject to civil authority. In short, Christian attitude toward the state can be described as critical solidarity.

Even if the critique of secular political authority was minimal and was nowhere directed to detailed matters of structure or practice, early Christians put forward radical ideas about the structure of power within the church itself. In Mark 10:42-45 Jesus is challenging the traditional power structure. And he links this challenge to the creation of a new community which has the character of an "alternative society", cf. "it is not so among you" (10:43).

It has been argued that the search for a just society was a crucial concern for the first Christians, but they did not achieve this goal by acting outside the community. Instead they aimed at constructing a community which in itself was an example of a just society.[55] As J. H. Yoder puts it, "The primary social structure through which the gospel works to change other structures is that of the Christian community."[56]

2. The mission of hope

Both 1 Peter and Revelation are reminders that Christian hope is an indispensable part of the mission of the church.[57] The words of 1 Pet 3:15 are of special interest which is underlined by an ecumenical study process in 70's: "Giving account of the hope that is within us". Christian groups and communities were asked to consider in which way Jesus Christ is to be experienced, interpreted and communicated in different cultures. It was maintained that giving account of the Christian hope can occur in many different ways: in liturgies, in situations of conflict, through proclaiming the gospel, through involvement in society, as the community of men and women etc.[58]

The study document states that a mission of hope embraces the entire life of the community with all its sufferings and all its activities. Four aspects are pointed out.[59] First *the proclamation of the gospel of hope*, especially to the poor, is considered to be the most important part of the all-embracing mission. Secondly, *the new community in Christ* made up by Jews and Gentiles, Greeks and barbarians, masters and slaves, men and women (Gal 3:28; Col 3:11) is itself a witness of the hope of Christ in the world. Thirdly, to complete the mission of hope, as well as proclamation and fellowship, *service* is required. Finally, the mission of hope is attested by the *glorification* of the Triune God.

The passage of 1 Pet 3:15 is like a little window, through which we can see how early Christian evangelism took place.[60] The author admonishes the Christians to be ready for a conversation with their non-Christian neighbours and fellow workers.

The usual way of perceiving evangelism is that Christians – especially those gifted for preaching – go out and tell the non-Christians about the good news. In 1 Pet 3:15, however, it is the non-Christians who begin the conversation. The readers are told that they will be questioned and challenged by their non-Christian neighbours and that they have to give account of their hope.

The hope of the early Christians was that Christ is Lord and that his cause would win. This hope became visible in their daily life. Their priorities obviously differed from those of the people surrounding them. They were even ready to suffer and die for that hope. Such a visible hope astonished or irritated their neighbours and colleagues. So questions arose, not only friendly questions, but also accusations. Christians were summoned before the judge.

In the early church mission was thus not only an organized activity by especially gifted persons such as Paul. It was much more the spontaneous and non-aggressive "gossiping of the gospel" by ordinary Christians in the course of their daily life. And the secret of it all was the hope which had become visible in the life of the Christians.

In this model of mission Christianity is presented as a "working man's religion". Lofty Christian concepts and virtues are brought down to earth and applied to everyday relationships, at work or at home. No sphere of life is to be exempt from obedience to Christ.[61]

The model of mission in 1 Peter is a challenge to contemporary forms of mission. As we go back into our daily neighbourhoods and jobs we must ask: "How today can our Christian hope become visible in our lives?"[62] To answer this question we must be ready to live out the story of Christ – each in our particular situation.[63]

Notes

1 Hahn 1965, 140.
2 Cf. Senior and Stuhlmueller 1983, 306-307.
3 For a more detailed analysis see Köstenberger 1998, 193-199.
4 Cf. Olsson 1994.
5 Cf. Elliott 1981; Senior and Stuhlmueller 1983, 297-298. *Contra* Winter 1994, 16, who maintains that it is only a theological description.
6 Elliott 1981, 221.
7 Elliott 1981, 220-221.
8 For criticism of Elliott's use of sociological models see Holmberg 1990, 92-96.
9 Cf. Köstenberger 1998, 202.
10 Cf. Piper 1980.
11 Cf. Winter 1994, 15-17.
12 Cf. Philips 1971, 27 and 49.
13 See also Goppelt 1972. Schottroff 1975, 215, notes: "Feindesliebe ist Appell zu einer missionarischen Haltung gegenüber den Verfolgern"; cf. Nissen 1980, 282.
14 Cf. Elliott 1981, 226-230.
15 Cf. Kee 1995, 124-129.
16 Cf. Blauw 1962, 128.
17 Cf. Senior and Stuhlmueller 1983, 299.
18 Cf. Krodel 1977, 72.
19 Cf. Winter 1994, 20.
20 Elliott 1966, 185: "Witness in word and in deed are not alternatives but compose a double task in which the latter complements and corroborates the former".
21 Cf. Senior and Stuhlmueller 1983, 301.
22 Senior and Stuhlmueller 1983, 302. See also Goppelt 1976, 508: "Der 1. Petrusbrief ist *die ntl. Schrift, die am stärksten das Zeugnis des Wortes mit dem Zeugnis der christlichen Präsenz in der Gesellschaft verbindet*" (his italics).
23 Olsson 1994, 74.
24 Cf. Collins 1984, 89-97; Hays 1997, 170.

25 Cf. Fiorenza 1985, 173. No sharp line can be drawn between the apocalyptic and prophetic elements; Miller 1998, 230

26 Cf. Fiorenza 1985, 140.

27 Hays 1997, 177.

28 Cf. Collins 1992, 706.

29 Cf. Fiorenza 1985, 187. See also Meeks 1987, 143-144.

30 Fiorenza 1993, 56; cf. Verhey 1984, 149.

31 Cf. Verhey 1984, 149.

32 Cf. Minear 1968, 276-277; Minear 1962, 23.

33 Cf. Meeks 1987, 147.

34 Cf. Verhey 1984, 151.

35 Cf. Rowland & Corner 1990, 151.

36 Cf. Senior and Stuhlmueller 1983, 304.

37 Barr 1984, 41.

38 Cf. Yoder 1972, 238.

39 Meeks 1987, 146, claims that the Book of Revelation is no call for revolutionary action, but for passive resistance, for disengagement and for quietism.

40 Hays 1997, 180.

41 Cf. Rowland & Corner 1990, 151. On the idea of witness in Revelation, see the survey in Trites 1977.

42 Hays 1997, 180-181.

43 Cf. Minear 1968, 276.

44 Senior and Stuhlmueller 1983, 305.

45 Cf. Schillebeeckx 1977, 558.

46 For this terminology see the instructive article by Heiligenthal 1983.

47 Cf. Mouw 1975, 53-59.

48 Cf. Rowland & Corner 1990, 88.

49 Cf. McDonald 1993, 243-244.

50 In 1985 a group of (white) South African theologians produced "The Kairos Document". This document is a self-critical analysis of the "State Theology" which used Rom 13 ideologically to support the apartheid regime. See also Rowland & Corner 1990, 173ff.

51 Cf. Rowland & Corner 1990, 146.

52 Cf. Fiorenza 1993, 128.

53 On these methodological problems see also Rowland & Corner 1990, 67, and my remarks in the introduction to this study.

54 Goppelt 1976, 500, speaks of a responsible and critical attitude to the institutions of the society; see also Heiene 1992.

55 See also Nissen 1994, esp. 231-233.

56 Yoder 1972, 157.

57 Cf. van Engen 1996, 259: "Hope is possibly the most explosive concept that missiology has to offer today."

58 Giving Account 1975, 26-27. This study process was carried out by the World Council of Churches.

59 Giving Account 1975, 46-47.
60 I owe the following description to Weber 1981, 257-259.
61 Cf. Köstenberger 1998, 205.
62 Weber 1981, 259.
63 This means, according to Russell 1978, 374, that we are challenged to live now as if we were fully part of God's new creation. "A crucial form of hermeneutics is living out the story and presence of the Coming One."

9.

Mission, culture, and dialogue:
New Testament perspectives and present challenges

Introduction

This final chapter is an attempt to encircle some of the problems which arise in the encounter between the New Testament texts and our modern experiences and questions. In order that this encounter can be a dialogue it is necessary that the world ("horizon") of the text and our world ("horizon") meet. Such a meeting can result either in a collision or a fusing of horizons.[1]

One of the preconditions for understanding is an openness on the part of the interpreter for the message of the text. As interpreters we should be aware of our own presuppositions. Otherwise, our "exegesis" easily will become an "eisegesis". We should also notice that the horizon of the text is not closed and fixed, but moves as the interpreter moves.[2] Therefore, it is indispensable to have a mutual challenge between the New Testament and today's mission. There is a demand for *a change of perspectives* which means that we should alternately attempt to see the problems from the perspective of the texts and from the perspective of our own time.

The outline of this chapter differs from the preceding ones. Throughout the chapter there is a change of perspectives from the texts to our questions. Among the contemporary currents in missiology I have selected three issues which are of specific importance in these years.[3] The first one is about plurality and unity in mission, the second one about gospel and culture, and the third one about the Bible and dialogue with people of other faiths.

I. Plurality and unity in mission

1. Incarnation and contextualization

The existence of different theologies of mission in the New Testament raises the question of unity in the midst of the variety. It also poses a question to our modern understanding since we have a tendency to focus on the unity and overlook the differences.

The reason why the New Testament contains not one but several models for mission has to be found in the fact that the texts speak to concrete situations, i.e. the situations in which the communities were living. The manifold character of the texts can be seen as an answer to the manifold needs in the communities. The ecumenical report from the meeting of Faith and Order in Bristol (1967) rightly notes that this diversity in the Bible reflects the diversity of God's actions in different historical situations. The report continues: "It is important that the scholar should not attach himself to one facet of Biblical thought, however central it seems to him to be, in such a way as to cut himself off from this variety and richness."[4] Thus, there is a diversity of traditions already found in the Bible. This also applies to mission theologies.

The Bible is received always as an interpreted text, a text already in interaction with a context. Each person reads it with their own context and spectacles.[5] The relationship between text and context should be a hermeneutical spiral, that is, a dynamic and creative tension and interaction between situation and Bible and vice-versa. No wonder, then, that the term "contextualization" has become crucial not only in biblical scholarship but also in mission theology.

The contextualization is the attempt to take the concrete human context in all its dimensions with the utmost seriousness. The *particularity* of each milieu becomes the starting point for both the questions and the answers which will shape the mission. What is the nature of the human condition for *these* people in *this* place? What *specific* problems do they face? What does the gospel say about *these* issues?[6]

The theological roots of contextualization are to be found in the incarnation.[7] In Jesus Christ God has taken a *human face*, becoming Emmanuel, "God with us".[8] In a sense it is true that Jesus can only be met through some texts. However, the basic reality is not "dead" texts, but a living person. The word was embodied, it became flesh (John 1:14), that is, God was revealed in a concrete historical context. The New Testament witnesses to the God who has been "heard", "seen" and "touched" with human hands, the God who has become himself "the word of life" (1 John 1:1) in human flesh.

In this sense the context is not just a matter of secondary importance. It is a part of the text. Precisely because God has revealed himself not in an abstract idea, but in a specific context, this context must be taken into consideration. From this fact comes the necessity of the historical-critical exegesis.

All theologies are the result of "contextualization". D. von Allmen has demonstrated that this also applies to the formation of theologies in New Testament time. To take just one example, Paul himself was a Judaeo-Christian, but the churches he founded were Pagano-Christian churches. The whole struggle of Paul in his letters was to protect these churches from "Christo-Paganism" (or syncretism), but also to defend them against the accusation of Judaeo-Christians in the "mother-church", that Pagano-Christianism is as such a "Christo-Paganism". The way in which the Hellenizing of Christianity took place in apostolic times (and the way it did not take place!) remains exemplary for our times.[9]

Thus, from the very beginning the missionary message of the Christian church incarnated itself in the life and world of those who had embraced it.[10] The African theologian J. Pobee has described this by means of the term *skenosis* which is used in John 1:14.[11] The literal meaning of the Greek word *eskenosen* is "it tabernacled".

The imagery of tabernacling underlines two crucial aspects of the operation: an eternal, non-negotiable divine aspect which may be referred to as the Word of God, on the one hand, and a temporary, contextual, contingent reality, on the other. Therefore, *skenosis* is and must be an on-going process of renewal.

2. The plurality of the Bible as a positive challenge

The contextualization is a reminder that we should not reduce mission in the Bible to one specific form, e.g. the "Great Commission" in Matt 28.

Even scholars who stress the importance of mission as contextualization can be criticized for some form of reductionism. So, for instance, D. Bosch in his magnificent work on *Transforming Mission* focuses on the contributions by Matthew, Luke and Paul, arguing that these three New Testament authors are "representative of first-century missionary thinking and practice".[12] However, in his exclusive focus on these three writers, he is more or less neglecting other important contributions to mission. This includes particularly the Gospel of John, but also such books as Colossians, Ephesians and 1 Peter.

Given this variety of types of mission we might be tempted to assign priority to one of these forms. But any choice we might make would have to proceed from an a priori judgment of our own of what mission ought to be. Instead we should be willing to be challenged by the rich variety of biblical data, including above all its unexpected elements. If there are biblical forms of mission that fail to correspond to our own idea of mission, then this is precisely where we should pause. In this way we can be forced to transcend our ready-made schemata and review our way of understanding mission in the Bible.[13]

The fact that the Bible offers various perspectives on a specific theme need not be interpreted negatively. The differences, if viewed as God taking history and culture seriously, can be regarded positively. Even statements that appear to be contradictions on the propositional level may be understood as evidence of the seriousness of the incarnation.[14] God is taking the risk of limiting his message to human history and experience.

The plurality in the Bible is seen by some people to be a threat against the unity of the Bible. They also fear that the authority of the Bible is being questioned. But their idea of both the unity and the authority of the Bible is too unilateral. As to the question of unity, the Bible is something like an orchestra in which there are different instruments, blending usually to be sure, but making distinctly different sounds.

As regards the authority of the Bible it cannot be based on some hypothetical "objective reading"; rather, it grows out of living encounters with Scripture.[15] There is a need for re-evaluation of authority itself. Authority is often seen as being something inflexible and hierarchical. True authority can never be imposed; it only works when offered, chosen and freely accepted. When applied from above, vertically, it is oppressive, but when it happens horizontally, it expands, "bursts" – not in an exclusive way but inclusively. The Word became words: stories, dialogues, lives, action – flesh. The early Christian community was involved in the shaping of the text itself, "living the Scripture" by telling and living its story in changing circumstances.[16]

The Bible as canon functions as framework of control in several ways:[17]

(1) It serves to stress the role of the community of faith in appropriating biblical resources.

(2) It reminds us of the on-going activity of God. Although every portion speaks with authority of God's presence as it was apprehended in a particular time and place, it is clear that no word is the final word concerning God's revealing of himself.

(3) As a corollary to the previous point, the canon helps prevent the absolutizing of the biblical text.

(4) The canon prevents the selecting of texts based on the predisposition of the selector.

(5) Emphasis on the canon helps avoid critical reductionism.

Finally, the variety of mission types in the Bible might also be helpful today where Christians are facing a variety of challenges.[18] The situation differs enormously between the mission addressed to the neopaganism of the lands of ancient Christendom and that directed to those whom the call of the gospel has not yet reached; between a mission intended for the people of solid, old religious cultures as in Asia, and one addressed to those who have been despoiled of their culture by a devastating colonialism, as in Latin America; between receptive milieus, as in tribal societies, and the context of the lands of Islam.

3. Some tendencies in recent mission theology

The variety of missiological perspectives in the New Testament corresponds to some extent to the variety in modern understandings of mission. To illustrate this point I shall characterize briefly three tendencies.[19]

The first tendency is *the evangelical movement*.[20] Since 1974 it has been organized by the Lausanne Committee for World Evangelization. In evangelical circles mankind is usually seen from the perspective of the Fall. The root of the world's problem is spiritual and has to be recognized as such. It is therefore inadequate to understand the gospel solely in terms of social and political liberation. Evangelicals tend to regard "mission" and "evangelism" as synonyms, defining both largely in terms of verbal proclamation. The biblical foundation for mission is found in the "Great Commission" in Matt 28 and the Pauline theology. "All have sinned and fall short of the glory of God" (Rom 3:23).

The second tendency is *the ecumenical movement* which has its basis in the World Council of Churches (WCC) and in the liberation theology. Ecumenicals tend to look at man from the perspective of creation. This has several consequences. Social involvement is not seen as something superimposed on the gospel, but as being inherent in it, and growing out of it. Furthermore, salvation is not only spiritual and the Kingdom of God is not only a future reality. Sin is not only an individual matter, but has also a social, structural, institutional aspect. Liberation theology speaks of integral liberation. Salvation is liberation from *any* form of alienation, misery, sin and death. The biblical foundation for this interpretation is mainly Luke 4:16-30.

In 1980 both of these movements held a world conference. There may be more than a grain of truth in the observation that Melbourne (WCC) used "Jesus language, Kingdom language," whereas Pattaya (the evangelical movement) showed a preference for "the language of the epistles."[21] The two movements also differ in their understanding of eschatology. While the evangelicals see mission in the light of the parousia of Christ and the final judgement,[22] the ecumenicals tend to emphasize the present aspect of eschatology.

The charismatic movement might be characterized as a third tendency. Here the Book of Acts plays a specific role. However, this movement is a not unambiguous entity. It is often marked by a strong fundamentalist bias and in many cases this is combined with political conservatism (so, for instance, a number of Pentecostals in the United States).[23] The social concern and the political involvement has been poor. However it is suggestive that Pentecostals in Latin America show interest not only for the spiritual salvation but also for social and political issues.

Christians in these movements have to ask the question: how do we read, quote and use the Bible? The differences are particularly clear between "evangelicals" and "ecumenicals". Both groups are in constant danger of using the Bible simply to confirm what they have been saying all the time, and hence the richness and depth of the whole Bible does not come to life.[24] It is perhaps the special gift and task of Christians in the South to facilitate bridging the gaps and differences "because their faith is usually evangelical and their sense of responsibility in the world is ecumenical."[25]

In recent years there have been some convergence between the "evangelicals" and the "ecumenicals".[26] This might be due not only to Christians in the South but also to the so-called radical evangelicals – Mennonites and others – who have made important contributions to social thinking and practice among evangelicals.

Convergence

4. Major lines in the New Testament understanding of mission
Even if mission in the New Testament is multidimensional, there are some direction finders and criteria which we should consider when giving profile to what

mission might be today. Following D. Bosch I shall point at six major "salvific events" which are important for the understanding of mission:[27]

(a) *The incarnation.* This motif is underlined by the Gospel of John (cf. 1:14). In the Gospels the earthly Jesus is pictured as one who sided with those who suffer. This practice of Jesus has indeed much to say about the nature and content of mission today.

(b) *The cross.* The importance of the cross is particularly emphasized by Paul. The cross also stands for reconciliation (Eph 2:14-16). The Fourth Gospel is another example of the meaning of the cross for mission, cf. the metaphor of the grain of wheat (John 12:24). The scars of the risen Lord do not only prove Jesus' identity, however; they also constitute a model to be emulated by those whom he commissions (John 20:21). "Mission under the cross" is a mission of self-emptying, of humble service (cf. 1 Cor 9:19-23).

(c) *The resurrection.* In the Gospels the missionary mandate is a consequence of the resurrection of Christ. The church is called to live the resurrection life in the here and now and to be a sign of contradiction against the forces of death and destruction – that is, called to unmask modern idols and false absolutes; see also the chapter on Colossians and Ephesians.

(d) *The ascension* is, preeminently, the symbol of the crucified and risen Christ: he now reigns as King (cf. Phil 2:9-11). Within this unjust world we are called to be a community of those committed to the values of God's reign, to concern ourselves with the victims of society and proclaim God's judgment on those who continue to worship the gods of power and self-love.

(e) *Pentecost.* The importance of the Holy Spirit is especially underlined by the Acts of the Apostles and the Gospel of John. The church in the power of the Spirit is a fellowship which actualizes God's love in its everyday life and in which justice and righteousness are made present and operative. The Spirit may not be held hostage by the church, as if his sole task were to maintain it and protect it from the outside world; cf. Acts 10:1-11:18. According to John 3:8 the Spirit blows where it chooses.

(f) *The parousia.* This motif underscores that mission should take place in a hurry. In the apocalyptic discourse mission is motivated by the coming of the end (Mark 13:10). This eschatological dimension seems also to be important for Paul's mission journeys and for his collection.

These salvific events may never be viewed in isolation from one another. In our mission, we proclaim the incarnate, crucified, resurrected, ascended Christ, present among us in the Spirit and taking us into his future. Unless we hold on to this, we will communicate to the world a truncated gospel.[28]

II. Gospel and cultures

The inter-relationship of the gospel and cultures has become a key concern in theology and mission today. Culture is often defined primarily by race or ethnicity. But this definition is too narrow. Instead culture can be defined as "what holds a community together, giving a common framework of meaning. It is preserved in language, thought patterns, ways of life, attitudes, symbols and presuppositions, and is celebrated in art, music, drama, literature and the like. It constitutes the collective memory of the people and the collective heritage which will be handed down to generations still to come."[29]

1. Inculturation

In recent years inculturation has become an important model of mission. According to this model the gospel needs to take root in every culture and the church must incarnate itself in every new culture. This is the basic condition for mission today. With it comes a certain diversity, for the one gospel in many cultures gives way to a certain plurality.[30]

Inculturation follows the model of incarnation.[31] The gospel needs to be "en-fleshed" or "em-bodied" in a people and its culture. Inculturation is a kind of *ongoing* incarnation. In this approach it is not so much a case of the church being *expanded*, but of the church being *born anew* in each new context and culture. This approach also breaks radically with the idea of the faith as "kernel" and the culture as "husk" – cf. the distinction between "content" and "form". A more appropriate metaphor may be that of the flowering of a seed implanted into the soil of a particular culture.

Sometimes the terms "accommodation" and "indigenization" are used almost in the same way as "inculturation". So, for instance, K. Koyama argues that the event and message of Jesus Christ, which was brought by the missionaries, must be rooted ("indigenized") in India, Thailand, Indonesia, Hong Kong etc. "It is not the transplantation of a grown tree, say from Amsterdam to Djakarta. Actually indigenization is a critical antithesis to this whole process of big-tree-trans-plantation. The shift from transplantation to rooting is a difficult and painstaking process."[32]

The link between incarnation and inculturation is characteristic of the New Testament. This is perhaps seen most clearly in the Acts:[33] This book is the story of the gospel being unfolded, opened up, its beauty increasingly revealed as it is appropriated and re-appropriated by culture after culture. It is through the encounter of the Jewish Christians with the cultures of people like Cornelius that the horizon of theology is expanded. It is in facing the religio-cultural milieu of Athens that Paul's grasp of the gospel is enriched.

Of special importance is the story in Acts 2. Through emphasizing that each heard the gospel in his or her own language, Luke indicates that the identities of the hearers were affirmed. In the presence of the Spirit, difference need not mean division. No longer can any group or place or time claim to be more "sacred" than another.[34]

Pentecost is the reversal of Babel. Babel offers a promise for all through one language, one culture. It allows no room for the identity of each language, each culture. By contrast, Pentecost holds together both "all" and "each". Local identities are affirmed within a larger community.

In its broadest sense the biblical story moves from the single to the multiple, from the uniform to the plural. At its deepest level, the vision is not one of uniformity: Christianity is not an ethnocentric religion. Gentiles need not become Jews; Chinese need not become Italian or Polish. The universalism of the gospel means that in faith one can find solidarity in and through the plurality of nations.[35]

Multiplicity and not uniformity is what characterizes Christianity.[36] The vision is one Gospel, diverse cultures, one community. People in different parts of the world speak different languages, see the world through different eyes and live their lives in different ways. But when people accept Jesus Christ, they become members of a new community, with a new identity and a new way of living. The question is: How can the various cultures encounter the gospel – and be transformed by it – without losing their distinctiveness and vitality? On the other hand, how can the distinctiveness and integrity of the Christian faith be lived in each culture?[37]

Authentic inculturation may view the gospel as the liberator of culture. However, the gospel can also become the prisoner of the culture. This means that we must ask to what extent the gospel affirms the existing culture and to what extent it rejects the culture.

Inculturation in the New Testament does not mean the total assimilation of the gospel into culture.[38] Confronted with new cultures the New Testament churches both accepted and denounced – condemning with no uncertain vigour all that was oppressive, dehumanizing and corrupt in them. So the book of Revelation is a sustained condemnation of the violent oppression of Roman Rule, and Paul's letters are full of vehement denunciations of the sex and violence of the Hellenistic world. "Such prophetic denunciation is as much a part of the New Testament Church as its readiness to adapt. Both indeed are integral parts of the finely discerning attitude with which it encounters the cultures of the 'world'. Because it was open to all cultures the New Testament was slave to none but confronted all as the redemptive judgment of God."[39]

2. Christ and culture

What response should Christians have to culture? In his famous book "Christ and Culture", H. Richard Niebuhr notes five different responses to culture within the Christian tradition. Where possible, he tries to identify a New Testament origin for each approach.[40]

The first response is *Christ against culture.* Culture is seen negatively, as something hostile to Christianity. In much of the early Church, and especially during the persecutions, it was natural that Christ and Christianity would be completely contrary to the culture. Niebuhr sees this "Christ against culture" expressed in 1 John. From our analysis it would be more natural to point to the "exclusive" stance in Revelation and the position of the weak in 1 Cor 8-10.

The second approach is the *Christ of culture* which sees the gospel and culture as being in harmony; there is neither tension nor opposition between the claims of Christ and culture. Christ is absorbed into culture. Niebuhr can identify no New Testament writing with this approach, but he cites the Ebionites, a group present within the early church as representative of it.

These first two paradigms are the two extremes. In between them Niebuhr sets three types of relationships.

The third paradigm is *Christ above culture.* Christ is neither opposed to the culture nor absorbed into it. Rather, Christ is seen as coming to perfect the culture. Although Christ is viewed as discontinuous with culture, he remains able to fulfill its aims and aspirations. This model is parallel to the fulfilment theory; cf. the section on "Bible and dialogue" in this chapter.

Niebuhr's fourth paradigm is *Christ and culture in paradox.* This is the dualist approach: Christ is good, and human culture is sinful and corrupt. Niebuhr argues that this motif can be found in Paul: The cross as a judgement to culture (cf. 1 Cor 1:18-23), and the resurrection as a resource to new life.

The fifth model is *Christ the transformer of culture.* This position is more hopeful about culture; culture is not inherently evil, although it is the locus of disorder and sin. What is needed is conversion or transformation of the culture. Niebuhr finds that the Gospel of John is an example of this model.[41] Another and perhaps better example would be Romans 6.

Niebuhr's typology is interesting but it is also open to criticism at several points. In the first place, he deals with the relation of church and culture within a single culture and does not raise the difficult and complicated questions which arise in the communication of the gospel from one culture to another.[42]

Secondly, Niebuhr's types are Constantinian, in that within their conceptuality it is impossible to imagine or enact the church as itself a culture. But this is precisely what is one of the most important things about the New Testament church. It is a "holy nation" (cf. 1 Pet 2:9).[43]

Thirdly, Niebuhr's placing of Paul in the fourth model is also open to criticism. "Rather than pigeon-hole Paul into a particular motif it seems better to note that his attitudes to culture are plural, and can vary from letter to letter (as is the case in his attitudes to circumcision). Underneath these variations, however, two principles can be detected which are common to his dealings with both pagan and Jewish culture: the soteriological and the pastoral."[44]

The most central of Niebuhr's models is undoubtedly "Christ the transformer of culture". A. Stauffer rightly notes that the church is called not only to inculturate, but also to be countercultural. Not everything in *any* given culture is worthy or appropriate of Christian worship. All that is human needs always to be critiqued by the light of the gospel. Ultimately, Christ came to transform all things human, including ourselves and our cultures. We are called not to conform to the world, in the final analysis, but to be transformed ourselves (Rom 12:2) and in turn, to transform the world.[45]

3. Church, cross and culture

In the encounter between gospel and cultures two principles are at work: on the one hand there is the "indigenizing" principle, which affirms that the gospel is at home in every culture and every culture is at home with the gospel. On the other hand there is the "pilgrim" principle, which warns us that the gospel will put us out of step with society.[46]

The encounter between these two principles can be illustrated by two different attitudes of the Christians to the culture (especially urban culture).[47] The one model is the Pilgrim's Progress Model where the emphasis is upon the decisive break by which the Christian separates himself from the world, flees from the "wicked city" and makes for his true home in another world. The other model is the Jonah Model. Here too there is a wicked city at the centre of the picture, but the command to God's servant is to go into the city. God pleads with Jonah for the city: Should I not have compassion on that great city which is surely full of wickedness, but also of innocent babes and animals?

Both these models have their roots in Scripture and both have played their part in the long history of the church. The interesting element is that they are united in the figure of Jesus. Luke tells that he "set his face to go to Jerusalem" (Luke 9:51) and yet he speaks of the "exodus" which he accomplished in Jerusalem (Luke 9:31; NRSV "departure"). Christian life and mission must somehow have room for them both. The cross is both the new Exodus, and at the same time the place at which the Son of God entered into the very heart of the world in all its wickedness. "The cross is in one sense an act of total identification with the world. But in another sense it is an act of radical separation. It is both things at the same time."[48]

Perhaps the greatest danger for the church is to be dominated too much by the "Pilgrim Progress" model. It prefers to live in a place of security, in a well-walled city. The effect is that it forgets its missionary commitment to the surrounding world. A few reflections on the "local church" might illustrate what I mean.

According to L. Newbigin the local church is essentially the church "*for that place*".[49] And the meaning of the preposition "for" must be determined christologically. The church in each place is the church for that place, in the sense in which Christ is *for* mankind and *for* the world. Christ is the one who has been made flesh, died and risen again in order to take away the sins of the world and to reconcile all to the Father.

There are two opposite dangers in relating the church to the place. The first danger is that the church may not be truly local in that its language, worship and style of life belong to another "place" and do not speak to the man of that place as the authentic call of God. The other danger is that the church may be so conformed to the "place" that it simply echoes and confirms the interests of its members and does not communicate to them the sovereign judgement and mercy of God. In that case the local church is not truly the church.

To be a church in mission the church has to manifest a critical solidarity.[50] Newbigin points out that to fulfill the task of being church for that place, a separation might be necessary, but separation is always for the sake of mission. Furthermore, it is emphasized that separation can never be the last word. Because the gospel is about God's purpose to unite *all* things in Christ. And the cross is the place at which all people of every kind and place are to be reconciled. Thus separation is always provisional.[51]

4. Criteria for discernment of the spirits

The various models of Niebuhr are interesting in that they point to the role of Christ in connection to the cultures. This, however, is also the limitation of his typology. Another approach would be to raise the question of the role of the Holy Spirit.

This approach has recently been favoured by many theologians. It is also the approach which had a decisive influence on the theme of the general assembly of the World Council of Churches in Canberra (1991): "Come, Holy Spirit – Renew the Whole Creation". The conference was an invitation to explore the presence and action of the Holy Spirit in all creation. As K. Stendahl notes: "When we call on the Holy Spirit to renew the whole creation, we become aware that God`s Spirit permeates the whole cosmos and the whole oikoumene in ways which cannot be controlled or manipulated by us."[52]

We have many instances from both the Old Testament and the New Testament that God or the Spirit is at work in all creation (Psalm 104) or among the pagans, cf. the story about Balaam in Num 23-24 and about Cyrus in Isa 44:24-38; 45:1. In the New Testament we have the story of Peter and Cornelius in Acts 10:1-11:18 and the story of Jesus and the Syrophoenician woman in Mark 7:24-30. Both stories reveal discernment of God's presence and action in the lives of people regarded as pagans.

The story in Acts 10 refers directly to the Holy Spirit, and the point is that pagans receive the Spirit before they are baptized, that is before becoming members of the church.

The Gospel of John in a similar way seems to affirm the concept of the Spirit at work in creation. The Spirit surely blows where it will (John 3:8). This is not an incidental spirit but the Word (Logos) known from the Prologue. The blowing of the Logos-Spirit is the precondition for an authentic dialogue which is crossing all barriers, cf. the story of the Samaritan woman in John 4.

The presence of the Spirit outside the believing community raises the question of how to distinguish between the Holy Spirit and other spirits.[53] This question is addressed in several passages in the New Testament. So, for instance, in 1 Thess 5:19-20 Paul says: "Do not quench the Spirit. Do not despise the words of prophets, but test everything...".

Furthermore, in 1 Corinthians Paul emphasizes the need for the Christians to treat the claims of religious experience critically, with discernment and employs several criteria by which the genuineness and value of charismata can be tested. Three important tests are:[54]

(a) The test of true or false inspiration is the confession: "Jesus is the Lord" (12:3).

(b) The criterion of spirituality is not the degree of inspiration but love (ch. 13).

(c) The community benefit (ch. 14).

These criteria are all based on the christological event. The close link between Christ and the Spirit is also highlighted in 1 John 4:1-3 "...By this you know the Spirit of God: Every spirit that confesses that Jesus Christ *has come in the flesh* is from God". These words are a critique of the Gnostics who do not accept Jesus as incarnated. At the last commission in John (20:19-23) the disciples receive the Spirit. At the same time they see the scars of Jesus in order that they can note the identity between the crucified and the risen Jesus. This point is that the Holy Spirit is not an incidental spirit, but the holy Spirit of the crucified Christ.[55]

Another important touchstone is the fruits of the Spirit. No one has ever seen the Spirit, but it can be discerned by virtue of its effects. In John's Gospel these effects are seen in the new way of life of the community (e.g. the mutual love).[56] Paul in a similar fashion emphasizes that love is the touchstone of all spiritual phenomena (1 Cor 13; Gal 5:22).

The conference in Canberra also discussed how to distinguish between the spirits. The report states that the Holy Spirit is "distinct from other 'spirits', benign or demonic"[57], and again that "Spirits must be discerned. Not every spirit is of the Holy spirit. The primary criterion for discerning the Holy spirit is that the Holy Spirit is the Spirit of Christ; it points to the cross and resurrection, and witnesses to the Lordship of Christ. The fruits of the Spirit, among them love, joy, and peace, is another criterion to be applied (Gal 5:22). We believe that these criteria should also operate when we encounter the profound spirituality of other religions".[58]

What, then, is the conclusion from this dialogue between the biblical texts and our experiences regarding the discernment of the spirits? It seems to me that there are two observations both of which have their validity.

The first observation is that if the Spirit is at work in all creation and among people of other faiths it is no longer theologically acceptable today, to look on other religions as Satanic. The experience of God's action must be seen to involve, on our part, a process of listening, without prejudice, of being open to the Spirit and expect the unexpected. We must see the activity of God as extending beyond the boundaries of our culture, our churches and confessions, and all human norms and structures. We must admit the impossibility of holding God captive within our human structures, and the limitation of human wisdom to fully comprehend divine transcendence.[59]

The second observation is that the Holy spirit in the Bible is the Spirit that uncovers and reveals all truth (cf. John 16:8-11). Christians therefore should witness to the liberating Spirit of God.[60] The New Testament reckons with a spiritual warfare. It shows a realistic appreciation of the depth of evil which the Spirit of God has to contend with.[61] It speaks of creation and history as the theatre also of the unfolding of a Satanic spirit. This is illustrated by the letter to the Ephesians (e.g. 6:12) and by the letter to the Colossians: The decisive battle is between the Spirit and the spirits through his death on the cross, Col 2:15. Another example is the Gospel of John which says that darkness is a reality in the world; it has to be reckoned with and contended with (John 1:5). The Holy Spirit gives the power for this spiritual resistance against the destructive powers.[62]

This struggle between the Holy Spirit and the spirits of this world, between truth and distortions of the truth, is going on *within* every religious community in history. S. Samartha reminds us that Christians should avoid the temptation to transform it into a struggle *between* Christianity and other religions in the world.[63] To discern the movement of the Spirit not only in the church but also in the communities of people outside the visible boundaries of the church is perhaps the most challenging demand of our time.

III. Bible and dialogue

1. Three models for dialogue

The central theological question is whether salvation is possible outside Christianity. The difficulties can be focused in relation to two traditionally held Christian axioms. The first states that salvation is through Jesus Christ alone (John 14:6; Acts 4:12). The second axiom is that God desires the salvation of all humankind (Acts 14:17; 1 Tim 2:4; Rom 2:6-7).[64] It appears that these two theological axioms are implicitly determinative of the three paradigms: exclusivism, inclusivism and pluralism.[65]

a. Exclusivism

This position is known both in a more radical form and a more moderate form.

According to *the radical exclusivism* Jesus is the only path to salvation. This is the traditional view of the church. The great majority of the evangelical movement also subscribes to this understanding.[66] References are often made to K. Barth who declared religion to be unbelief. Religion is the opposite of revelation. There are no points of contact in humanity for the gospel. However, this statement is directed primarily not at the other religions, but at Christianity. Man is an "idol factory", and the idol thus manufactured is religion, Christian or otherwise.[67]

The modified exclusivism likewise says that Christ is the only path to salvation, but adds that God is continually at work and present in the creation. He has not left himself without witness – see Romans 1-2; Acts 14:15-17 and John 1:4. But people are caught up in sin and so reject what they can know of God. They use their religiosity to elude God. All humans are the objects of God's wrath, dead through trespasses and sins (cf. Eph 2:1-3).

This modified exclusivism is represented among others by P. Althaus who refers to a "primeval" revelation ("Ur-Offenbarung"). Another representative is E. Brunner who reckons with a natural theology which, however, has been perverted by the sin.[68]

b. Inclusivism

This approach affirms the salvific presence of God in non-Christian religions. At the same time it maintains that Christ is the definitive and authoritative revelation of God.

Jesus occupies a unique place in salvation history as Saviour of all the world. Of all humanity he alone is of universal significance. But the claim to uniqueness and exclusivism, to the universality and absoluteness of the Christian faith, cannot mean that only Christians – to the exclusion of others – are recipients of God's saving grace and thus alone know him in the fullness of his truth. All of salvation history is directed toward Christ and is completely "christocentric" in nature. From creation on humankind has been called by God to redemption in Jesus Christ.

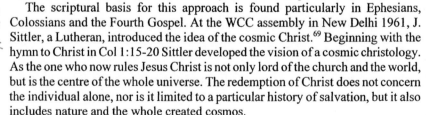

The scriptural basis for this approach is found particularly in Ephesians, Colossians and the Fourth Gospel. At the WCC assembly in New Delhi 1961, J. Sittler, a Lutheran, introduced the idea of the cosmic Christ.[69] Beginning with the hymn to Christ in Col 1:15-20 Sittler developed the vision of a cosmic christology. As the one who now rules Jesus Christ is not only lord of the church and the world, but is the centre of the whole universe. The redemption of Christ does not concern the individual alone, nor is it limited to a particular history of salvation, but it also includes nature and the whole created cosmos.

Dialogue is only possible if we proceed from the belief that we go expecting to meet the God who has preceded us and has been preparing people within the context of their own culture and convictions. God has already removed the barriers. His Spirit is constantly at work in ways that pass human understanding. We do not have him in our pocket, so to speak, and do not just "take" him to the others.

The paradigm of inclusivism is often linked to *the theory of fulfilment* which was put forward at the beginning of the past century and is related to the idea of evolution which dominated in the nineteenth century. Other religions could prepare the way for Christianity.[70] This can be compared to the relationship between Judaism and Christianity. Jesus did not come to abolish the religions, but to fulfill them, cf. Matt 5:17. The gospel fulfills the longings of the non-Christian religions and answers their questions. Christ is already present everywhere, including other religions ("Christian presence"). This being so, it is presumptuous of the Christian missionary to talk of "bringing" Christ with him; what he does is to "find" Christ already there and then help to "unveil" him.

Prominent mission theologians have developed the model of inclusivism in relation to the great world religions, e.g. K. Cragg in relation to Islam, and K. L. Reichelt in relation to Buddhism. The inclusive position has had great influence on Catholic mission theology since Vatican II. K. Rahner, in particular, has played a significant role. He argues that the adherent of a non-Christian religion should be regarded as an "anonymous Christian".[71]

c. Pluralism

According to this view all religions provide ways of salvation which are equally valid, that is Christianity cannot claim to be either the only path (exclusivism) or the fulfilment of other paths (inclusivism). This position is taken by theologians with different backgrounds, for instance J. Hick (Protestant), W. Ariarajah (Protestant) and P. Knitter (Catholic).

The difference between this model and the previous two has been explained by P. Knitter.[72] The first model holds to an *exclusive uniqueness* and maintains that the Christ event is *constitutive* of any true encounter with God, anywhere in history. The second model proposes an *inclusive uniqueness* for Jesus. Jesus remains, if not constitutive of, at least *normative* for, all religious experience, for all times. The third model is theocentric; it proposes what can be called a *relational uniqueness* for Jesus. In other words, Jesus is unique, but not exclusive or normative.

The pluralist model is *theocentric*. It underlines that Christianity should move from christocentrism to theocentrism. Both Knitter and Ariarajah argue that the original message of Jesus was theocentric. His mission and person were profoundly kingdom-centred, which means God-centred. "All his powers were to serve this God and this kingdom; all else took second place".[73] In the Synoptic Gospels Jesus never called himself the Son of God, but son of man. His own life was entirely God-centred, God-dependent and God-ward. In the New Testament there is a significant shift from the theocentric attitude that characterizes Jesus' own teaching to the Post-Easter confessions. Gradually Jesus comes to the centre and God is pushed to the periphery.[74]

What then about the exclusive statements? They are all statements of faith about Jesus the Christ. They derive their meaning in the context of faith, and have no meaning outside the community of faith. They are confessions, but they are not definitive.[75]

According to this understanding the exclusive statements are not philosophical texts (universal statements) but texts of confession. They only have a meaning within their own context.[76] Ariarajah illustrates this point by means of a metaphor: When his daughter tells him that he is the best daddy in the world, she is speaking the truth. For this comes out of her experience. But of course it is not true in another sense, because in the next house there is another little girl who also thinks that her daddy is the best father in the whole world. And she too is right. "It is impossible to compare the truth content of the statements of the two girls. For here we are dealing not with absolute truths, but with the language of faith and love".[77]

The "pluralists", then, argue that Jesus is normative for Christians. To speak of Jesus as unique is to speak the language of faith. But exclusive uniqueness was not the intent of this language of faith.

2. The uniqueness and the universality of Christ

This brief survey of different models for approaching other religions indicate that we have to do with a most complicated issue. There is no comprehensive solution available from the Bible, but it does offer some leads.

Two major traditions can be found in the Bible. P. Rossano has described them as two "economies":[78] on the one hand is the economy of the covenant, that is, the covenant granted to Israel and to the Christians. On the other hand is the "sapiental economy" in which all people are embraced. The Wisdom literature describes the action of God through Wisdom. This idea is also found in other parts of the Old Testament as well as in New Testament writings. The important thing is that both economies, that of the Mosaic covenant and that of Wisdom, are, in a New Testament perspective, joined and fused in Jesus. He is the "elect," the "beloved of God," and the "Son," in whom Israel is resumed. But he is also the "Wisdom of God," present throughout the universe.

The first of the two traditions is the narrow, particular and exclusivist tradition that emphasizes a radical *discontinuity* between Christian revelation and the whole range of non-Christian experience. The other tradition is the broad, inclusive tradition that emphasizes the *continuity* of God's activity in Christ with his activity among all persons everywhere. Both of these traditions must be affirmed and maintained, but this is difficult to do "when some persons affirm continuity with doubtful uniqueness and others affirm uniqueness without continuity. What is needed in our theology of religion is uniqueness *with* continuity".[79]

The ambiguous character of religion is testified by the Bible. On the one hand, religious experience has a positive value. Several New Testament texts show sympathy for the God-fearing pagans. The Magi have a vision of the star, a religious experience that draws them to Israel (Matt 2:1-12). The centurion already has faith that puts God's people to shame (Matt 8:5-13). Even before baptism Cornelius was "a devout man who feared God with all his household" (Acts 10:2). Paul and other biblical writers acknowledged the possibility of "natural religion" whereby the true God could be detected in the order of his creation (cf. Romans 1). Paul is presented by Luke as acknowledging with respect the Athenians' cult to the "unknown God" (Acts 17:22).[80]

On the other hand, although some biblical writers did recognize genuine religious experience in individual pagans, in no instance was a religious "system" other than Judaism and Christianity considered to have any validity. As was the case with Judaism, explicit evaluations of other religions tended to be negative. Gentiles suffered from "ignorance" and were considered to be caught in a life of idolatry and futility.[81] There are also demonic expressions found in the religions. Paul on more than one occasion exorcised demons (Acts 16:18; 19:12). This too is part of the biblical approach to religions. Religions in and of themselves do not save, they may in fact enslave.[82]

The attitude of the Bible to people of other faiths is thus a complicated phenomenon. If we shall do full justice to this fact, neither the pluralist position nor the exclusivist position (at least in its radical form) are acceptable.[83]

Evangelical particularity and catholic universality are both inherent in the biblical picture of the historical Jesus of Nazareth as the resurrected Christ of God. C. Braaten rightly notes that the exclusive claim is not a footnote to the gospel; it is the gospel itself. Not part of the husk, but the very kernel. On the other hand, the uniqueness of Christ lies in his universality. Therefore, Braaten argues for a position between the Scylla of evangelicalism without the universality of Jesus Christ and the Charybdis of universalism without the uniqueness of Jesus Christ.[84]

The task, then, is to held together the uniqueness of Christ and his universality. John's Gospel is one of the best examples in the Bible of the uniqueness *and* universality of Christ. The Gospel is important to the question of the religions in that "the Johannine Jesus takes words upon himself that were originally spoken in a context of many claims to divinity by foreign deities."[85] At the same time, the core of John's christology is the affirmation that Jesus Christ is the unique revealer of the living God.

John's Gospel is addressed to a first century context of conflicting religious claims and has particular relevance in our own pluralistic setting today. In this Gospel we have an exclusiveness which at the same time is inclusive.[86] This can be illustrated by the "I am" sayings.[87] These sayings are no dogmatic demarcations, but *universal invitations* to discipleship. There are no limits to the range of the Christ-event – just as there are no limits to a light shining in the darkness.

3. A trinitarian approach to mission

A narrow theo-centric approach to other religions will lead to pluralism or even syncretism. Conversely, a narrow christo-centric approach will lead to a radical exclusivism. Finally, an inclusive understanding of the Spirit makes it difficult to distinguish between the Spirit of God and the spirits of the world.

We therefore have to ask: How is it possible to prevent creation from becoming sheer romanticism and spirituality from becoming religious fanaticism? Only by insisting that the Spirit of the triune God is at work in creation. A proper starting point for a theology of religion is the trinitarian confession. *Missio Dei* – the mission of God – is the mission of the triune God.[88] There are three aspects of a trinitarian understanding of mission:[89]

First, a trinitarian approach to a theology of religion is based on the concept of God as the Father and Creator of this world. This means that we and our non-Christian neighbours share a common nature as those who have been created by the one God who is the Father of all. We meet as children of one Father, regardless of whether or not our partners have accepted their sonship. We must reckon with the fact that the Creator of heaven and earth is alive and leaves no living person without a witness to his existence (Acts 14:17).

Second, this approach insists on the importance of Jesus Christ. God has sent many "servants", but in Jesus Christ, he himself has come. Cross and resurrection are of particular significance.[90] In 1 Cor 1-2 Paul describes Jesus' cross as the divine judgment upon all human religiosity while at the same time both cross and resurrection are the power for liberation and redemption for all peoples. In the death and resurrection of Jesus something so decisive happened that its dimensions are indeed cosmic and its importance extends to human beings of every religious stripe. In the crucified and resurrected Lord, God is reaching forth his hand to the whole cosmos and to people of all religions (cf. 2 Cor 5). The old is past; the new has begun.

Third, the Holy Spirit has a crucial role in a trinitarian approach to the dialogue. We should expect that the Holy Spirit can and will use this dialogue to do its own sovereign work, to glorify Jesus by converting to him both partners in the dialogue. The Spirit is not the possession of the church but is Lord over the church guiding it from its limited, partial and distorted understanding and embodiment of the truth into the fullness of the truth in Jesus who is the one in whom all things consist (Col 1:17). Following M. Warren we may speak of a "theology of attention".[91] This means that we walk humbly and honestly with men of other faiths and keep our eyes open for any evidence of the Spirit's work among them.

4. Mission on the way

Mission is not just church extension. It is something more costly and more revolutionary. It is the action of the Holy Spirit who in sovereign freedom both convicts the world (John 16:8-11) and leads the Christians toward the fullness of the truth which they have not yet grasped (John 16:12-15).[92]

It is a matter of dispute whether Jesus is the 'end' of revelation. The words in John 16:13 – "guide you into all the truth" – point to a deepening and on-going understanding of truth. The Spirit is not the exclusive property of the Christian church but it is intimately related and ultimately indivisible with Christ and the Father. In the sense that Jesus is the definitive revelation of God in history – the decisive norm by which all subsequent and previous revelations are judged and related – in this sense only can Christ be said to be the end of revelation. Although the Christian may believe that Jesus is the "end" of revelation, this belief does not preclude the universal workings of the Spirit, which "blows where it chooses" (John 3:8).[93]

The church has yet much to learn. To be a disciple is to be on the way; it is to be in a process of learning. We have already seen that this aspect plays a significant role in the Gospel of Mark.[94]

To be on the way is also a central motif in Luke's writings. Pilgrimage seems to be a key to interpreting his portrayal of both Jesus and the earliest disciples. According to M. Forward Luke makes use of the theme of faith as pilgrimage in order to impart the Christian message. "In Luke's view the journey of faith requires *metanoia*, repentance, a change of orientation, a seeking to hear and do God's will, rather than taking a relationship with him for granted as a static event and an assured status."[95]

The Gospel of Matthew offers interesting insights in what it means to be a disciple. The main point in the "Great Commission" is the making disciples. The method of instruction was to teach by example. Making disciples involves one's whole life. Mission is to live a precarious existence; it is to live at the frontier. The final words of Jesus "I am with you always, to the end of the age" reflect that Jesus' presence is permanent. Even if Matthew does not mention the Holy Spirit in 28:20, Jesus' presence with his disciples is to be understood pneumatologically.[96]

The image of way is crucial to the Gospel of John. Those who follow Jesus are promised that they will never walk in darkness but will have the light of life (8:12). They might be unsure and say like Thomas: "Lord, we do not know where you are going. How can we know the way?" (14:5). To this Jesus said: "I am the way, and the truth, and the life" (14:6). Here there is no distinction between means and end. The opening up of the way and the coming of Jesus Christ are one and the same.[97] K. Cracknell comments: "So be it. We will follow that Way, that Truth, that Life now, in the midst of our religious plural world. We will ourselves assuredly see the marks of the nails, for dialogue is an element of the cross, we are called to bear".[98]

Modern documents on the dialogue with people of other faiths often use the concept of pilgrimage. Thus in the WCC "Guidelines on Dialogue with People of Living Faiths and Ideologies" (1979) it is said: "We feel able with integrity to assure our partners in dialogue that we come not as manipulators but as genuine fellow-pilgrims, to speak with them of what we believe God to have done in Jesus Christ."[99]

Wild Goose

This metaphor is helpful, for it reminds us that we ourselves are Abrahamic people, still looking for "a city that has foundations, whose architect and builder is God" (Hebr 11:10). "Such a self-conception belongs to the heart of Christian understanding: we are not to be a settled community, living on the traditions of the past, but rather are those who realize that 'here we have no abiding city'..."[100]

People search for the truth or for God. This search is seen as something positive in the Bible (Acts 17:27; John 1:38). The decisive point, however, is that regardless of humanity's religious search for God, God is coming to us. With this everything begins. This is the essence of the Bible.[101]

Again and again the synoptic Gospels tell how Jesus is searching for those who are the miserable ones, the marginalized, the small. This is the crucial point in the parable of the lost son (Luke 15:11-32).

The Gospel of John in a similar way describes God as one who is searching for human beings. When the Samaritan woman asks for the right place to worship, Jesus answers that "the true worshippers will worship the Father in spirit and truth, for the Father *seeks* such as these to worship him" (John 4:23). The point is that he seeks such worshippers by sending his Son.

It was in the "excess" of his humanity that Christ showed us his divinity. He was not more God by being less of a man, but rather, in being human to the utmost degree he showed that he was God. John wanted to make this clear by saying: "Having loved his own who were in the world, he loved them to the end" (John 13:1). As Y. Raguin says: "This is the Christian way that transcends the ways of other religions at which the Incarnation is not the complete key to life".[102]

The ultimate theological foundation of mission is this movement of God toward human beings. Mission is first and foremost the God who comes.[103] Moreover, God's mission is the invasion of love in history.[104] The important thing is that God finds us in Jesus Christ. Jesus Christ is God in search of man. It is this image of the searching God – the Word which became flesh and lived among us – which makes the decisive difference between Christianity and the other religions.

Notes

1   For a more detailed discussion of this problem see the introductory chapter.
2   Thus, the horizon is something into which we move and that moves with us; cf. Thiselton 1980, 307.
3   For a survey of the contemporary currents see Jongeneel & van Engelen 1995, 446-457. One of the important issues which is not discussed separately in this chapter is mission as liberation. See, however, my book "Poverty and Mission" from 1984.
4   Bible 1980, 32.
5   Cf. Bible 1980, 51: "Just as the biblical writers responded to a particular situation, so contemporary interpretation is also determined by our own situation".
6   Cf. Taber 1983, 119-120.

7   There is a close link between incarnation, communication and contextualization; cf. Sugdon 1981, 111-117.
8   Cf. Costas 1979, 25-26.
9   von Allmen 1975, 37-38.
10   Cf. Bosch 1991, 421.
11   Pobee 1986, 7.
12   Bosch 1991, 55.
13   Cf. Legrand 1990, 151.
14   Cf. Swartley 1983, 232.
15   Cf. The Authority of Scripture 1980, 108-113.
16   Cf. The Authority of Scripture, 1980, 110.
17   Cf. Birch & Rasmussen 1976, 182-184.
18   Cf. Legrand 1990, 151.
19   I have in mind particularly the situation among Protestants. Similar tendencies, however, might be found in the Catholic church. For other ways of describing the present situation see also Jongeneel & van Engelen 1995, 446-447. For a discussion of the Pope John Paul II's encyclical, *Redemptoris Missio*, see Bevans 1993.
20   For a comparison between the evangelical movement and the ecumenical movement see, among others, Bosch 1980b; Bosch 1981; Verstraelen 1980.
21   Bosch 1980b, 24 (with reference to W. Scott).
22   Cf. the theme of Lausanne II (conference in Manila 1989): "Proclaim Christ Until He Comes" – which is a reference to Mark 13:10.
23   On the Pentecostal understanding of Scripture see Hollenweger 1972, esp. 291-310. The author demonstrates that this theological conservatism often runs parallel to a social and political blindness (pp. 296-297).
24   Verstraelen 1980, 46.
25   Verstraelen 1980, 47.
26   The same applies to the relationship between Pentecostalism and the ecumenical movement; cf. Hollenweger 1972, 442ff.
27   Bosch 1991, 512-516; cf. Missiologi 1994, 438-440. The survey of the six "salvific events" is a way of answering the question: *Why* mission? See the introductory remarks on the biblical grounding of mission in chapter 1.
28   Bosch 1991, 518.
29   Gathered 1983, 32; see also King 1997, 85. Similarly, Lathrop defines culture as "the symbolic-expressive dimensions of social life" (Lathrop 1994, 17).
30   Cf. Mortensen 1998, 220.
31   Cf. Bosch 1991, 454; Amalorpavadass 1978, 18-22.
32   Koyama 1975, 67-68.
33   Duraisingh 1996, 37.
34   Cf. Spirit 1995, 11.
35   Cf. Senior & Stuhlmueller 1983, 344.
36   See also Arendt 1994, 31-32. Notice the difference between Christianity and Islam as regards the concept of universality and uniformity. While Christianity underlines the multiplicity, Islam tends to underline the uniformity: its language of devotion is Arabic; the same applies

to its holy scripture: the translation of the Koran into other languages is in principle unacceptable. Cf. Arendt 1994, 20-39.

37 Cf. Spirit 1995, 32.

38 According to Koyama (1975, 54-69) the same is valid of the term "accommodation". One has to distinguish between accommodation and syncretism. Bosch 1991, 447-450, however, is more hesitant in using the term "accommodation".

39 Soares-Prabhu 1976, 282.

40 Niebuhr 1951. For a review of his typology see, a.o., A. Stauffer 1994, 9-10; King 1997, 86ff.

41 Niebuhr 1951, 197: John "undertakes not only to translate the gospel of Jesus Christ into the concepts of its Hellenistic readers, but to lift these ideas about Logos and knowledge, truth and eternity, to new levels of meaning by interpreting them through Christ".

42 Cf. Newbigin 1978, 164.

43 Cf. Clapp 1996, 58 and 65.

44 King 1997, 97. "In other words, he does not have one attitude to culture; he has, rather, *different* responses to *different* cultures" (p. 89).

45 Stauffer 1994, 15.

46 Cf. Bosch 1991, 455.

47 Cf. Newbigin 1974, 99-100.

48 Newbigin 1974, 101.

49 Newbigin 1977. See also the reflections in Newbigin 1978, 163-164.

50 See also the analysis of 1 Peter in chapter 8 of this study. For the use of the term "critical solidarity" see Nissen 1984, 127-129.

51 Newbigin 1977, 124.

52 Stendahl 1990, 49.

53 This controversial question came into focus at the Canberra Assembly of the WCC, with the keynote address on the Holy Spirit by the Korean theologian Chung Hyun Kyung (Chung 1991). She linked Christian theology with elements of popular religiosity. Many understood her to equate the Holy Spirit with the "spirits full of *Han*," associated in Korea with the wandering spirits of those who have died unjustly. For a review and discussion see, among others, Thunberg 1992; Anderson 1993, 204-205.

54 Cf. Dunn 1977, 192-194.

55 Cf. A.M. Aagaard 1991, 261-262.

56 On this issue see Nissen 1999.

57 Signs 1991, 112.

58 Signs 1991, 117.

59 Cf. Ukpong 1989, 422-424.

60 Cf. the theme of section II in Canberra. "Spirit of Truth – Set us Free!"; Signs 1991, 244-248.

61 Cf. Thomas 1990, 218-219.

62 On the Spirit of truth see also chapter 5, section I.3.

63 Samartha 1990, 260.

64 Cf. D'Costa 1986, 4.

65 For a review of these positions see, a. o., van Lin 1995, Bosch 1991, 478-483, Romarheim 1983, 126ff.; Lande 1994.

66 At Lausanne the evangelicals declared that "it is impossible to be a biblical Christian and a universalist simultaneously" (Let the Earth Hear 1975, 76). Yet, in "Proclaim Christ" 1990, 181, it is said that the evangelicals do not all agree when they come to work out the implications of the exclusivist standpoint. Some evangelicals are sympathetic to the inclusivist standpoint.

67 For a discussion of Barth's understanding of religion and its importance for missiology see Thomas 1987, 50-58.

68 For the dissent between Barth and Brunner see Klaiber 1997, 86-87.

69 Cf. The New Delhi Report 1962, 15.

70 But it remains the "crown", as J. N. Farquhar argued in his famous study on *The Crown of Hinduism* (1913). Cf. Bosch 1991, 478.

71 For a fuller description and a discussion of Rahner's viewpoint see, among others, D'Costa 1986, esp. 80-116.

72 Knitter 1985, 171.

73 Knitter 1985, 173.

74 Ariarajah 1985, 21.

75 Cf. Ariarajah 1985, 23.

76 Cf. Knitter 1985, 184-186.

77 Ariarajah 1985, 26.

78 Rossano 1981, 28-29.

79 Anderson 1993, 205-206.

80 Cf. Senior & Stuhlmueller, 331-332.

81 Cf. Senior & Stuhlmueller, 345.

82 Cf. Hedlund 1993, 329-330. "Religion is under the judgement of God. That includes *Christian* religion as it was true of the Hebrew religion of the Old Testament...Religion does not save...It is Jesus Christ who saves" (330). This is the truth in Barth's viewpoint.

83 For a fuller discussion and critique of the pluralist position see D'Costa 1986. See also the discussion of Knitter's approach in the Dutch periodical *Wereld en Zending* 15 (1986), Vol. 2 (a number of articles) and the discussion of Ariarajah's approach in Arendt 1987, 84-95.

84 Braaten 1981, 75-78 and 87.

85 Ball 1991, 53.

86 See Nissen 1991.

87 Klaiber 1997, 65, notes that precisely the strict exclusiveness of a statement like John 14:6b ("No one comes...") serves the universality of the sentence preceding it in which Jesus respond to the question about the way to God ("I am the way...").

88 Cf. Aagaard 1973, 21-92; Thunberg 1993, 106.

89 Cf. Verkuyl 1978, 354-362; Newbigin 1978, 197-214. On the use of the concept of *Missio Dei* see Jongeneel & van Engelen 1995, 447-448. – Cf. also Verkuyl 1993, 71-81, where he argues for a Kingdom-oriented dialogue with people of other faiths.

90 As Newbigin 1978, 200, has put it: "The message of Jesus, of the unique incarnate Lord crucified by the powers of law, morals, and piety and raised to the throne of cosmic authority, confronts the claim of every religion with a radical negation".

91 Warren 1971.
92 Cf. Newbigin 1978, 66.
93 Cf. D'Costa 1986, 135.
94 Cf. also Via 1985, 191: "A person is put *on the way*, a way which surprisingly affords new beginnings."
95 Here quoted from Cracknell 1986, 190, note 49.
96 Cf. Bosch 1983, 243-244.
97 Cf. Wieser 1982, 225.
98 Cracknell 1986, 152.
99 Guidelines on Dialogue 1979, 11.
100 Cracknell 1986, 147.
101 Cf. J. Aagaard 1991, 45.
102 Raguin 1979, 95. The author continues: "The more Christ shows Himself man, the more He loves, gives Himself and "dies" in His humanity for those He loves, so much the more does He show Himself to be God".
103 Cf. Legrand 1990, 152.
104 Cf. Castro 1985, 86ff.

Bibliography

Aagaard, A. M. 1973. *Helligånden sendt til verden*. Aarhus: Aros.

Aagaard, A. M. 1985. "Gudsrigets Gud: Latinamerikansk befrielsesteologi", in S. Pedersen (ed.): *Gudsbegrebet*. Copenhagen: Gad, 247-255.

Aagaard, A. M. 1991. *Identifikation af kirken*. Copenhagen: Anis.

Aagaard, J. 1983. "Den religiøse dimension i kirkens mission," *Mission and Evangelism* 1/2:1-23.

Aagaard, J. 1985. "Eksklusivitet og inklusivitet missionsteologisk belyst", *Nordisk Missionstidsskrift* 96:146-171.

Aagaard, J. 1987. "The Double Apostolate (Part 1)", *Areopagos* 1/2:15-18.

Aagaard, J. 1991. "Christian Faith and the Religions," *Areopagos* 4/3:45-46.

Aagaard, J. 1992. "Dialog and apologetics," *Update and Dialog* 1/1:13.

Aano, K. 1985. *Men jeg siger jer. Mødet mellem religion og kristendom på Madagascar*. Copenhagen: DMS forlag.

Abraham, M. V. 1977. "Paul: the Unique Apostle," *The Indian Journal of Theology* 26:63-72.

Achtemeyer, P. J. 1980. *The Inspiration of Scripture: Problems and Proposals*. Philadelphia: The Westminster Press.

Ahn, Byung Mu. 1981. "Jesus and the Minjung in the Gospel of Mark," in Kim Yong Bock (ed.), *Minjung Theology: People as the Subjects of History*. Singapore: Christian Conference of Asia, 136-151.

Albertz, R. 1983. "Die 'Antrittspredigt' Jesu im Lukasevangelium auf ihrem alttestamentlichen Hintergrund," *Zeitschrift für die neutestamentlichen Wissenschaft* 74:182-206.

Allen, R. 1956. *Missionary Methods: St. Paul's or Ours?* London: World Dominion Press (first published in 1912).

Allen, R. 1962. *The Mission of the Spirit. Selected Writings by Roland Allen*, ed. D.M. Paton. Grand Rapids: Eerdmans.

Amalorpavadass, D. S. 1978. *Gospel and Culture: Evangelization, Inculturation and "Hinduisation"*. Bangalore: National Biblical Cathechetical And Liturgical Centre.

Anderson, G. H. 1993. "Theology of Religions and Missiology: A Time of Testing," in C. van Engen & D. S. Gilliland & P. Pierson (eds.), *The Good News of the Kingdom: Mission Theology for the Third Millenium* (FS A. F. Glasser). Maryknoll, NY: Orbis Books, 200-208.

Arendt, N. H. 1987. "Gud hedder Kristus," i *Bibel, dialog og mission*. (Nyt synspunkt No. 27). Copenhagen: DMS forlag, 84-95.

Arendt, N. H. 1994. *Gud er stor: Om islam og kristendom*. Copenhagen: Anis.

Ariarajah, W. 1985. *The Bible and People of Other Faiths*. Geneva: World Council of Churches.

Arias, M. 1982. "Centripetal Mission or Evangelization by Hospitality," *Missiology: An International Review* 10:69-81.

Arias, M. & Johnson, A. 1992. *The Great Commission: Biblical Models for Evangelism*. Nashville: Abingdon Press.

Arnold, C. E. 1989. *Ephesians: Power and Magic. The Content of Power in Ephesians in Light of its Historical Setting*. Cambridge: Cambridge University Press.

Authority of Scripture. 1980. "The Authority of Scripture in Light of New Experiences of Women, Amsterdam, December 1980," in W. H. Lazareth (ed.), *The Lord of Life*. Geneva: World Council of Churches, 101-115.

Bakke, R. 1987. *The Urban Christian*. London: MARC Europe.

Ball, D. M. 1991. "'My Lord and my God': The Implications of the 'I Am' Sayings for Religious Pluralism", in A. D. Clarke & B. C. Winter (eds.), *One God, One Lord in a World of Religious Pluralism*. Cambridge: Tyndale House, 53-71.

Banks, R. 1980. *Paul's Idea of Community: The Early House Churches in their Historical Setting*. Exeter: The Paternoster Press.

Barr, D. L. 1984. "The Apocalypse as a Symbolic Transformation of the World: A Literary Analysis," *Interpretation* 33:39-50.

Barrett, C. K. 1968. *A Commentary on the First Epistle to the Corinthians*. London: Adam & C. Black.

Barrett, C. K. 1978. *The Gospel According to John*. London: SPCK, 2nd. edn.

Barrett, C. K. 1979. "Light from the Holy Spirit on Simon Magus (Acts 8:4-25)," in J. Kremer (ed.), *Les Actes des Apôtre. Tradition, rédactions, théologie*. Gembloux/Geneve: J. Duculot, 86-108.

Barth, M. 1959. *The Broken Wall: A Study of the Epistle to the Ephesians*. Valley Forge: The Judson Press.

Barth, M. 1968. "Jews and Gentiles: The Social Character of Justification in Paul," *Journal of Ecumenical Studies* 5:241-267.

Barth, M. 1974. *Ephesians*. 2 Volumes (Anchor Bible 34 & 34A). Garden City, NY: Doubleday & Co.

Barth, M. 1982. "Christ and All Things," in M. D. Hooker & S. G. Wilson (eds.), *Paul and Paulinism* (FS C. K. Barrett). London: SPCK, 160-172.

Beker, J. C. 1980. *Paul the Apostle: The Triumph of God in Life and Thought*. Philadelphia: Fortress Press.

Berkhof, H. 1962. *Christ and the Powers*. Scottdale: Herald Press.

Best, E. 1986. *Disciples and Discipleship: Studies in the Gospel According to Mark*. Edinburgh: T. & T. Clark.

Bevans, S. 1993. "The Biblical Basis of the Mission of the Church in *Redemptoris Missio*," in C. van Engen, D. S. Gilliland, P. Pierson (eds.), *The Good News of the Kingdom: Mission Theology for the Third Millenium* (FS A. F. Glasser). Maryknoll, NY: Orbis Books, 37-46.

Bible. 1980. *The Bible: Its Authority and Interpretation in the Ecumenical Movement*, ed. by E. Flesseman-van Leer. Geneva: World Council of Churches.

Bieder, W. 1965. *Gottes Sendung und der missionarischen Auftrag der Kirche nach Matthäus, Lukas, Paulus und Johannes*. Zürich: EVZ-Verlag.

Birch, B.C. & Rasmussen, L. L. 1976. *Bible and Ethics in the Christian Life*. Minneapolis: Augsburg Publishing House.

Blauw, J. 1962. *The Missionary Nature of the Church: A Survey of the Biblical Theology of Mission*. London: Lutterworth.

Blaser, K. 1972. *Wenn Gott schwarz wäre...: Das Problem des Rassismus in Theologie und christlicher Praxis*. Zürich & Freiburg: Theologischer Verlag & Imba Verlag.

Blount, G. 1998. *Go Preach! Mark's Kingdom Message and the Black Church Today*. Maryknoll, NY: Orbis Books.

Boer, H. 1961. *Pentecost and Missions*. London: Lutterworth.

Boomershine, T. E. 1981. "Mark 16:8 and the Apostolic Commission," *Journal of Biblical Literature* 100:225-239.

Bornkamm, G. 1964. "Der Auferstandene und der Irdische, Mt 28:11-20," in E. Dinkler (ed.): *Zeit und Geschichte*. Tübingen: Mohr Siebeck, 171-191.

Bornkamm, G. 1966. "The Missionary Stance of Paul in 1 Corinthians and Acts," in L. E. Keck & J. L. Martyn (eds.), *Studies in Luke-Acts* (FS P. Schubert). Nashville, NY: Abingdon Press, 194-207.

Bosch, D. J. 1980a. *Witness to the World: The Christian Mission in Theological Perspective.* Atlanta: John Knox.

Bosch, D. J. 1980b. "Behind Melbourne and Pattaya: A Typology of Two Movements," *IAMS Newsletter* 16-17: 21-33.

Bosch, D. J. 1981. "In Search of Mission: Reflections on ' Melbourne' and ' Pattaya'", *Missionalia* 9-1:3-18.

Bosch, D. J. 1983. "The Structure of Mission: An Exposition of Matthew 28:16-20 ", in W. R. Shenk (ed.), *Exploring Church Growth.* Grand Rapids: Eerdmans, 218-248.

Bosch, D. J. 1986. "Towards a Hermeneutic for Bible Studies and Mission," *Mission Studies* III-2:65-79.

Bosch, D. J. 1991. *Transforming Mission: Paradigm Shifts in Theology of Mission.* Maryknoll, NY: Orbis Books.

Braaten, C. 1981. "The Uniqueness and Universality of Jesus Christ," in G. H. Andersen & T. F. Stransky (eds.), *Faith Meets Faith* (Mission Trends No. 5). New York & Grand Rapids: Paulist Press & Eerdmans, 69-89.

Brown, R. E. 1966-1970. *The Gospel According to John.* 2 Volumes (Anchor Bible 29 & 29A). Garden City, NY: Doubleday & Co.

Brown, R. E. 1979. *The Community of the Beloved Disciple: The Life, Loves and Hates of an Individual Church in New Testament Times.* New York: Paulist Press.

Brown, R. McAfee. 1984. *Unexpected News: Reading the Bible with Third World Eyes.* Philadelphia: Westminster Press.

Brown, S. 1977. "The Mission to Israel in Matthew's Central Section (Mt 9:35-11:1), *Zeitschrift für die neutestamentliche Wissenschaft* 69:73-90.

Bultmann, R. 1968. *Das Evangelium des Johannes.* Göttingen: Vandenhoek & Ruprecht. 19th. edn. (1941).

Bultmann, R. 1951. *Theology of the New Testament.* Vol 1. New York: Charles Scribner's Sons.

Burrows, W. R. 1998. "Reconciling All in Christ: The Oldest New Paradigm for Mission," *Mission Studies* XV-1:79-98.

Bussmann, C. 1971. *Themen der paulinischen Missionspredigt auf dem Hintergrund der spätjüdische-hellenistische Missionsliteratur.* Bern: Herbert Lang.

Bühner, J.-A. 1977. *Der Gesandte und sein Weg im 4. Evangelium: Die kultur- und religionsgeschichtliche Entwicklung.* Tübingen: Mohr Siebeck.

Cahill, P. J. 1976. "The Johannine LOGOS as Center," *Catholic Biblical Quarterly* 38:54-72.

Castro, E. 1985. *Sent Free: Mission and Unity in the Perspective of the Kingdom.* Geneva: World Council of Churches.

Chadwick, H. 1954-55. "All things to all men," *New Testament Studies* 1:261-275.

Chappuis, J.-M. 1982. "Jesus and the Samaritan Woman: The Variable Geometry of Communication," *Ecumenical Review* 34:8-34.

Chung, Hyun Kyung. 1991. "Come, Holy Spirit – Renew the Whole Creation," in M. Kinnamon (ed.), *Signs of the Spirit.* Official Report. Seventh Assembly. Geneva: World Council of Churches, 37-47.

Clapp, R. 1996. *A Peculiar People: The Church as Culture in a Post-Christian Society.* Downers Grove, Il: InterVarsity Press.

Collins, A. Y. 1984. *Crisis and Carthasis: The Power of the Apocalypse.* Phildelphia: Fortress Press.

Collins, A. Y. 1992. "Revelation, Book of", *The Anchor Bible Dictionary* 5:694-708.

Comblin, J. 1979a. *The Meaning of Mission: Jesus, Christians, and the Wayfaring Church.* Dublin: Gill and MacMillan.

Comblin, J. 1979b. *Sent from the Father: Meditations on the Fourth Gospel.* Dublin: Gill and MacMillan.

Conn, H. 1993. "A Contextual Theology of Mission for the City," in C. van Engen, D. S. Gilliland & P. Pierson (eds.), *The Good News of the Kingdom: Mission Theology for the Third Millenium* (FS A. F. Glaser). Maryknoll, NY: Orbis Books, 96-106.

Conzelmann, H. 1964. *The Theology of Saint Luke.* London: Faber & Faber, 3. impr.

Costas, O. 1979. "Contextualization and Incarnation," *Journal of Theology for Southern Africa* 29:23-30.

Costas, O. 1989. *Liberating News: A Theology of Contextual Evangelism.* Grand Rapids: Eerdmans.

Cracknell, K. 1986. *Towards a New Relationship: Christians and People of Other Faith.* London: Epworth Press.

Crafton, J. A. 1997. *The Agency of the Apostle: A Dramatic Analysis of Paul's Responses to the Conflict in 2 Corinthians.* Sheffield: Sheffield Academic Press.

Crosby, M. 1977. *Thy Will Be Done: Praying the Our Father as Subversive Activity.* Maryknoll, NY: Orbis Books.

Crosby, M. 1988. *House of Disciples: Church, Economics, and Justice in Matthew.* Maryknoll, NY: Orbis Books.

Cullmann, O. 1976. *The Johannine Circle.* Philadelphia: Westminster Press.

Dahl, N. A. 1965. "Das Geheimnis der Kirche nach Eph. 3,8-10," in E. Schlink & A. Peters (eds.), *Zur Auferbaung des Leibes Christi* (FS P. Brunner). Kassel: Johannes Stauda-Verlag, 63-75.

Dahl, N. A. 1974. "The Nations in the New Testament," in M. E. Glasswell et al. (eds.), *New Testament Christianity and the World* (FS H. Sawyeer). London: SPCK, 54-68.

Dahl, N. A. 1977. *Studies in Paul: Theology for the Early Christian Mission.* Minneapolis: Augsburg Publishing House.

D'Costa, G. 1986. *Theology and Religious Pluralism: The Challenge of Other Religions.* Oxford: Basil Blackwell.

Degenhardt, H. J. 1965. *Lukas. Evangelist der Armen: Besitz und Besitzverzicht in den lukanischen Schriften. Eine Traditions- und redaktionsgeschichtlichen Untersuchung.* Stuttgart: Katholisches Bibelwerk.

Donahue, J. R. 1978. "Jesus as the Parable of God in the Gospel of Mark," *Interpretation* 32:369-386.

Donaldson, T. L. 1996. "Guiding Readers – Making Disciples: Discipleship in Matthew's Narrative Strategy", in R. N. Longenecker (ed.): *Patterns of Discipleship in the New Testament.* Grand Rapids: Eerdmans, 30-49.

Donaldson, T. L. 1997. *Paul and the Gentiles: Remapping the Apostle's Convictional World.* Minneapolis: Fortress Press.

Doohan, L. 1986. *Mark: Visionary of the Early Christianity.* Santa Fe, NM: Bear and Co.

D'Sa, F. X. 1984. "Sehen – Glauben – Innewohnen: Joh 1 als hermeneutischer Modell," in G. M. Soares-Prabhu (ed.), *Wir werden bei ihm wohnen: Das Johannesevangelium in indischer Deutung.* Freiburg: Herder, 99-121.

Dunn, J. D. G. 1970. *Baptism in the Holy Spirit: A Reexamination of the New Testament Teaching on the Gift of the Spirit in Relation to Pentecostalism Today.* London: SCM Press.

Dunn, J. D. G. 1975. *Jesus and the Spirit: A Study of the Religious and Charismatic Experience of Jesus and the First Christians as Reflected in the New Testament.* London: SCM Press.

Dunn, J. D. G. 1977. *Unity and Diversity in the New Testament: An Inquiry into the Character of Earliest Christianity.* London: SCM Press.

Dupont, J. 1979. "Le discours à l'Areópag (Ac 17,22-31), lieu de rencontre entre christianism et hellénism," *Biblica* 60:530-546.

Duraisingh, C. 1996. "The Day of Pentecost: Acts 2:1-13", in H. S. Wilson (ed.), *Gospel and Cultures: Reformed Perspectives.* Geneva: World Alliance of Reformed Churches, 37-43.

Elliott, J. H. 1966. *The Elect and the Holy: An Exegetical Examination of 1 Peter 2.4-10 and the Phrase basileion hierateuma.* Leiden: E. J. Brill.

Elliott, J. H. 1981. *A Home for the Homeless: A Sociological Exegesis of 1 Peter. Its Situation and Strategy.* Philadelphia: Fortress Press.

Erdmann, M. 1998. "Mission in John's Gospel and Letters," in W. J. Larkin & J. F. Williams (eds.), *Mission in the New Testament: An Evangelical Approach.* Maryknoll, NY: Orbis Books, 207-226.

Escobar, S. 1993. "A Pauline Paradigm of Mission: A Latin American Reading," in C. van Engen, D. S. Gilliland & P. Pierson (eds.), *The Good News of the Kingdom: Mission Theology for the Third Millenium* (FS A. F. Glasser). Maryknoll, NY: Orbis Books, 56-66.

Fiorenza, E. S. 1983. *In Memory of Her: A Feminist Theological Reconstruction of Christian Origins.* London: SCM Press.

Fiorenza, E. S. 1985. *The Book of Revelation: Justice and Judgment.* Philadelphia: Fortress Press.

Fiorenza, E. S. 1993. *Revelation: Vision of a Just World.* Edinburgh: T. & T. Clark.

Flender, H. 1967. *St. Luke – Theologian of Redemptive History.* Philadelphia: Fortress Press.

Ford, J. M. 1983. "Reconciliation and Forgiveness in Luke's Gospel," in R. J. Cassidy & P. J. Scharper (eds.), *Political Issues in Luke-Acts.* Maryknoll, NY: Orbis Books, 80-98.

Francis, F.F. 1977. "The Christological Argument of Colossians," in J. Jervell & W. A. Meeks (eds.), *God's Christ and His People* (FS N. A. Dahl). Oslo: Universitetsforlaget, 192-208.

Frankemölle, H. 1982. "Zur Theologie der Mission im Matthäusevangelium," in K. Kertelge (ed.), *Mission im Neuen Testament.* Freiburg: Herder, 93-129.

Freyne, S. 1989. *Galilee from Alexander the Great to Hadrian, 325 B.C.E. to 135 C.E.* Wilmington, Del.: Michael Glazier.

Fung, R. 1989. "Mission in Christ's Way," *International Review of Mission* 78:4-29.

Furnish, V. P. 1968. *Theology and Ethics in Paul.* Nashville & New York: Abingdon Press.

Gadamer, H.-G. 1990. *Truth and Method.* 2d. ed. New York: Crossroad.

Gathered. 1983. *Gathered for Life.* Official Report. VI Assembly, ed. by D. Gill. Geneva & Grand Rapids: World Council of Churches & Eerdmans.

Georgi, D. 1986. *The Opponents of Paul in Second Corinthians.* Philadelphia: Fortress Press.

Giving Account. 1975. *Giving Account of the Hope.* Geneva: World Council of Churches.

Goppelt, L. 1972. "Prinzipien neutestamentlicher Sozialethik nach dem 1. Petrusbrief," in H. Baltensweiler & Bo Reicke (eds.), *Neues Testament und Geschichte* (FS O. Cullmann), Zürich & Tübingen: Theologischer Verlag & Mohr Siebeck, 285-296.

Goppelt, L. 1976. *Theologie des Neuen Testaments I-II.* Göttingen: Vandenhoek & Ruprecht.

Gospel and Cultures. 1995. *Study Process on Gospel and Cultures: Suggested Guidelines for Study Groups*. Programme Unit II: Churches in Mission, Health, Education, Witness. Geneva: World Council of Churches.

Grassi, J. A. 1965. *A World to Win: The Missionary Methods of Paul the Apostle*. Maryknoll, NY: Orbis Books.

Green, J. B. 1995. "The Practice of Hearing the New Testament," in J. B. Green (ed.), *Hearing the New Testament: Strategies for Interpretation*. Grand Rapids & Carlisle: Eerdmans & The Paternoster Press, 411-427.

Guidelines. 1979. *Guidelines on Dialogue with People of Living Faiths and Ideologies*. Geneva: World Council of Churches.

Haas, O. 1971. *Paulus der Missionar: Ziel, Grundsätze und Methoden in der Missionstätigkeit der Apostels Paulus nach seinen eigenen Aussagen*. Münsterschwarzach: Vier-Türme Verlag.

Haenchen, E. 1971. *The Acts of the Apostles: A Commentary*. Oxford: Basil Blackwell.

Hahn, F. 1965. *Mission in the New Testament*. Naperville Il. & London: Alec R. Allenson & SCM Press.

Hammar, K. G. 1975. *Dialog i kyrkan: Synpunkter på predikan*. Lund: Håkan Ohlssons Förlag.

Hanks, T. D. 1983. *God So Loved the Third World: The Biblical Vacabulary of Oppression*. Maryknoll, NY: Orbis Books.

Hartman, L. 1985. "Universal Reconciliation (Col 1,20)," *Studien zum Neuen Testament und Seiner Umwelt* 10:109-121.

Hartman, L. 1994. "Dop och ande – nio frågor," in R. Hvalvig & H. Kvalbein (eds.), *Ad Acta. Studier til Apostlenes Gjerninger og urkristendommens historie* (FS E. Larsson). Oslo: Universitetsforlaget, 86-108.

Hartman, L. 1995. "Humble and Confident. On the So-called Philosophers in Colossae," in D. Hellholm, H. Moxnes & T. K. Seim (eds.), *Mighty Minorities? Minorities in Early Christianity: Positions and Strategies* (FS J. Jervell). Oslo: Scandinavian University Press, 25-39.

Hays, R. H. 1997. *The Moral Vision of the New Testament: Community, Cross, New Creation*. Edinburgh: T. & T. Clark.

Hedlund, R. E. 1993. "The Biblical Approach to Other Religions," in J. Kavunkal & F. Hrangkhuma (eds.), *The Bible and Mission in India Today*. Bombay: St. Pauls, 308-335.

Heiene, G. 1992. "En analyse av 1 Pet 2,13-17 med henblikk på tekstens aktualitet for politisk etikk," *Tidsskrift for Teologi og Kirke* 63:17-31.

Heiligenthal, R. 1983. "Strategien konformer Ethik im Neuen Testament am Beispiel von Röm 13,1-7," *New Testament Studies* 29:55-61.

Hengel, M. 1983. "The Origins of the Christian Mission," in Hengel, *Between Jesus and Paul: Studies in the Earliest History of Christianity*. London: SCM Press, 48-64.

Hock, R. 1980. *The Social Context in Paul's Ministry: Tentmaking and Apostleship*. Philadelphia: Fortress Press.

Hollenweger, W. 1972. *The Pentecostals*. London: SCM Press.

Hollenweger, W. 1973. *Evangelisation gestern und heute*. Stuttgart: J. F. Steinkopf, 9-24.

Hollenweger, W. 1979. *Erfahrungen der Leibhaftigkeit: Interkulturelle Theologie I*. Munich: Chr. Kaiser Verlag.

Holmberg, B. 1990. *Sociology and the New Testament: An Appraisal*. Minneapolis: Fortress Press.

Howell, D. N. 1998. "Mission in Paul's Epistles: Theological Bearings," in W. J. Larkin & J. F. Williams (eds.), *Mission in the New Testament: An Evangelical Approach*. Maryknoll, NY: Orbis Books, 92-116.

Hultgren, A. J. 1985. *Paul's Gospel and Mission*. Philadelphia: Fortress Press.

Hurtado, L. W. 1996. "Following Jesus in the Gospel of Mark – and Beyond," in R. N. Longenecker (ed.): *Patterns of Discipleship in the New Testament*. Grand Rapids: Eerdmans, 9-29.

Jeremias, J. 1958. *Jesus' Promise to the Nations*. London: SCM Press.

Jeremias, J. 1971. *Neutestamentliche Theologie I: Die Verkündigung Jesu*. Gütersloh: Gütersloher Verlagshaus Gerd Mohn.

Jervell, J. 1978. *Ingen har større kjærlighet. Om Johannesevangeliets Jesusbilde*. Oslo: Universitetsforlaget.

Jongeneel, J. A. B. & van Engelen, J. M. 1995. "Contemporary Currents in Missiology," in A. Camps et al. (eds.), *Missiology: An Ecumenical Introduction*. Grand Rapids: Eerdmans, 438-457.

Joseph, M. J. 1977. "A leap into the 'Slavery of Paul' from an Indian angle," *The Indian Journal of Theology* 26:73-85.

Kairos. 1986. *The Kairos Document: Challenge to the Church = A Theological Comment on the Political Crisis in South Africa*, introduced by J. W. de Gruchy. Grand Rapids: Eerdmans.

Kappen, S. 1977. *Jesus and Freedom*. Maryknoll, NY: Orbis Books.

Kasting, H. 1969. *Die Anfänge der urchristlichen Mission*. Munich: Kaiser Verlag.

Kavunkal, J. 1993. "Mission in the Fourth Gospel," in J. Kavunkal & F. Hrangkhuma (eds.), *Bible and Mission in India Today*. Bombay: St. Pauls, 117-146.

Keck, L. E. 1976. *The New Testament Experience of Faith*. St. Louis, Missouri: The Bethany Press.

Keck, L. E. 1979. *Paul and his Letters* (Proclamation Commentaries). Philadelphia: Fortress Press.

Kee, H. C. 1990. *Good News to the Ends of the Earth: The Theology of Acts*. London & Philadelphia: SCM & Trinity Press.

Kee, H. C. 1995. *Who are the People of God? Early Christian Models of Community*. New Haven & London: Yale University Press.

Kelber, W. 1974. *The Kingdom in Mark*. Philadelphia: Fortress Press.

Kelber, W. 1985. "Apostolic Tradition and the Form of the Gospels," in F. F. Segovia (ed.) *Discipleship in the New Testament*. Phildelphia: Fortress Press, 24-46.

King, F. 1997. "St. Paul and Culture," *Mission Studies* XIV-1/2: 84-101.

Kjær-Hansen, K. 1995. *Apostlenes Gerninger*. Copenhagen: Bibelselskabet.

Klaiber, W. 1997. *Call and Response: Biblical Foundations of a Theology of Evangelism*. Nashville: Abingdon Press.

Klauck, H.-J. 1985. "Gemeinde ohne Amt? Erfahrungen mit der Kirche in den johanneischen Schriften," *Biblische Zeitschrift* 29:193-220.

Knitter, P. 1985. *No Other Name? A Critical Survey of Christian Attitudes Toward the World Religions*. Maryknoll, NY: Orbis Books.

Koenig, J. 1979. *Jews and Christians in Dialogue: New Testament Foundations*. Philadelphia: Fortress Press.

Koenig, J. 1985. *New Testament Hospitality: Partnership With Strangers as Promise and Mission*. Philadelphia: Fortress Press.

Koester, C. R. 1995. *Symbolism in the Fourth Gospel: Meaning, Mystery, Community*. Minneapolis: Fortress Press.

Koyama, K. 1975. *Theology in Contact*. Madras: CLS.

Koyama, K. 1979. *Three Mile an Hour God*. London: SCM Press.

Koyama, K. 1980. "The Crucified Christ Challenges Human Power," in *Your Kingdom Come: Mission Perspectives*. Report on the World Conference on Mission and Evangelism, Melbourne 12-25 May,1980. Geneva: World Council of Churches, 157-170.

Krodel, G. 1977. "First Peter", in G. Krodel (ed.) *Hebrews-James-1 and 2 Peter-Jude-Revelation* (Proclamation Commentaries). Philadelphia: Fortress Press, 50-80.

Kysar, R. 1976. *John: The Maverick Gospel*. Atlanta: John Knox Press.

Kuhl, J. 1967. *Die Sendung Jesu und der Kirche nach dem Johannes-Evangelium*. St Augustin: Steyler.

Kuhn, K. G. 1954. "Das Problem der Mission in der Urchristentum," *Evangelische Missions-Zeitschrift* 11:161-167.

Käsemann, E. 1958. "Ephesierbrief", *Religion in Geschichte und Gegenwart*. Tübingen: Mohr Siebeck. II:517-520.

Käsemann, E. 1966. *Jesu letzter Wille nach Johannes 17*. Tübingen: Mohr Siebeck.

Köstenberger, A. J. "Mission in the General Epistles", in W. J. Larkin & J. F. Williams (eds.), *Mission in the New Testament: An Evangelical Approach*. Maryknoll, NY: Orbis Books, 189-206.

Lande, Aa. 1982. "Identitet og åbenhed," in *Kristendommen og de andre religioner*. Copenhagen: DMS forlag, 7-8.

Lande, Aa. 1994. "Pluralistisk religionsteologi?" *Nordisk Missionstidsskrift*, 105-3: 8-11.

Larkin, W. J. 1998. "Mission in Acts," in W. J. Larkin & J. F. Williams (eds.), *Mission in the New Testament: An Evangelical Approach*. Maryknoll, NY: Orbis Books, 170-186.

Lathrop, G. W. 1994. "Baptism in the New Testament and its Cultural Settings," in S. A. Stauffer (ed.), *Worship and Culture in Dialogue*. Geneva: The Lutheran World Federation, 17-38.

Legrand, L. 1990. *Unity and Plurality: Mission in the Bible*. Maryknoll, NY: Orbis Books.

Let the Earth Hear. 1975. *Let the Earth Hear His Voice*. International Congress on World Evangelization, Lausanne, Switzerland, ed. by J. D. Douglas. Minneapolis, Minn: World Wide Publications.

Levison, J. R. & Pope-Levison, P. 1995. "Global Perspectives on New Testament Interpretation," in J. B. Green (ed.), *Hearing the New Testament: Strategies for Interpretation*. Grand Rapids & Carlisle: Eerdmans & The Paternoster Press, 329-348.

Liebschner, S. 1979. "Die Armen im Evangelium", *Zeitschrift für Mission* 5:136-142.

Longenecker, R. N. 1984. *New Testament Social Ethics for Today*. Grand Rapids: Eerdmans.

Maccini, R. G. 1996. *Her Testimony is True: Women as Witnesses According to John*. Sheffield: Sheffield Academic Press.

Mar Osthathios, G. 1995. "Mission and the Uniqueness of Jesus Christ," *Mission Studies* XII-1:79-94.

Marshall, I. H.: *Luke: Historian and Theologian*. Exeter: The Paternoster Press, 1970.

Martin, R. P. 1981. *Reconciliation: A Study of Paul's Theology*. London: Marshall, Morgan & Scott.

Matson, D. L. 1996. *Household Conversion Narratives in Acts: Pattern and Interpretation*. Sheffield: Sheffield Academic Press.

Matthey, J. 1980. "The Great Commission According to Matthew", in *International Review of Mission* 69:161-173.

MacRae, G. W. 1970. "The Fourth Gospel and *Religionsgeschichte*," *Catholic Biblical Quarterly* 32:13-24.

McDonald, J. I. H. 1993. *Biblical Interpretation and Christian Ethics*. Cambridge: Cambridge University Press.

McGavran, D. A. 1970. *Understanding Church Growth*. Grand Rapids: Eerdmans.

McPolin, J. 1969. "Mission in the Fourth Gospel," *Irish Theological Quarterly* 36:113-122.

Meeks, W. A. 1972. "The Man from Heaven in Johannine Sectarianism," *Journal of Biblical Literature* 91:44-72.

Meeks, W. A. 1977. "In One Body: The Unity of Humankind in Colossians and Ephesians," in J. Jervell & W. A. Meeks (eds.), *God's Christ and his People* (FS N. A. Dahl). Oslo: Universitetsforlaget, 209-221.

Meeks, W. A. 1980. "The Urban Environment of Pauline Christianity," *Society of Biblical Literature: Seminar Papers*. No. 19 (ed. P. Achtemeyer), 113-122.

Meeks, W. A. 1983. *The First Urban Christians: The Social World of the Apostle Paul*. New Haven: Yale University Press.

Meeks, W. A. 1987. *The Moral World of the First Christians*. London: SPCK.

Meyer, B. F. 1986. *The Early Christians: Their World Mission and Self-Discovery*. Wilmington: Michael Glazier.

Meyer, R. P. 1971. *Kirche und Mission im Ephesierbrief*. Stuttgart: Verlag Katholisches Bibelwerk.

Michel, O. 1950/51. "Der Abschluss des Matthäusevangeliums", in *Evangelische Theologie* 10:16-26.

Miguez-Bonino, J. M. 1975. "The Struggle of the Poor and the Church", *The Ecumenical Review* 27:36-43.

Miller, J. V. 1998. "Mission in Revelation," in W. J. Larkin & J. F. Williams (eds.), *Mission in the New Testament: An Evangelical Approach*, Maryknoll, NY: Orbis Books, 227-238.

Minear, P. S. 1962. "The Cosmology of the Apocalypse," in W. Klassen & F. G. Snyder (eds.), *Current Issues in New Testament Interpretation* (FS O. A. Piper). New York: Harper, 23-37.

Minear, P. S. 1968. *I Saw a New Earth*. Washington, DC: Corpus Books.

Missiologi. 1994. *Missiologi i dag* (ed. by J.-M.Berentsen, T. Engelsviken & K. Jørgensen). Oslo: Universitetsforlaget.

"Mission and Evangelism – An Ecumenical Affirmation". 1982. *International Review of Mission* 71:427-451.

Moloney, F. J. 1991. *Disciples and Prophets: A Biblical Model for Religious Life*. Bombay: St. Pauls.

Mortensen, V. 1998. "Mission: Identity in Conflict," in M. L. Pandit et al. (eds.), *Identity in Conflict: Classical Christian Faith and Religio Occulta*. (FS J. Aagaard). New Delhi Munshiram Manoharlal Publ., 219-228.

Mouw, R. J. 1975. *Political Evangelism*. Grand Rapids: Eerdmans.

Moxnes, H. 1986-1987. "Meals and the new community in Luke," in *Svensk Exegetisk Årsbok* 51-52:158-167.

Moxnes, H. 1988. *The Economy of the Kingdom: Social Conflict and Economic Relations in Luke's Gospel*. Philadelphia: Fortress Press.

Moxnes, H. 1995. "'He saw that the city was full of idols' (Acts 17:16): Visualizing the World of the First Christians," in D. Hellholm, H. Moxnes & T. K. Seim: *Mighty Minorities? Minorities in Early Christianity: Positions and Strategies*. (FS J. Jervell). Oslo: Scandinavian Univ. Press, 107-131.

Murphy-O'Connor, J. 1978. "Freedom or the Ghetto," *Revue Biblique* 85:543-574.

Murphy-O'Connor, J. 1979. *1 Corinthians*. Wilmington: Michael Glazier.

Myers, C. 1988. *Binding the Strong Man: A Political Reading of Mark's Story of Jesus*. Maryknoll, NY: Orbis Books.

Müller-Fahrenholz, G. 1995. *God's Spirit: Transforming a World in Crisis*. New York & Geneva: Continuum & World Council of Churches.

Månsus, H. 1983. *Shalom jord: Om fred, helhetssyn och jordens framtid*. Örebro: Libris.

New Delhi Report. 1962. *The New Delhi Report*. The Third Assembly of the World Council of Churches. 1961. London: SCM Press.

Newbigin, L. 1974. *'The Good Shepherd': Meditations on Christian Ministry in Today's World*. Madras: CLS.

Newbigin, L. 1977. "What is 'a local church truly united'?," *Ecumenical Review* 29:115-128.

Newbigin, L. 1978. *The Open Secret: Sketches for a Missionary Theology*. London: SPCK.

Newbigin, L. 1987. *Mission in Christ's Way: Biblical Studies*. Geneva: World Council of Churches.

Nicholls, B. 1977. "The particularity and the universality of the gospel," in *Faith in the Midst of Faiths: Reflections on Dialogue in Community*. Geneva: World Council of Churches, 117-122.

Niebuhr, H. R. 1951. *Christ and Culture*. New York: Harper & Row.

Nissen, J. 1980. "Suffering and Ethics in the New Testament," in E. A. Livingstone (ed.), *Studia Biblica III: Papers on the Gospels*. Sheffield: Sheffield Academic Press, 277-287.

Nissen, J. 1984. *Poverty and Mission: New Testament Perspectives on a Contemporary Theme*. Leiden-Utrecht: Interuniversitair Instituut voor Missiologie en Oecumenica.

Nissen, J. 1988. "Firmness and Flexibility: Paul's Mission to the Greeks," in L. Thunberg et al. (eds.), *Dialogue in Action* (FS J. Aagaard). New Delhi: Prajna Publications, 56-84.

Nissen, J. 1989. "Den sociale hermeneutik," in S. Pedersen (ed.), *Skriftsyn og metode*. Aarhus: Aarhus Universitetsforlag, 247-288.

Nissen, J. 1991. "Inklusiv og eksklusiv kristologi i Johannesevangeliet," in J. Aagaard (ed.), *Religiøsitet og religioner*. Copenhagen: Anis, 137-56.

Nissen, J. 1992. "Gnosis og holisme i Johannesevangeliet," *Præsteforeningens Blad* 82:361-371.

Nissen, J. 1993. "Rebirth and Community: A Spiritual and Social Reading of John 3,1-21," in P. Bilde et al. (eds.), *Apocryphon Severini* (FS S. Giversen). Aarhus: Aarhus University Press, 121-139.

Nissen, J. 1994. "Jesus, the People of God, and the Poor: The Social Embodiment of Biblical Faith," in S. Pedersen (ed.), *New Directions in Biblical Theology*. Leiden: E. J. Brill, 222-242.

Nissen, J. 1997. "Unity and Diversity: Biblical Models for Partnership," *Mission Studies* XIV-2:121-146.

Nissen, J. 1998. "Mission in Christ's Way: The Temptation in the Desert and Christian Mission," in M. L. Pandit et al. (eds.), *Identity in Conflict: Classical Christian Faith and Religio Occulta*. (FS J. Aagaard). New Delhi: Munshiram Manoharlal Publ., 41-51.

Nissen, J. 1999. "Community and Ethics in the Gospel of John," in J. Nissen & S. Pedersen (eds.), *New Readings in John: Literary and Theological Perspectives*. Sheffield: Sheffield Academic Press, 194-212.

Nolan, A. 1977. *Jesus Before Christianity: The Gospel of Liberation*. London: Darton, Longman & Todd.

Nürnberger, K. 1978. "The Economics of Paul," in K. Nürnberger (ed.), *Affluence, Poverty, and the Word of God*. Durban: Lutheran Publishing House, 163-178.

Okure, T. 1988. *The Johannine Approach to Mission: A Contextual Study of John 4:1-42.* Tübingen: Mohr Siebeck.

Ollrog, H. 1979. *Paulus und seine Mitarbeiter.* Neukirchen-Vluyn: Neukirchener Verlag.

Olsson, B. 1974. *Structure and Meaning in the Fourth Gospel: A Text-Linguistic Analysis of John 2:1-11 and 4:1-42.* Lund: Gleerup.

Olsson, B. 1994. "Misjon hos Paulus og Peter," in J. M. Berentsen et. al. (eds.): *Missiologi i dag.* Oslo: Universitetsforlaget, 65-76.

Onuki, T. 1984. *Gemeinde und Welt im Johannesevangelium: Ein Beitrag zur Frage nach der theologischen und pragmatischen Funktion des johanneischen "Dualismus".* Neukirchen-Vluyn: Neukirchener Verlag.

Paoli, A. 1973. *Freedom to be Free.* Maryknoll, NY: Orbis Books.

Park, Eung Chun. 1995. *The Mission Discourse in Matthew's Interpretation.* Tübingen: Mohr Siebeck, 1995.

Patmury, J. 1993. "Concepts and Strategies of Paul's Mission", in J. Kavunkal & F. Hrangkuma (eds.): *Bible and Mission in India Today.* Bombay: St. Pauls, 147-171.

Patro, S. K. 1974. "The Fourth Gospel and Its Relevance in India," in C. Duraisingh & C. Hargreaves (eds.), *India's Search for Reality and the Relevance of the Gospel of John.* Mysore: ISPCK, 134-138.

Perkins, P. 1982. *The Love Commands in the New Testament.* New York: Paulist Press.

Pesch, R. 1980. *Das Markusevangelium.* Vol I. Freiburg: Herder.

Philips, K. 1971. *Kirche in der Gesellschaft nach dem ersten Petrusbrief.* Gütersloh: Gütersloh Verlagshaus Gerd Mohn.

Piper, J. 1980. "Hope as the Motivation of Love: 1 Peter 3:9-12," *New Testament Studies* 26:212-231.

Pobee, J. 1986. "*Skenosis* – The Tabernacling of the Word," *Mission Studies* III-2:4-13.

Pobee, J. 1987. *Who are the Poor? The Beatitudes as a Call to Community.* Geneva: World Council of Churches.

Popkes, W. 1978. "Zum Verständnis der Mission bei Johannes," *Zeitschrift für Mission* 4:63-69.

Proclaim. 1990. *Proclaim Christ Until He Comes: Calling the Whole Church to Take the Whole Gospel to the Whole World.* ed. by J. D. Douglas. Minneapolis: World Wide Publications.

Rader, W. 1978. *The Church and Racial Hostility: A History of Interpretations of Ephesians 2:11-22.* Tübingen: Mohr Siebeck.

Rademakers, J. 1974. *La Bonne Nouvelle selon Marc.* Bruxelles: Institut d'Études Théologique.

Raguin, Y. 1979. *The Depth of God.* Wheathampstead Hertfordshire: Anthony Clarke.

Raiser, K. 1991. *Ecumenism in Transition: A Paradigm Shift in the Ecumenical Movement?* Geneva: World Council of Churches.

Rebell, W. 1987. *Gemeinde als Gegenwelt: Zur soziologischen und didaktischen Funktion des Johannesevangeliums.* Frankfurt a. Main: Verlag Peter Lang.

Reichelt, L. 1939. "The Johannine Approach," in *The Authority of Faith.* (International Missionary Council meeting at Tambaram, Madras, December 12th to 29th, 1938). Oxford & London: Oxford University Press & Humphrey Milford, 90-101.

Rensberger, D. 1989. *Overcoming the World: Politics and Community in the Gospel of John.* London: SPCK.

Richardson, P. 1979. *Paul's Ethic of Freedom.* Philadelphia: Fortress Press.

Ricoeur, P. 1973. *Hermeneutik und Strukturalismus: Der Konflikt der Interpretationen I.* Munich: Chr. Kaiser Verlag.

Rika och fattiga. 1993. *Rika och fattiga*. Ett brev från Svenska kyrkans biskopar om rättfärdighet och moral i global ekonomi. Stockholm: Svenska Kyrkans Information.

Ringe, S. 1985. *Jesus, Liberation, and the Biblical Jubilee: Images for Ethics and Christology*. Philadelphia: Fortress Press.

Robinson, G. 1978. "A New Economic Order: The Challenge of the Biblical Jubilee," in S. Amirtham (ed.), *A Vision of Man* (FS R. Chandran). Madras: CLS, 363-379.

Romarheim, A. 1983. "Kristendommens syn på seg selv i forhold til andre religioner", in I. Asheim (ed.), *For kirke og skole* (FS O. Modalsli). Oslo: Universitetsforlaget, 124-132.

Rossano, P. 1981. "Christ's Lordship and Religious Pluralism," in G. H. Anderson & T. F. Stransky (eds.), *Faith Meets Faith* (Mission Trends No. 5). New York & Grand Rapids: Paulist Press & Eerdmans, 20-35.

Rowland, C. 1985. *Christian Origins: An Account of the Setting and Character of the Most Important Messianic Sect of Judaism*. London: SPCK.

Rowland, C. & M. Corner. 1990. *Liberating Exegesis: The Challenge of Liberation Theology to Biblical Studies*. London: SPCK.

Rowland, C. 1995. "In This Place: The Center and the Margins in Theology", in F. F. Segovia & M. A. Tolbert (eds.): *Reading from this Place: Social Location and Biblical Interpretation*, Vol 2. Philadelphia: Fortress Press, 169-182.

Ruiz, M. R. 1987. *Der Missionsgedanke des Johannesevangeliums: Ein Beitrag zur johanneischen Soteriologie und Ekklesiologie*. Würzburg: Echter Verlag.

Russell, L. M. 1978. "Called to Account", *Ecumenical Review* 30:369-375.

Russell, L. M. 1982. *Becoming Human*. Philadelphia: The Westminster Press.

Samartha, S. J. 1981. *The Lordship of Jesus Christ and Religious Pluralism* (with responses from A. Glasser and R. Schreiter and a reply by the author). Madras: CLS.

Samartha, S. J. 1990. "The Holy Spirit and People of Other Faiths," *Ecumenical Review* 42:250-263.

Sanders, J. A. 1975. "From Isaiah 61 to Luke 4," in J. Neusner (ed.): *Christianity, Judaism and Other Greco-Roman Cults*. Part I (FS M. Smith). Leiden: E. J. Brill, 75-106.

Sandnes, K. O. 1981. "Fra Jerusalem til jordens ender: En lukasstudie til hedningemisjonens basis,"*Norsk tidsskrift for misjon* 36:123-134.

Sandnes, K. O. 1994. "Omvendelse og gjestevennskap,", in R. Hvalvig & H. Kvalbein (eds.): *Ad Acta: Studier til Apostlenes Gjerninger og urkristendommens historie* (FS E. Larsson). Oslo: Universitetsforlaget, 325-346.

Santa Ana, J. de, 1977. *Good News to the Poor: The Challenge of the Poor in the History of the Church*. Geneva: World Council of Churches.

Schillebeeckx, E. 1977. *Christus und die Christen: Die Geschichte einer neuen Lebenspraxis*. Freiburg: Herder.

Schlier, H. 1958. *Der Brief an die Epheser*. Düsseldorf: Patmos, 2d. edn.

Schneider, G. 1981. "Anknüpfung, Kontinuität und Widerspruch in der Areopagusrede," in P. G. Müller & W. Stenger (eds.), *Kontinuität und Einheit* (FS F. Mussner). Freiburg: Herder, 173-178.

Schneiders, S. M. 1991. *The Revelatory Text: Interpreting the New Testament as Sacred Scripture*. San Francisco: HarperCollins Publishers.

Schottroff, L. 1975. "Gewaltverzicht und Feindesliebe in der urchristlichen Jesustradition," in G. Strecker (ed.), *Jesus Christus in Historie und Theologie* (FS H. Conzelmann). Tübingen: Mohr Siebeck, 197-221.

Schottroff, L & Stegemann, W. 1986. *Jesus and the Hope of the Poor*. Maryknoll, NY: Orbis Books.

Schreiter, R. 1981. "Response" in S. J. Samartha, *The Lordship of Jesus Christ and Religious Pluralism*. Madras: CLS, 36-46.

Schreiter, R. 1992. *Reconciliation: Mission and Ministry in a Changing Social Order*. Maryknoll, NY: Orbis Books.

Schweizer, E. 1963. "The Church as the Missionary Body of Christ," in E. Schweizer, *Neotestamentica* (Deutsche und Englische Aufsätze). Zürich: Zwingli Verlag, 317-329.

Schweizer, E. 1976. *Der Brief an die Kolosser*. Zürich: Benziger.

Schweizer, E. 1988. "Slaves of the Elements and Worshippers of Angels: Gal 4:3,9 and Col 2:8,18,20," *Journal of Biblical Literature* 107:455-468.

Scroggs, R. 1977. *Paul for a New Day*. Philadelphia: Fortress Press.

Scroggs, R. 1980-81. "The Sociological Interpretation of the New Testament: The Present State of Research," *New Testament Studies* 29:164-179.

Seim, T. K. 1987. "Roles of Women in the Gospel of John," in L. Hartman & B. Olsson (eds.), *Aspects on the Johannine Literature*. Uppsala: Almqvist & Wiksell International, 56-73.

Seim, T. K. 1995. *The Double Message: Patterns of Gender in Luke-Acts*. Edinburgh: T. & T. Clark.

Senior, D. & Stuhlmueller, C. 1983. *The Biblical Foundations for Mission*. London: SCM Press.

Signs, 1991. *Signs of the Spirit. Official Report. Seventh Assembly*, ed. by M. Kinnamon. Geneva: World Council of Churches.

Sider, R. 1977. *Rich Christians in an Age of Hunger: A Biblical Study*. Downers Grove, Ill.: InterVarsity Press.

Sloan, R. B. 1977. *The Favorable Year of the Land: A Study of the Jubilary Theology in the Gospel of Luke*. Austin: Schola.

Smyth, B. T. 1980. *Paul: Mystic and Missionary*. Maryknoll, NY: Orbis Books.

Soards, M. 1994. *The Speeches in Acts: Their Content, Context, and Concerns*. Louisville, Kentucky: Westminster/John Knox.

Soares-Prabhu, G. M. 1976. "The New Testament as a Model of Inculturation," *Jeevadhara* 33:268-282.

Soares-Prabhu, G. M. 1978. "Good News to the Poor: The Social Implications of the Message of Jesus," *Biblebhashyam* 4:193-212.

Soares-Prabhu, G. M. 1982. "Jesus the Teacher: The Liberative Pedagogy of Jesus of Nazareth", *Jeevadhara* 12:243-256.

Soares-Prabhu, G. M. 1986. "Missiology or Missiologies?", *Mission Studies* III-2:85-87.

Soares-Prabhu, G. M. 1993. "Following Jesus in Mission: Reflections on Mission in the Gospel of Matthew," in J. Kavunkal & F. Hrangkhuma (eds.): *Bible and Mission in India Today*. Bombay: St. Pauls, 64-92.

Soares-Prabhu, G. M. 1994. "The Church as Mission", *Jeevadhara* 34:271-281.

Spindler, M. R. 1980. "Indian Studies of the Gospel of John: Puzzling Contextualization," *Exchange* 27:1-55.

Spindler, M. R. 1995. "The Biblical Grounding and Orientation of Mission," in A. Camps, L. A. Hoedemaker, M. R. Spindler & F. J. Verstraelen (eds.), *Missiology: An Ecumenical Introduction*. Grand Rapids: Eerdmans, 123-143.

Spirit. 1995. *Spirit, Gospel, Cultures: Bible Studies on the Acts of the Apostles*. Geneva: World Council of Churches.

Stam, J. 1979. "The Hermeneutics of Liberation Theology," *Bangalore Theological Forum* 11:122-141.

Stambaugh, J. & Balch, D. 1986. *The Social World of the First Christians*. London: SPCK.

Stauffer, A. 1994. "Christian Worship: Toward Localization and Globalization," in A. Stauffer (ed.), *Worship and Culture in Dialogue*. Geneva: The Lutheran World Federation, 7-15.

Stendahl, K. 1966. *The Bible and the Role of Women: A Case Study in Hermeneutics.* Philadelphia: Fortress Press.

Stendahl, K. 1977a. "It took a miracle to launch the mission to the Gentiles: the Cornelius story," in S. Samartha (ed.): *Faith in the midst of faiths.* Geneva: World Council of Churches, 124-125.

Stendahl, K. 1977b. *Paul Among Jews and Gentiles.* London: SCM Press.

Stendahl, K. 1980. "Your Kingdom Come: Notes for Bible Study," in *Your Kingdom Come: Mission Perspectives.* Report on the World Conference on Mission and Evangelism. Melbourne 12-25 May, 1980; Geneva: World Council of Churches, 72-82.

Stendahl, K. 1990. *Energy for Life: Reflections on the Theme 'Come, Holy Spirit – Renew the Whole Creation'.* Geneva: World Council of Churches.

Sugden, C. 1981. *Radical Discipleship.* London: Marshalls.

Swartley, W. M. 1983. *Slavery, Sabbath, War, and Woman: Case Issues in Biblical Interpretation.* Scottdale: Herald Press.

Synnes, M. 1994. "Hvor viktig er 'tegn og under' i Lukas' misjonshistorie?" in R. Hvalvig & H. Kvalbein (eds.): *Ad Acta. Studier til Apostlenes Gjerninger og urkristendommens historie* (FS E. Larsson). Oslo: Universitetsforlaget, 362-378.

Taber, C. 1983. "Contextualization", in W. R. Shenk (ed.), *Exploring Church Growth.* Grand Rapids: Eerdmans, 117-131.

Thelle, N. 1991. *Hvem kan stoppe vinden? Vandringer i grenseland mellom Øst og Vest.* Oslo: Universitetsforlaget.

Theissen, G. 1975. "Legitimation und Lebensunterhalt: Ein Beitrag zur Soziologie urchristlicher Missionare," *New Testament Studies* 21:192-221.

Theissen, G. 1977. *Soziologie der Jesusbewegung: Ein Beitrag zur Entstehungsgeschichte des Urchristentums.* Munich: Chr. Kaiser Verlag.

Thiselton, A. C. 1980. *The Two Horizons: New Testament Hermeneutics and Philosophical Description with Special Reference to Heidegger, Bultmann, Gadamer, and Wittgenstein.* Grand Rapids & Exeter: Eerdmans & The Paternoster Press.

Thomas, M. M. 1987. *Risking Christ for Christ's Sake: Towards an Ecumenical Theology of Pluralism.* Geneva: World Council of Churches.

Thomas, M. M. 1990. "The Holy Spirit and the Spirituality for Political Struggles," *Ecumenical Review* 42:216-224.

Thunberg, L. 1992. "Kris i Kyrkornas världsråd?" in E. Block & E. Ignestam (eds.), *Kom, heliga Ande! Canberra 1991* (Tro & Tanke No. 9). Uppsala: Svenska kyrkans forskningsråd, 41-45.

Thunberg, L. 1993. "Kristen helligåndsteologi i mødet med anderledes troende – nogle adspredte refleksioner," in H. Thomsen (ed.), *Du som går ud fra den levende Gud.* Copenhagen: Anis, 98-120.

Tidball, D. 1983. *An Introduction to the Sociology of the New Testament.* Exeter: The Paternoster Press.

Tillich, P. 1959. *Theology of Culture.* New York: Oxford University Press.

Tolbert, M. A. 1989. *Sowing the Gospel: Mark's World in Literary-Historical Perspective.* Minneapolis: Fortress Press.

Trites, A. A. 1977. *The New Testament Concept of Witness.* Cambridge: Cambridge University Press.

Ucko, H. 1997. (ed.) *The Jubilee Challenge – Utopia or Possibility: Jewish and Christian Insights.* Geneva: World Council of Churches.

Ukpong, J. S. 1989. "Pluralism and the Problem of the Discernment of Spirits," *Ecumenical Review* 41:416-425.

Ukpong, J. S. 1996. "The Parable of the Shrewd Manager (Luke 16:1-13): An Essay in Inculturation Biblical Hermeneutic," in G. West & M. W. Dube (eds.), *"Reading With": An Exploration of the Interface Between Critical and Ordinary Readings of the Bible. African Overtures* (Semeia 73). Atlanta, GA: Scholars Press, 189-210.

Wagner, C. P. 1979. *Our Kind of People: The Ethical Dimensions of Church Growth in America.* Atlanta: John Knox.

Walter, N. 1979. "Christusglaube und heidnische Religiosität in paulinischen Gemeinden," *New Testament Studies* 25:422-442.

Warren, M. 1971. *A Theology of Attention.* Madras: CLS.

Weber, H.-R. 1971. *The Invitation: Matthew on Mission.* New York: The United Methodist Church.

Weber, H.-R. n.d. "Interpretations of Interpretations," in *The Holy Bible: The Politics of Bible Study.* Pamphlet publ. by the Student Christian Movement, Anandale, London, 12-17.

Weber, H.-R. 1979. "Kingdom = Glory = Service. Notes by Weber to 'The Crucified Christ Challenges Human Power'", in *Your Kingdom Come: Ten Bible Studies.* Sidney: Australian Council of Churches, 24.

Weber, H.-R. 1980. "The First Interchurch Aid Project," in *Empty Hands: An Agenda for the Churches.* Geneva: World Council of Churches, 35-36.

Weber, H.-R. 1981. *Experiments with Bible Study.* Geneva: World Council of Churches.

Weber, H.-R. 1986. *Living in the Image of Christ.* Geneva & Valley Forgy, PA: World Council of Churches & Judson Press.

Weber, H.-R. 1989. *Power: Focus for a Biblical Theology.* Geneva: World Council of Churches.

Weeden, T. J. 1971. *Mark – Traditions in Conflict.* Philadelphia: Fortress Press.

Wieser, T. 1982. "The Way of Life," *Ecumenical Review* 34:221-227.

Wilckens, U. 1974. *Die Missionsreden der Apostelgeschichte: Form- und Traditionsgeschichtliche Untersuchungen.* Neukirchen-Vluyn: Neukirchener Verlag (3rd enlarged edn.; 1st edn. 1961).

Wilder, A. N. 1965. "Reconciliation – New Testament Scholarship and Confessional Differences," *Interpretation* 19:203-216 and 312-326.

Williams, J. F. 1998. "Mission in Mark," in W. J. Larkin & J. F. Williams (eds.) *Mission in the New Testament: An Evangelical Approach.* Maryknoll, NY: Orbis Books, 137-151.

Willis, W. L. 1985. *Idol-Meat in Corinth: The Pauline Argument in 1 Corinthians 8 and 10.* Chico, CA: Scholars Press.

Wilson, S. G. 1982. "Paul and Religion," in M. D. Hooker & S. G. Wilson (eds.), *Paul and Paulinism* (FS C. K. Barrett). London: SPCK, 339-354.

Wink, W. 1984. *Naming the Powers: The Language of Power in the New Testament.* Philadelphia: Fortress Press.

Winn, A. C. 1981. *A Sense of Mission: Guidance from the Gospel of John.* Philadelphia: Westminster Press.

Winter, B. W. 1994. *Seek the Welfare of the City: Christians as Benefactors and Citizens.* Grand Rapids & Carlisle: Eerdmans & The Paternoster Press.

van Canghe, J. 1972. "La Galilée dans l'évangile de Marc: un lieu theologique?" *Revue Biblique* 79:59-75.

van Engen, C. 1996. *Mission on the Way: Issues on Mission Theology.* Grand Rapids: Bakers Books.

van Lin, J. 1995. "Models for a Theology of Religion," in A. Camps & L. A. Hoedemaker & M. R. Spindler & F. J. Verstraelen (eds.), *Missiology: An Ecumenical Introduction*, Grand Rapids: Eerdmans, 177-193.

Vanhoozer, K. J. 1995. "The Reader in New Testament Interpretation," in J. B. Green (ed.), *Hearing the New Testament: Strategies for Interpretation*. Grand Rapids & Carlisle: Eerdmans & The Paternoster Press, 301-328.

Vandana, Sister. 1981. *Waters of Fire*. Madras: CLS.

Vellanickal, J. 1980. "Discipleship According to the Gospel of John," *Jeevadhara* 56:131-147.

Vellanickal, J. 1982. "The Gospel of John in the Indian Context," *Jeevadhara* 68:140-155.

Verkuyl, J. 1978. *Contemporary Missiology: An Introduction*. Grand Rapids: Eerdmans.

Verkuyl, J. 1993. "The Biblical Notion of Kingdom: Test of Validity for Theology of Religion," in C. van Engen & G. S. Gilliland & P. Pierson (eds.), *The Good News of the Kingdom: Mission Theology for the Third Millenium* (FS A. F. Glasser). Maryknoll, NY: Orbis Books, 71-81.

Verhey, A. 1984. *The Great Reversal: Ethics and the New Testament*. Grand Rapids: Eerdmans.

Verstraelen, F. J. 1980. "After Melbourne and Pattaya: Reflections of A Participant Observer," *IAMS Newsletter* 16-17:34-49.

Via, D. O. 1985. *The Ethics of Mark's Gospel – In the Middle of the Time*. Philadelphia: Fortress Press.

Vivekananda Swami 1953. *The Yogas and Other Works*, ed. by Swami Nikhilananda. New York.

Vogel, H.-J. 1983. "Nicodemus – Bible Study of John 3:1-21," in G. Köberlin (ed.), *Before the Cock Crows: Biblical and Theological Reflection in the Student Christian Movements in Europe Today*. Madras: CLS, 74-86.

von Allmen, D. 1975. "The Birth of Theology," *International Review of Mission* 44:37-55.

Yoder, J. H. 1972. *The Politics of Jesus: Vicit Agnus Noster*. Grand Rapids: Eerdmans.

Zeller, D. 1982. "Theologie der Mission bei Paulus," in K. Kertelge (ed.), *Mission im Neuen Testament*. Freiburg: Herder, 164-189.